James Payn

Report on the Irish Diatomaceae

James Payn

Report on the Irish Diatomaceae

ISBN/EAN: 9783744759700

Printed in Europe, USA, Canada, Australia, Japan

Cover: Foto ©ninafisch / pixelio.de

More available books at **www.hansebooks.com**

XXXVII.—REPORT ON THE IRISH DIATOMACEÆ. By the Rev. EUGENE O'MEARA, M. A. Part I. (With Plates 26 to 35.)

[Read June 28, 1875.]

IT is now just a century, since in 1773, O. F. Müller discovered the first known diatomaceous form; nor was it till ten years after, the same distinguished author was able to add two new forms to the list. In the year 1824 Agardh published his "Systema Algarum;" and then the number of species was forty-nine, comprehended under eight genera. But if in this province of Natural Science the progress was slow during the first half century, it has been very rapid in the last, owing not only to the number of eminent labourers in this field of research, but also to the greatly improved means of investigation. The number of species in Europe alone, as computed by Rabenhorst in his index, is about 4000. This may be beyond the mark, but certainly Pfitzer is far short of it when he fixes the total number of known species at about 1000. It is not necessary to enumerate the many authors to whose useful labours the students of this branch of Science are indebted, but special notice should be made of Kützing, who explored the whole surface of the globe; and of Ehrenberg, who, not content with the same ample field of investigation, extended his researches into the bowels of the earth. But no authors, perhaps, have contributed so much to the extent and accuracy of our knowledge, as those who have restricted their labours to some special families, or to the collection and examination of the forms incidental to some country or district. The treatise on the Diatomaceæ of the Clyde has earned for Gregory an imperishable name. The Austrian forms have been described by Grunow. The Prussian by Schuman. The Danish by Heiberg. Those of Sweden and Norway by Cleve, and those of Great Britain by Smith in his admirable Synopsis.

No country would appear more favourable to the growth of these forms than our own, with its extensive sea-coast indented with numerous bays, its rivers and lakes, and mountain ranges. And yet it is strange that Smith, an Irishman, at least labouring professionally in Ireland, should have done but little in exploring its resources, as appears from the fact that, in the case of 389 forms figured and described by him as British, there are not more than about one hundred for which Irish localities have been assigned. Hence it might be supposed that the climate of Ireland is not favourable to the growth of Diatomaceous forms—an impression which is not justified by the fact, as I hope to prove by the present work.

For many years the intervals of professional engagements had been devoted by me to the collection and study of the Irish Diatomaceæ; and a large amount of material had been gathered and arranged when

I was favoured with the request of the Royal Irish Academy to prepare a list of the forms to be met with in this country—a request with which I unhesitatingly complied. Had I been content with furnishing an inventory of the forms I had found, the task I had undertaken might have been speedily performed; but my anxiety was to render the work as complete and as useful to my fellow-students as I could, and as worthy of the reputation of the Royal Irish Academy as it was possible for me to make it. With this view I determined to explore new localities, and to search more carefully, districts I had previously examined. I was anxious also to avail myself of the labours of the most distinguished authors on the subject, and was therefore obliged to acquire a knowledge of languages with which I was previously unacquainted.

For all this, time was required, and I refer to the subject for the purpose of showing that the long period that has elapsed since the task was undertaken has been busily, and I hope not fruitlessly, occupied. No authentically named specimens were available; and this proved to me a source of much additional labour and delay. Those who are practically acquainted with the Diatomaceæ are aware how difficult it is sometimes under the most favourable circumstances to identify a form. The difficulty is enhanced in cases in which the original form, observed under the disadvantage of inferior instruments, has been inadequately described; and when a mistake has been made in the figure or the description, the only satisfactory means of identification is the inspection of the specimen. Hence some idea may be formed of the difficulty and delay arising from the circumstance of there being no authentic specimens preserved in any of the Collections or Herbaria of Dublin. Many are the friends who have kindly assisted me in the prosecution of this work, but special acknowledgments on my part are due to Professor E. Perceval Wright, M.D., not only for the loan of collections but also of books and objectives, to Rev. Maxwell H. Close, and A. G. More, Esq., whose collections have added numerous forms to my list, as well as new localities for many others; and also to Dr. David Moore, whose many and valuable collections were kindly placed at my disposal.

The name of Bacillariaceæ was employed to designate this group of organisms at a time when little of their structure and habits, except their outward form, was known; and Pfitzer maintains that this designation should be retained because of its priority: but I have adopted the more modern name of Diatomaceæ, not only because it is more pronounceable, but specially because it is more characteristic and more generally known.

The question, what is the proper position of the Diatomaceæ in the classification of organized beings, has been variously answered. The first known species were by their discoverers included amongst the Confervaceæ; the extraordinary movements, however, of Bacillaria paxillifer, noticed by Müller, induced that author to identify it with the genus Vibrio; and the position assigned to this form, as well as the rapid motion by which it is characterised, may have insensibly inclined succeeding observers to assign to the Diatomaceæ generally a place in the Animal Kingdom. This theory is supported by the authority of the illustrious Ehrenberg, who regarded the numerous globules noticeable in the cells as so many stomachs, and therefore gave to a group embracing these and other forms the general designation of Polygastriceæ. But notwithstanding the deference justly due to so great an authority, more recent observers are, I may say, unanimously of opinion that the Diatomaceæ belong to the Vegetable Kingdom—an opinion sustained by the analogy which the forms of this group exhibit as regards their general structure, and more especially by the mode of reproduction which they possess in common with other organisms generally regarded as vegetable.

The Motion of the Diatomaceæ.

One of the first phenomena which attracts the notice of the students of the Diatomaceæ is the extraordinary power of motion with which the frustules are endowed. To account for this motion, various theories have been suggested, reducible to two general classes. By some it has been supposed that in the process of imbibing water containing nourishment and expelling what is superfluous, currents are produced which have the effect of propelling the frustules backwards and forwards through the water. As concerns this hypothesis, I quite concur with the opinion expressed by Ralfs, that it should be regarded rather as a figment of the imagination than founded on the observation of facts. Others have suggested that the frustules are furnished with special organs of locomotion. The occurrence of hair-like processes on the frustules has afforded a colourable reason for such a statement; they are, however, only occasional, and have the appearance of parasitic growth, rather than of normal organs of the plant. Ehrenberg conceived that a pedal organ was extruded from what he regarded as an orifice in the centre of the valve: but so far from the existence of such an organ having been satisfactorily sustained, the fact that what that eminent observer, as well as others of deservedly high reputation, considered to be an opening, is now generally regarded as a thickening of the silicious plate, is fatal to the theory. So while the motion of the Diatomaceæ continues to excite attention, it must be confessed that the mechanical agency by which the motion is effected remains unexplained.

Structure of the Cell.

There is one remarkable feature in the structure of the Diatomaceæ which distinguishes them from cognate organisms, that is, the fact that the cell is invested with a silicious covering, consisting of two distinct plates, more or less parallel to one another, and held together by a rim or hoop. This silicious covering has been appropriately assimilated to a pill-box, consisting of the box itself and the cover which slips over it; and if we suppose the cover to be of the same depth as the box, or nearly so, we have a structure on a large scale which nearly resembles the silicious covering of such Diatomaceous species as possess a circular form, and which with some modification may be taken to illustrate the general plan on which the silicious part of the cell of Diatoms is constructed. In the larger forms it may easily be noticed that one valve of the frustule, with its accompanying rim or hoop, is smaller than the other into which it fits, as the slides of a telescope fit into one another. It has been supposed that in the parent frustule the two valves are of the same size, and that the diminution in the dimensions of one valve is owing to the fact of its being developed within the rim of the primary valve, and is consequently smaller than it by the thickness of the rim. Pfitzer, however, has remarked that in some cases at least the difference in size is noticeable in the mother cell, in which one valve is secreted in the first instance, and then the opposite valve is formed within the former. This remark is worthy of notice and should be borne in mind when cases of conjugation come under view, in order to ascertain whether the occurrence is casual, or whether the same process takes place in the other species of Diatomaceæ. To the distinguished author just named belongs the merit of having contributed more than any other to the extent and accuracy of our knowledge concerning the various parts and disposition of the cell-contents. There is first the plasm-sac, consisting of a fine colourless plasm, forming a closed sac of the shape of the cell, and in which the cell-contents are enveloped. It is often very difficult for the observer to make himself certain of the existence of this sac, because its refractive power differs but slightly from that of water, but the structure becomes apparent immediately on the application of dilute hydrochloric acid. The effect of this re-agent is to produce an instantaneous contraction of the sac, which at first, as it recedes from the cell-wall, preserves the form of the cell and still maintains connexion with it by means of a few pellucid threads, but after some time it becomes contracted into a round mass. This result is accomplished most effectively by the use of osmic acid at the strength one per cent. Iodine gives a bright yellow colour to the plasm-sac. Within the plasm-sac, and in close proximity to it, is the structure to which Pfitzer has given the name of Endochromeplates, varying in number and position in the various genera. Some possess two of these plates, others only one. In the Naviculæ these plates, two in number, lie one at either side, the middle of the plate corresponding with the middle of the hoop or connecting band, whence they pass on either side towards the median line, leaving a small narrow space down the middle of the valve free; in other genera there is but one such plate, variously disposed. They consist of a thick substance, and are of the same colour thoroughout, varying from light yellow to dark yellowish brown. The plasm of which these plates consist differs in density from the plasm which forms the plasm-sac and the structure which is called the middle-mass. In case the normal condition of the cell-contents be disturbed by fracture of the silicious epiderm, the endochrome plates go together, and never commingle with the material of the plasm-sac. If the colouring matter be discharged by alcohol, the demarcation of the endochrome plate from the rest of the plasm can be readily distinguished. Within the folds of the endochrome plates is found in some a collection of plasm, which Pfitzer calls the "middle plasm-mass," described by Ehrenberg as resembling "the embyro in an egg;" in the Naviculæ it forms generally an irregular quadrangle. Vacuoles and oil globules occur imbedded in this middle plasm-mass, and appear distinctly in consequence of their strong refractive power. In the middle of this plasm-mass a central vesicle is observable in some genera, but is not equally distinct in all species. And although in some cases it cannot be discovered, even with the most skilful management, Pfitzer considers that nevertheless the statement of Lüders may be correct, that no Diatomaceous cell is destitute of such a vesicle, because although in many cases no such structure can be detected by ordinary means, it becomes apparent by the application of re-agents, the most effective for the purpose being dilute hydrochloric acid.

Besides the parts already specified, there have been observed in some of the Diatomaceæ a water-like fluid substance, and oil-globules, varying in size. These latter occur swimming freely in the cell, but in greater number upon the inner surface of the plasm-sac. In consequence of their strong refractive power they strike the eye at once, and are changed into a black colour by the use of osmic acid. As they readily combine, they have no investing pellicle. It is thought that in proportion as the oil-globules abound, the cells have suffered from the want of pure water, and that the appearance of the larger oil-globules is a sign that the cell has attained its full maturity, and that its resources have been exhausted. The oil-globules afford a means of answering the question whether the cell contents are of a watery or of a gelatinous consistency. In favour of the former view, Pfitzer refers to the fact that very weak acid produces an immediate shrinking of the plasm-sac, and also to his observation that the oil-globules can be moved about with facility, which could not occur if the surrounding matter were of a gelatinous thickness. And this opinion of Pfitzer has been corroborated by Föcke, who discovered that the oil-globules, in consequence of their light specific gravity, accumulate on the upper surface of the cell, and change their position in case the frustule is turned upside down.

The Reproduction of the Diatomaceæ

Is a subject of deep interest, requiring some explanatory remarks. The ordinary mode of increase is by self-division, as it has been termed. The cell-contents within the enclosure of the silicious epiderm separate into two distinct masses. As these develop they push the valves of the mother-cell more and more widely asunder. A new silicious valve is secreted by each of the two masses, on the side opposite to the original valves. And, when this process has been completed, two distinct frustules are formed, the silicious valves in each being one of the valves of the parent-cell, and a newly secreted valve apposed to it. During the active life of the cell this process of self-division is continued, and is rapidly completed. On this subject Smith observes, " I have been unable to ascertain the time occupied in a single act of self-division; but, supposing it to be completed in twenty-four hours, we should have as the progeny of a single frustule the amazing number of one thousand millions in a single month—a circumstance which will, in some degree, explain the sudden, or, at least, rapid appearance of these organisms in localities where they were, but a short time previously, either unrecognised or sparingly diffused."—British Diatomaceæ, vol. i., p. 25.

It seems probable that the Diatomaceæ are sometimes reproduced by zoospores. Rabenhorst records his having observed a specimen of Melosira varians, in which, from the sporangial frustule, there issued what appeared to be germs, and has described the process. Die Susswasser Diatomaceen, T. x., fig. 18 c. A similar occurrence was noticed by myself in 1858, in the case of Pleurosigma Spencerii: and Castracane has recorded two or three observations of the same kind. So far as I am aware, the development of these zoospores, if such they be, has in no case been traced through its successive stages to its ultimate result; but there is nothing unreasonable in the presumption that the phenomenon may be a phase of the reproductive process.

Another mode of reproduction in the Diatomaceæ is by conjugation, of which, according to Smith, there are four distinct phases. First. The union of two parent frustules issues in the formation of two sporangia. Second. Two parent frustules produce only one sporangium. Third. A single frustule develops a single sporangium. Fourth. A single parent frustule produces two sporangia. In the first stage of the conjugative process, a mucous sac is secreted by the parent frustules, within which the sporangia are developed; these sporangia, in some cases, lie parallel, and in other species at an angle with the parent frustules or valves, as the case may be. A phase of conjugation, quite distinct from the four just referred to, came under my notice, many years ago, in the case of Diatoma vulgare.* I observed numerous instances of the long chain of concatenated frustules in their normal condition with a sudden jerk fold themselves into a solid mass. In a very brief period a mucous sac was seen to develop itself, inclosing the whole mass of frustules, and in some cases enveloping forms of a different species which happened to be in immediate proximity. By degrees the mucous sac pushed itself forward, sometimes in a single projection, sometimes in two, and into these prolongations the cell-contents of the

---

* Natural History Review, 1859, vol. vi., page 50, Pl. ix.

frustules were poured; the prolongations became gradually more and more constricted at the base, until ultimately they were completely cut off from the mucous sac, in which the frustules remained folded, in a state of perfect inanition. The process described was completed within the space of a few hours, so that in innumerable instances I was able to trace it from beginning to end—that is, from the commencement of conjugation up to the formation of the sporangia. Smith refers to cases of Cocconema cistula, and also of Synedra radians, having been found aggregated in great numbers and enclosed in mucous sacs similar to what has been described in the case of Diatoma vulgare; and all three cases seem to me to represent the same phase of conjugation: and I am disposed to think that, as in Diatoma vulgare, so in the other two cases, the encysted frustules were not, as Smith considered them, young frustules in course of development from a sporangium, but parent frustules preparing to produce sporangia.

Instances of conjugation in any of its varied forms are rarely to be met with. When Smith published his Synopsis, in 1856, cases had been observed in thirty species, included in seventeen distinct genera; and during the interval of fifteen years that had elapsed when Pfitzer published his work, "Uber Bau und Entwicklung der Bacillariaceen," only twenty-eight cases had been added to the list, exclusive of that of Diatoma vulgare, making a total of sixty-one. This remarkable fact Smith thus endeavours to account for: "During conjugation the process of self-division is arrested, the general mucous envelope or stratum produced during self-division is dissolved, and the conjugating pairs of frustules become detached from the original mass; they are thus more readily borne away and dispersed in the surrounding currents, or by the movements of worms or insects, and their detection becomes in consequence more casual and difficult." It is not improbable, however, that the mode of collecting, and the time that is often suffered to elapse before the collection is submitted to investigation, may have more to do with the fact. And, in confirmation of this view, I would mention that, although I have for very many years been engaged in the study of the Diatomaceæ, and have made innumerable collections at all seasons of the year, I have not been so fortunate in observing instances of conjugation as some friends whose collections have been made with a view to the discovery of other organisms. Their gatherings are usually made in large bottles containing a considerable quantity of water, by which the specimens may be preserved for a long time in their normal state—my gatherings being put up in minute bottles with little water, so that the vigour of the frustules is greatly abated before an opportunity of examining them may be afforded. As to the seasons of the year in which conjugation is most likely to occur, the facts hitherto accumulated do not afford much information. Besides the case of Diatome vulgare which I observed in conjugation in the month of August, seventy-two observations, with specification of date, have been recorded, making seventy-three in all. Of these, twenty-three occurred in spring, twenty in summer, twenty-four in autumn, and only six in winter. The paucity of such observations during the winter may, however, be traceable to the fact that then, in consequence of the inclemency of the weather, fewer gatherings are made, than because the process of conjugation is of less frequent occurrence during the season.

Classification.

In the various systems of classification, the several authors have treated the facts they had to arrange as Procrustes is said to have dealt with his guests : " Qui ad lectum hospites emensus breviores extendebat longiores decurtabat." How just this observation is will be obvious if we consider Pfitzer's fair criticisms on the anomalies of the systems of classification hitherto propounded. All systems are artificial; and when we consider the immensity and variety of Nature's productions, we cannot wonder if in every group some organisms will be found to exist which cannot, without violence, be reduced into the order proposed. Every plan of arrangement will be liable to objection; and that may be regarded as the best which is the most obvious, the most simple, the most comprehensive, and productive of the fewest anomalies.

Pfitzer considers that the imperfections of the existing systems are traceable to the fact that the ground-plan has been laid down on a single line, and as a remedy suggests a system of classification based on several concurrent lines, the principal of which are the character and number of the endochrome-plates, the structure of the sporangia, and the symmetrical or unsymmetrical form of the frustules in their several aspects. Upon these lines Pfitzer has skilfully constructed a most ingenious system of arrangement; but however great its merits as a philosophical abstraction, it appears to me liable to objection on practical grounds. The dislocation of analogous species chargeable on former systems, so far from being avoided, is scarcely, if at all, diminished by the proposed plan. Here we have the Nitzschieæ brought into close contact with the Naviculeæ; the symmetrical Synedriæ and the unsymmetrical Eunoticæ are placed side by side, and in near proximity to the Surirelleæ. The symmetrical Fragilarieæ are severed from the symmetrical Synedriæ, and associated with the unsymmetrical Meridieæ. The Tabellarieæ are separated from the Fragilarieæ and ranged with the Lichmophoreæ. The character of the endochrome-plates seems to me a condition of too recondite a nature to admit of practical application; besides, the induction of facts on the subject is, as yet, far too limited to justify its adoption. As to the reproductive process and its results, if our knowledge on the subject were sufficiently comprehensive, it would furnish most valuable help towards the construction of a satisfactory arrangement of the Diatomaceæ; but, unhappily, in the great dearth of authentic facts illustrative of the subject, we are not warranted in using the knowledge we have as a ground plan of a general systematic arrangement.

The reproductive process has not been observed in more than about sixty-five species, and in some of these cases there is a difference of opinion as to the facts. A system, therefore, in which this process constitutes an important part of the ground plan, is practically objectionable, as founded on hypothesis.

The system which appears to me to have most to recommend it is that which has been matured by Heiberg, founded on the symmetrical or unsymmetrical structure of the frustules in their various aspects. There are two principal aspects in which a diatomaceous frustule may be regarded—the front view, in which the hoop or connecting band is presented to the eye, and the side view, in which one or other of the two valves is under observation; and in both these positions the longitudinal and transverse axes are to be considered. If in these two positions, and in these varied views, exact symmetry obtains, the frustule is said to be symmetrical in all its aspects; but if the two opposite valves are not uniform, or the portions of the valves on either side of the transverse or longitudinal axis, on side view or front view, do not exhibit the same proportions or outline, the frustule is said to be unsymmetrical on that view or axis on which the difference of form is observable. Such is the ground plan of Heiberg's systematic arrangement, and which I have adopted in the present report. It is not, indeed, wholly free from the objections to which other systems are liable, and, possibly, may be open to others peculiarly its own; but still the principle on which the arrangement is based commends itself as being at once most simple, most comprehensive, and most easily applied.

There are, however, two very important yet subordinate features of Heiberg's system, in regard to which I cannot adopt the views of that distinguished author. He ranges the numerous Cuneate species as aberrant varieties of the families which in other respects they most closely resemble; for example, Meridion and Asterionella are associated with the Fragilarieæ, under the distinctive appellation of Fragilarieæ cuneatæ; Podosphenia with the Striatilleæ, as Striatilleæ cuneatæ; Gomphonema and Cocconeis with the Naviculeæ, as Naviculeæ cuneatæ; whereas I have collected the numerous species with a cuneate outline, under the one general group of Cuneatæ. Again, the numerous species of Diatomaceæ, as is well known, exhibit various normal phases of growth. Some species are normally free, others attached by a short gelatinous cushion, or a larger or shorter stipes; the frustules in some genera are simple, while in others, after self-division, they remain in concatenate or ribbon-like filaments; in some genera the frustules are naked, while in others they are enveloped in mucous fronds, of which some are indefinite, others definite, forming simple or composite tubes. These peculiarities of growth Heiberg treats as of little significance; and accordingly, the genera Schizonema, Berkleya, and Colletonema, the frustules of which are included in tubes; Dickiea, the frustules of which are imbedded in a less definite mucous mass; Diadesmis, the frustules of which are united in short filaments; and Brebissonia Boeckei = Doryphora Boeckei, in which the frustules are stipitate, are notwithstanding these peculiarities of growth included as species under the genus Navicula. If Smith and others attached too much value to these subordinate features, and therefore separated the forms which exhibited them very far from the Naviculeæ, with which, as regards the general structure of the frustules, they are intimately related, Heiberg, on the other hand, I consider, has made a mistake in ignoring these peculiarities altogether. Recognising these various normal modes of growth as generic distinctions, I have included the forms as separate genera of the group Naviculeæ.

On the Distribution of the Diatomaceæ.

Some species are found only in fresh water, some only in salt water, while others select as their normal habitat places in which salt and fresh water habitually or occasionally commingle. I have indeed frequently found fresh water species in the stomachs of Ascidians dredged from a considerable depth in the sea; but their occurrence therein indicates the influx of fresh water in the immediate neighbourhood. And when marine forms are found in fresh water, as occasionally they may be, they indicate that the place is within the range of tidal influence.

An experienced observer will be able at a glance to ascertain whether a gathering is marine, or made in fresh or brackish water; and not only so, but will be able to discriminate the lacustrine and alpine forms from those incidental to other situations.

It is not possible to ascertain for what period the life of the Diatomaceæ continues, but when their course, be it long or short, is ended, the silicious covering sinks into the sediment: and when in the process of ages the sediment is solidified into rock, the exuviæ of the Diatoms that lived in the water during the period of deposition continue unaltered in their stony shroud. If the rock be decomposed by natural or artificial agencies, they may be extracted, and subjected to inspection; and if found in sufficient number, the species discovered may serve to illustrate the circumstances under which the deposit was formed.

Irrespective of the variety and symmetrical beauty of the Diatomaceæ, there is another circumstance which invests them with a peculiar interest: it is this, that no existing organism, whether it be vegetable or animal, can boast of so ancient a lineage. Countless have been the genera and species of living beings which flourished during the several geological periods, and of which no representatives survived the vicissitude which brought their epoch to a conclusion; but so far back in the annals of the earth as research has been able to trace the Diatomaceæ, the species which have been discovered are identical with those we have living at the present time. Numerous are the fossil or subfossil diatomaceous deposits which have been discovered in all parts of the globe; some the accumulations of marine, others of fresh water growth. Among these latter, the Irish deposits of Lough Mourne, Lough Islandreavy, Toombe Bridge, and Tollymore Park, are distinguished for the number and beauty of the species they contain: and we are indebted to the industry and intelligence of Mr. Gray, of Belfast, for the discovery of several sub-peat collections in various parts of the country. Nearly all the species contained in these various deposits have been found living at the present day; and it is a noteworthy fact, that the forms of these numerous species, however remote from one another in time and space, exhibit no appreciable divergency. As an illustration I may mention a few facts. Through the kindness of Mr. Kitton, of Norwich, I was supplied with a sample of a fresh water deposit from California, which contained numerous specimens of Synedra amphirhynchus, in no respect differing from the specimens of the same species I had found living a few days before, in a ditch not far from my residence in the county Dublin. Another deposit discovered by Dr. Moss, R. N., at Vancouver's Island, was sent to me for examination; and in it, among many other well-known forms, I found in great number, specimens of Navicula Americana, in all respects identical with forms of that species collected by my friend the Rev. George Davidson, from a deposit at Lough Canmore, in the north of Scotland, and those I had myself gathered some time ago in a living state on the borders of Lough Neagh. Count Castracane is of opinion that Diatoms must have existed even in the remote ages of the Palæozoic period. It remains to be proved whether this was so or not; but in his researches in the lignite formation of Urbino he has traced existing species so far back as the earlier epoch of the Tertiary formation. The specimen of lignite examined by this distinguished Italian naturalist was furnished by Professor Mici, who considered it to belong unquestionably to the Miocene period. This result is confirmed by the statement of Pfitzer, that all the fresh water, as well as marine forms hitherto discovered in the deposits of the Tertiary period, belong to existing genera and species. The generations of a Diatom in the space of a few months far exceed in number the generations of man from the earliest time to the present day; and yet we find that the individuals now living retain without alteration the characteristics which distinguished the species at the remotest time to which their existence can be traced. It might be alleged in this case that the silicious valves within which the valves of successive generations are developed necessarily impress the characters of the parent on the offspring; and that, therefore, any tendency to variation, however powerfully it might operate, would be checked by the irresistible force of external pressure. But the sporangia before the soft skin has become solidified by the secretion of silex are of a more plastic character, and afford a facility for variation if the cell-contents were endowed with any such tendency. And although the formation of sporangia has been observed in but very few instances, yet the frequent recurrence of this process of reproduction is forced on our acceptance as a necessary inference from the fact of the continuous existence of numerous species, despite of the law which regulates their multiplication by the process of self-division. As in each successive act of fission the newly-formed valves are smaller than those within which they have been secreted, the species would soon become extinct, were there not a provision made for its perpetuation in the process of sporangial reproduction. All the circumstances considered, I am led to regard the Diatomaceæ as a group of organism on which the Creator has impressed certain distinctive characteristics from which, through countless, successive ages, they have shown no tendency to depart.

LIST OF SPECIES.

A. *Frustules symmetrical.* 1. *Valves circular.*

FAMILY I. MELOSIREÆ, Kütz.

Frustules simple, or adhering in filaments. Circular on side view.

This family, since the adoption of it by Kützing, has undergone considerable modification in respect to the genera included within it. If we omit the ill-defined genus Pyxidicula, the forms he embraced within it, with the exception of Cyclotella, belonged to those genera distinguished by the filamentous character of their growth. Kützing recognised the analogy between these genera and those of which Coscinodiscus may be regarded as the type, but placed them widely apart, principally on the ground of the areolate striation of the latter. This character, however, is by no means universal, and even if it were, could scarcely justify so great a dislocation. Grunow, therefore, who is followed by Heiberg, includes among the Melosireæ all the symmetrical forms circular on the side view, irrespectively of their peculiarities of striation; thus establishing a very distinct and well-defined group which I adopt—my only difficulty in doing so arising from the fact that in the genus Cyclotella, some of the included species are waved on the front view, and for this reason can scarcely be considered as symmetrical in all aspects, in the sense of Grunow and Heiberg.

Genus I. MELOSIRA, Agardh.

Frustules filamentous. Convex at the ends, filaments free.

Melosira borrerii, (Greville.) Marine or brackish water.

Valves sub-hemispherical; girdlebands marked with conspicuous circles of cellules; filaments varying in breadth; colour of the desiccated filaments, a rich brown. (Pl. 26, fig. 1.)

Greville, in Hooker's Brit. Flora,* p. 401. Wm. Sm. B. D., Vol. ii., p. 56; Pl. L., fig. 330. Heiberg, De Danske Diat., p. 28.—M. moniliformis, Kütz. Bac., p. 53, T. iii., fig. 2. Raben. Fl. Eur., p. 38. Ralfs, in Pritch., p. 817, Pl. v., fig. 71.

River Slaney, near Killurin, Co. Wexford. Brackish ditch near Wexford town. Malahide, Dollymount strand, Howth, Co. Dublin. Sea weeds, Giants' Causeway, Co. Antrim. Brackish ditch near the town of Wicklow. R. Nannywater, Laytown, Co. Meath.

Melosira subflexilis, (Kütz.) Fresh or brackish water.
Frustules usually narrow elongate, slightly inflexed upon the margin. (Pl. 26, fig. 2.)
Kütz. Bac., p. 53, T. ii., fig. 13. Wm. Sm., B.D., Vol. ii., p. 57, Pl. LI., fig. 331. Heiberg, De Danske Diat., p. 28. Rab. Fl. Eur., p. 39.

Considerable diversity of opinion exists as to the habitat of this species. According to Kützing it belongs to the fresh water forms, having been found by him in rapid brooks. "In schnell fliessenden Bächen." Bac., p. 54. Still more precisely does Rabenhorst assign to it a fresh water habitat. "Hab. in rivulis Sporadice per totam Europam e planitie usque in regionem montanam superiorem, Fl. Eur., p. 39. While Smith gives it either a fresh water or brackish locality, Heiberg makes it a marine species. His remarks are worthy of notice. "Smith attributes the authorship of this species to Kützing, but Kützing's figure can hardly be identified with certainty, and seems to be more properly referrible to Melosira varians. Kützing's Melosira Jurgensii more nearly resembles Smith's species, and so Pritchard accepts it. But Pritchard calls the species Melosira Jurgensii, and represents Melosira subflexilis Sm. as a synonym; but in any case this ought to be reversed, inasmuch as Smith was the first to define the species so that it could be identified with certainty." "Smith assigns it to fresh water, but as the localities mentioned are near the mouths of rivers, the species possibly has been borne out along with the floods." De Danske Diat., pp. 28, 29. In addition, I have only to say that the localities in which the species has been found by me in Ireland are marine, but still liable to the access of fresh water.

Lough Foyle, Bellarena, Co. Derry. Greystones, Co. Wicklow.

Melosira varians, (Agardh.) Fresh water.
Ends of the frustules not so convex as in the preceding species. Kütz. Bac., p. 54, T. ii., fig. 10. Rab. Die Süssw Diat., p. 13, T. ii., fig. 4. Wm. Sm. B.D., Vol. ii., p. 57, Pl. LI., fig. 332. Ralfs,

---

* For explanation of contractions and list of references, *vide* List at end of Report.

in Pritch., p. 817, Pl. xv., fig. 32. Heiberg, De Danske Diat., p. 27.—Gallionella varians, Ehr. Inf. T. x., fig. 4.

Very common in streams and fresh springs.

Melosira distans, (Kutz.) Fresh water.
Frustules short, but slightly convex at the ends, distinctly punctate. (Pl. 26, fig. 3.)
Kütz. Bac., p. 54, T. ii., fig. 12. Rab. Die Süssw Diat., p. 13, T. ii., fig. 9. Wm. Sm. B.D., Vol. ii., p. 58, Pl. LXI., fig. 385. Ralfs, in Pritch., p. 818.—Gallionella distans, Ehr. Inf., p. 170, T. xxi., fig. 4.

Smith describes this species as "obscurely cellulate," and distinguishes it on this ground from his Melosira nivalis, which he characterises as "distinctly cellulate," but remarks that "this character is probably insufficient to justify their separation." B.D., Vol. ii., p. 58. The forms occurring in the Bilin Polirschiefer, one of the localities assigned by Kützing to Melosira distans, are most distinctly punctate; I am therefore disposed to consider that Smith's species, Melosira nivalis, cannot be sustained.

Killikee, Dundrum, Co. Dublin. Kilcool, Co. Wicklow. Pond near Armagh.

Genus II. LYSIGONIUM, Link.

Frustules globose or cylindrical, valves furnished with an elevated keel which runs parallel with the sutures; in other particulars as in Melosira.

I have adopted this genus in deference to the authority of Heiberg, who, referring to Lysigonium nummuloides, remarks, "This species, which by all the more recent authors has been assigned to the genus Melosira, in my judgment ought to constitute a type of a new genus to which Melosira Westii Wm. Sm., which does not occur in our country, may also be referred. The name Lysigonium was in the first instance applied by Link. to O. F. Muller's Conferva moniliformis, with which in all probability this species is identical; and for this reason it seems most convenient to re-establish the genus to receive it." De Danske Diat., p. 29. Heiberg further remarks, "that the known species form shorter or longer filaments, attached or free;" but I have never seen any of the filaments attached.

Lysigonium nummuloides, (Lyngbye, Kütz.) Marine.
Ordinary frustules, globose. Keel thin, in front view appearing as lines projecting like horns. (Pl. 26, fig. 4.)
Heiberg, De Danske Diat., p. 29.—Melosira nummuloides, Kütz.

Bac., p. 52, T. iii., fig. 3. Wm. Sm., B. D., Vol. ii., p. 55. Pl. xlix., fig. 329. Ralfs, in Pritch., p. 816, Pl. v., fig. 64 and Pl. xi., fig. 14.

There is considerable difference of opinion as to the founder of this species; Smith assigns it to Kützing, Ralfs to Dillwyn and Agardh. On this subject Heiberg says, " As above mentioned, O. F. Muller was probably the first to discover this species, and describe it under the name of Conferva moniliformis, or strand-necklace, but that cannot be ascertained with certainty. The present specific name is attributable to Dillwyn, who in 1809 described a Conferva nummuloides, which Lyngbye cites as a synonym under his Fragillaria nummuloides. But as meanwhile there do not appear to be any original specimens of Dillwyn's species, and his figures can only be approximately identified, while the numerous specimens of Lyngbye which still exist are all attributable to our species, it seems most proper to name Lyngbye as the author." De Danske Diat., p. 29.

Brackish ditch near Wexford, Malahide, Dollymount, Northwall, Co. Dublin. Salt ditch near Wicklow, and many other places too numerous to mention.

Lysigonium Westii, (Wm. Sm.) Marine.
Frustules somewhat conical, furnished with two keels, one at the suture, another near the end, considerably thicker than the similar structure in Lys. nummuloides, and not projecting upwards to the same extent.

Melosira Westii, Wm. Sm., B. D., Vol. ii., p. 59, Pl. lii., fig. 333. Ralfs, in Pritch., p. 817. Rab. Fl. Eur., p. 38.

Dollymount, Oyster beds, Howth, Co. Dublin. Near Wicklow. Stomachs of Ascidians, Roundstone Bay, Co. Galway.

Lysigonium Wrightii, (O'Meara.) Marine.
Frustules rounded at the ends, narrow, surrounded by a broad keel, which curving slightly outwards and upwards, then bending inwards and downwards to the surface of the valve, forms round it a crown-like rim. In the front view two nodules are observable in the central portion of the valve; the frustule is perfectly hyaline, without sculpture of any kind.

O'Meara, Q. J. M. S., Vol. ix., Pl. xii., fig. 3.

Arran Islands, Co. Galway.

Genus III. PODOSIRA, Ehr.

Filaments attached by a distinct stipes, and generally short, consisting of a few frustules.

Heiberg regards the character on which this genus is founded as "wholly destitute of a scientific basis." De Dansko Diat., p. 27. Most other authors have, however, decided in favour of its validity. Smith's supposition that the apices of the valves are destitute of silex, with Heiberg and Ralfs, I consider is founded on imperfect observation.

Podosira Montagnei, (Kütz.) Marine.
Filaments usually consisting of two frustules. Frustules large, cylindrical, globose at the ends. (Pl. 26, fig. 5.)
Kütz. Bac., 52, T. xxix., fig. 85. Wm. Sm. B. D., Vol. ii., p. 53, Pl. xlix., fig. 326. Ralfs, in Pritch., p. 815, Pl. v., fig. 61. Rab. Fl. Eur., p. 37.

Arran Islands, Co. Galway.

Podosira hormoides, (Kütz.) Montagne. Marine.
Frustules small, compressed. Valve with distinct umbilicus, obscurely punctate.
Smith and Ralfs attribute the species to Kutzing; Heiberg, and Rabenhorst, Fl. Eur., to Montagne.
Kütz. Bac., p. 52, T. xxviii., fig. 5, and T. xxix., fig. 84. Wm. Sm., B. D., Vol. ii., p. 53, Pl. xlix., fig. 327. Ralfs, in Pritch., p. 815, Pl. ii., fig. 45. Rab. Fl. Eur., p. 37.—Melosira hormoides, Heiberg, De Danske Diat., p. 29.—Podosira nummuloides, Ehr.

Bannow, Co. Wexford. Salt ditch, near Wexford. Malahide. Piles on Strand, Clontarf, Co. Dublin.

Podosira maculata, (Wm. Sm.) Marine.
Frustules globose, distinctly punctate; puncta divided by radiate bands of a deeper colour, which latter do not reach the centre. Valves having a distinct umbilicus. (Pl. 26, fig. 5a.)
Wm. Sm., B. D., Vol. ii., p. 54, Pl. xlix., fig. 328. Ralfs, in Pritch., p. 815. Rab. Fl. Eur., p. 37.

Sea weeds, Bannow. Salt ditch, near Wexford. Arran Islands, Stomachs of Ascidians, Roundstone Bay, Co. Galway.

Genus IV. ORTHOSIRA, Thwaites.

Frustules attached in filaments; without stipes, plane on the side view, ornamented with a circlet of puncta parallel with the suture; junction surfaces spinous.

The genus Orthosira was originally established by Thwaites, for the purpose of distinguishing the filamentous species with level end surfaces from those included in Melosira, the end surfaces of which are more or less arched, and thus defined it has been adopted by most succeeding authors. Ralfs and Rabenhorst, however, abandoning the generic distinction, have relegated the several species of Orthosira to the genus Melosira. Heiberg, on the contrary, recognises the distinction of Thwaites, but includes the species of Cyclotella in the genus Orthosira, and establishes a new genus, Paralia, to receive the single species Orthosira marina (Wm. Sm.), on the ground that the frustule possesses an elevated keel similar to that which characterises the genus Lysigonium. It is a question, then, whether the distinction of Thwaites should be recognised, as most authors since his time have done, or discarded, as Rabenhorst has considered it ought to be; and the following observations of Pfitzer seem to supply a reasonable solution. Having referred to the original distinction, he adds, "A far more important distinction exists in the mode of developing Auxospores. Although the Orthosiræ in their mode of growth agree thoroughly with Melosira, have the same structure of the primordial cell, and the same mode of cell-division, they differ in this respect, that in the process of spore-formation from a single cell, the valves of which are pushed away from one another, the contents enveloped in a mucous investment come out free, and are then, without being in contact with the mother-cell, developed into a single Auxospore in which the firstling cell is so situated that the plane of division crosses that of the mother-cell, whereas in Melosira it is parallel to it. Thwaites had observed this feature in the case of Orthosira aurichalcea, and Smith refers to the peculiarity as an important generic distinction. But only one species had been observed in this aspect, and so it was questionable whether all the Orthosiræ obeyed the same law. Fr. Schmitz has succeeded in proving this in respect to another species, Orthosira roeseana (Rab.), = O. spinosa (Grev.)." Ueber Bau und Entwicklung der Bac., p. 134. If then the mode of developing Auxospores be regarded, as I consider it ought to be, of importance as a generic distinction, the conclusion is inevitable that the genus Orthosira should not be merged in Melosira, as Ralfs and Rabenhorst have treated it. And also, forasmuch as in those species of Cyclotella in which the formation of Auxospores has been noticed, the daughter-cell is parallel to the mother-cell, for this reason, as well as on the old ground of distinction, the species of Cyclotella should not with Heiberg be included in the genus Orthosira.

Orthosira arenaria, (D. Moore.) Fresh water.
Frustules very large; cell-cavity sub-spherical. Spines on juncture surfaces short, broad, and close. Striæ, on side view punctate, radiate, stronger at the margin, and loosing their radiate arrangement as they approach the centre. Striæ on front view punctate, transverse. (Pl. 26, fig. 6.)
Wm. Sm., B. D., Vol. ii., p. 59, Pl. lii., fig. 334. Heiberg, De Danske Diat., p. 31. Ralfs, in Ann. N. Hist., Vol. xii., p. 349, Pl. ix., fig. 4.—Melosira arenaria, Kütz. Bac., p. 55, T. xxi., fig. 27. Rab. Süssw. Diat., p. 14, T. ii., fig. 5.

Besides the localities specified by Smith, namely, near Belfast and Lough Mourne deposit, I have found the species in the following places :—River Erne, Crossdoney, Co. Cavan; ditch near Wexford; Vernor's-bridge, Co. Armagh; Killakee, Co. Dublin; stream near Kilcool, Co. Wicklow; L. Neagh, near the town of Antrim; surface of rock near Glenarm, Co. Antrim.

Orthosira sulcata, (Ehr. Kütz.)   Marine.
Spines of junction surfaces large, short, and more distant than in the former species. Striæ on side view linear, radiate, distinct at the margin, attenuated towards the centre, which they do not reach; puncta at the suture large; striæ on front view linear, direct, parallel (Pl. 26, fig. 7.)

Melosira sulcata, Kütz. Bac., p. 55, T. ii., fig. 57. Ralfs, in Pritch., p. 819; Pl. ix., fig. 131; Plate xi., fig. 26. Rab. Fl. Eur. p. 41.—Orthosira marina, Wm. Sm., B. D., Vol. ii., p. 59; Pl. liii., fig. 338.—Gallionella sulcata, Ehr.—Paralia marina, Heiberg, De Danske Diat., p. 33.

Although this species has been described and figured by Kützing as identical with Gallionella sulcata of Ehrenberg, Heiberg attributes it to Wm. Smith. The latter indeed has figured it more perfectly than Kützing has done; still, Kützing's figure, imperfect as it is, seems to me unmistakable; and all uncertainty as to the species indicated is removed by his reference to the Richmond deposit in which the form abounds. For this reason I have followed Ralfs and Rabenhorst in assigning the species to Ehrenberg and Kützing, as well as restoring the original specific designation. And as I have not been able to trace any keel similar in structure and position to that of Lysigonium, instead of adopting Heiberg's new genus, Paralia, I leave the species where Smith placed it in the present genus.

Cork and Kinsale Harbours, Wm. Smith. Bannow, River Slaney, Killurin, Co. Wexford. Near Wicklow. Malahide. Dalkey, Co. Dublin.

Orthosira Dickieii, (Thwaites.)   Fresh water.
Cell-cavity sub-spherical. Sutural puncta small and distant. Spines on junction surfaces absent. Striæ, both on front and side view, minutely punctate. Puncta on front view arranged in lines parallel to the suture.

Thwaites, Ann. N. H., 2 series, Vol. i., p. 168, Pl. xii. Wm. Sm., B.D.,Vol. ii.,p. 60, Pl.liii., fig.335.—Melosira Dickieii, Kütz. Sp. Alg., p. 889. Ralfs, in Pritch., p. 820, Pl. xv., fig. 29. Rab. Fl. Eur., p. 43.

This species is remarkable for the abnormal growth of frustule within frustule, so fully described by Smith, B. D., Vol. ii., Pl. lii., fig. 335. Thwaites regarded this peculiarity as a mode of developing sporangia, while Smith considered it an abnormal development similar to what he had noticed in Meridion circulare and M. constrictum, Himantidium Soleirolii, Odontidium anomalum, and Achnanthes subsessilis. I add the interesting description given by Pfitzer of an anomalous procedure noticed by Fr. Schmitz in the development of Orthosira spinosa, as likely to throw some light on the subject. " A separation of the firstling-cell followed, not immediately, but a deviation occurred analogous to what has been described in the case of Navicula ambigua. First one girdleband was developed, the length of which was about that of the radius of the cell. This girdleband, according to Fr. Schmitz, was attached only to one valve; that which ought to have been connected with the other valve, if it existed at all, was only rudimentary. Then the plasm moved about only in that half of the cell to which the girdleband adhered, and secreted a new valve, which, as might be expected, was parallel to the original one destitute of the girdleband. In the cell so originating, division then took place in the normal manner, only that the one end-cell of the filament in course of formation, instead of two valves possessed three. Inasmuch as a small portion of the plasm remained behind, between the two parallel valves, and then died off, Fr. Schmitz was inclined to think the procedure was an abortive attempt at self-division, one portion of the plasm being too small to develop itself into a daughter-cell." Ueber Bau und Entwicklung der Bac., p. 135.

Ditch on bank of Royal Canal, near Kilcock, Co. Kildare. It is likely this species is more common than it appears from the few localities assigned to it, as in its normal condition it may be easily confounded with Melosira varians.

Orthosira orichalcea, (Wm. Sm.) Freshwater.
The circle of puncta that in most of the species of this genus runs parallel with the suture is not observable in this. Spines on junction surfaces distinct ; valve not striated on the side view, except on the margin, where the points of the spines appear as small puncta. Frustules striated on front view. Striæ fine, punctate, parallel. (Pl. 26, fig. 8.)

Ralfs and Rabenhorst have referred this species to Mertens on the authority of Kützing, who has figured and described a form under this specific designation. The figure of Melosira orichalcea, Bac., T. ii., fig. 14, is by no means definite, and one feature in the description suggests the impression that he had quite a different species in view. " Sub epidermide silicea leviter bis contractis," Bac. p. 54, may possibly refer to Orthosira spinosa, but not to Orthosira orichalcea, as figured by Smith, to whom Heiberg considers the species should be attributed, as he was the first to give a description and figure by which it could be satisfactorily identified. Heiberg makes the following shrewd observation under Orthosira orichalcea :—" The figure by which Smith describes the process of conjugation in the species under consideration, and which he copied from Thwaites' original delineation, deviates so much from the normal appearance of the species, that one may almost take it for certain that it represents a very different form, for a difference of so much importance could scarcely have arisen from inadvertence."—De Dansko Diat., p. 31. In Thwaites' original description of Aulocoseira crenulata, Kütz. = Melosira orichalcea, Ralfs (and Orthosira orichalcea, Wm. Sm.), both the generic definition and the figure are inapplicable to the present species as figured by Smith. "*Aulacoseira* cellulis cylindricis, *bisulcatis*, extremitatibus plus minusve rotundatis, in filamenta concatenatis." Ann. of Nat. Hist. March, 1848, p. 7, most correctly describes Orthosira Roeseana, Rab. = O. spinosa (Wm. Sm.). The frustules, as described ib. Pl. xi., B., figs. 1, 2, and 3, are greatly more like that form than any other species, and the side view, as represented in the sporangial frustule, is precisely as the side view of that species is described by Smith, B. D., Vol. ii., p. 62, Pl. lxi., fig. 386. I am therefore disposed to think that it was not Orthosira orichalcea, but Orthosira Roeseana, which Thwaites observed in the process of forming sporangia, or, as Pfitzer designates them, Auxospores.

Smith's Irish localities are—Well at Seven Churches; Clonmacnoise; Moanarone, County Cork; Lough Mourne deposit; to which I have to add the following:—River Erne, Crossdoney, County Cavan; Lough Islandreavy, County Down; Lough Neagh, near the town of Lurgan, County Armagh; Killakee and Glenchree, County Dublin.

Orthosira punctata, (Wm. Sm.) Fresh water.
This species is distinguished from the preceding chiefly by the fact that in this the puncta are very much larger, and more regularly arranged; they are parallel to the suture, and so regularly placed that they sometimes appear to run spirally. Heiberg remarks that "Smith's species is easily recognised by the obvious rows of puncta crossing one another, which run in oblique spirals from the suture up to and over the side view."—De Danske Diat. p. 31. These last words seem to imply that the side view is punctate like the front view; if so, then the species must be regarded as certainly distinct from the preceding. Smith does not figure the side view, and, in consequence of the length of the frustule, it is difficult to turn it over so as to get it under observation. In one case only could I get a view of it, and then only obliquely; in this aspect it appeared strongly punctate. The circle of spines at the suture is absent in this species as in the last.

Ralfs, in Pritchard, p. 820, makes this species synonymous with Melosira granulata = Gallionella granulata, Ehr. and Rabenhorst, Fl. Eur., p. 43, adopts the same course; but so much uncertainty characterises Ehrenberg's figures of that species, I prefer, with Heiberg, to adopt the precise figure of Smith, and attribute the species to him.

Ulster Canal, near Poyntzpass. Lough Neagh, near Lurgan, County Armagh.

Orthosira Roeseana, (Rab.) Fresh water.

Inner surface of cell sub-spherical; frustule sulcate on either side of suture; spines at the junction surfaces very distinct and long; circlet of puncta parallel with suture absent. Striæ on side view radiate, distinct, with three large puncta placed triangularly at the centre. On front view striæ finely punctate, and parallel with suture. (Pl. 26, fig. 9.)

Smith, in 1856, describes this species as new, under the name of Orthosira spinosa. Wm. Sm., B. D., Vol. ii., p. 62, Pl. lxii., fig. 386. But it had been already described by Rabenhorst, Süssw. Diat., p. 13, T. x., fig. 5, in 1853, as Melosira Roeseana, and with sufficient accuracy, both as respects the figure and the description, as to render identification certain. Melosira Roeseana, Ralfs, in Pritch., p. 818, Pl. v., fig. 67.

Killakee, County Dublin. Ulster Canal, near Poyntzpass. Lough Neagh, near Lurgan, County Armagh. Ditch at side of Royal Canal, near Kilcock, County Kildare.

Genus V. CYCLOTELLA, Kütz.

Frustules normally single, narrow; sometimes slightly waved on the front view; on the side view having the valves more or less distinctly divided into two concentric portions.

It is extremely difficult to define this genus by words so precisely as to distinguish it with certainty from others nearly allied; yet still the forms included within it constitute a tolerably distinct group. So much so, that almost all authors have agreed to mark their peculiarity by a distictive generic name.

Heiberg and Cleve have included the several species under the genus Orthosira, with which they are closely allied; but I consider them entitled to stand by themselves, not only on account of their different modes of growth, but also on account of the distinctive characters of their sporangia.

It would appear at first view that the generic name Discoplea should, on account of its priority, be preferred to the more recent name of Cyclotella. As Ehrenberg has given no verbal diagnosis of his genus Discoplea, we have no means of ascertaining its characteristics, otherwise than by the figures, and in these no sufficiently distinctive feature is discernible. Not only are forms that seem to belong to different species included under the same specific name, but more than this, species belonging to Orthosira, on the one hand, and more closely resembling Coscinodiscus, on the other, are included in the genus Discoplea. Kützing's diagnosis of his genus Cyclotella, although sufficient to distingush it from Orthosira, on the one hand, is not clear enough, so far as words are concerned, to prevent confusion with Coscinodiscus, on the other. Yet his figures, however obscure in minute details of structure, distinctly mark the separation of the valves into two well-defined concentric parts.

Walker-Arnott confounded the distinction between this genus and Orthosira, when he identified Cyclotella dallasiana with the Cyclotella radiata of Brightwell, which should rather be included in Orthosira. There is great confusion as to the synonomy of the several species; nor is this surprising, as the earlier descriptions and figures are by no means satisfactory; and, in order to avoid consequent perplexity, I consider there is no more satisfactory plan than to follow the line marked out by the figures of Wm. Smith, which are so distinct as to be easily recognised.

Cyclotella Kützingiana, (Thwaites.) Fresh water.
Frustules undulate; striæ delicate, marginal, scarcely one half of the radius in length; the central portion of the valve unstriate. (Pl. 26, fig. 10.)

Smith attributes this species to fresh or brackish water, and with this opinion Rabenhorst concurs. Walker-Arnott alleges he has never seen the true species from fresh water. Cleve makes it an essentially brackish water species, and Heiberg on the contrary, a fresh water form. This difference of opinion may arise from mistake as to identity; but speaking of the form described by Smith as C. Kützingiana, I have to say that though I have sometimes found it in water slightly brackish, it has been commonly discovered by me in localities far remote from marine influences, so that I think it is to be considered an essentially fresh water species.

The slightly undulate outline which this species presents on the front view may possibly arise from the sinking in of the valve in the centre, and the consequent projection of the outline of the dip upon the plane of observation. Thus Wm. Smith accounts for the appearance, and his opinion on the subject is supported by that of Heiberg.

Wm. Sm., B.D., Vol. i., p. 27, Pl. v., fig. 47. Raben. Fl. Eur., p. 32.—Orthosira Kützingiana, Heib. De Danske Diat., p. 31.

Stream, Crossdoney, Co. Cavan. Stream near Larne, Co. Antrim. Tacumshane, Co. Wexford. Ditch on banks of River Liffey, Co. Kildare, near Ballymore Eustace. Tarbert, Co. Kerry. Ditch, Kilcool, Co. Wicklow.

Cyclotella Meneghiniana, (Kütz.) Fresh water.
Frustules not undulate on the front view; striæ on the valves much coarser than in the former species, more distant, and considerably longer. (Pl. 26, fig. 11.)

Walker-Arnott regards this species as identical with C. rectangula, De Bréb, and the greater weight attaches to his opinion as it was adopted after examination of specimens "from De Brébisson himself,

and a portion of the only gathering he ever made of it (near Paris.)" Q. J. M. S., Oct., 1860, p. 245. Subsequently De Brèbisson found the same form at Falaise, and gave a figure of it which is confirmatory of the opinion of Walker-Arnott. "Notes on some French Diatomaceæ," Journal of Queckett Mic. Club for April, 1870, fig. 6. Kützing states that this species is adnate. I have never seen it so.
Kütz. Bac., p. 50, T. xxx., fig. 68. Rab. Süssw. Diat., p. 11. T. ii., fig. 2. Possibly this species may be identical with C. Kützingiana, var. B. Wm. Sm., B. D., Vol. i., p. 27; and if so, it is not the same that Ralfs has figured as C. rectangula (De Brèb.) Ralfs, in Pritch., Pl. v., fig. 54; the latter being undulate on the front view, whereas the present species is rectangular.

Lucan. Feather-bed mountain, Co. Dublin. Kilcool, Co. Wicklow.

Cyclotella operculata, (Kütz.) Fresh water.
Marginal striæ short, fine, linear; central part of valve covered with distinct moniliform striæ radiately arranged. (Pl. 26, fig. 12.)
Though Smith, who is followed by Ralfs, describes the striæ in this species as obscure and very short, the figure in both cases is too clear to admit of any doubt as to identification.
Kütz. Bac., p. 50, T. i., figs. 1, 12, and 15. Wm. Sm., B.D., Vol. i., Pl. v., fig. 48. Ralfs, in Pritch., p. 811, Pl. v., fig. 53.— Orthosira operculata, Heiberg, De Danske Diat., p. 32. Cleve, Om Svenska och Norska Diat., p. 217. This form is not identical with that described by Walker-Arnott under this name, with the centre destitute of striæ, but probably is the same as the variety he identifies with C. minutula, Kütz. See Arnott on Cyclotella, Q. J. M. S. for Oct., 1860, pp. 246, 247.

Lower Lake, Killarney, Co. Kerry. Derrylane Lake, Co. Cavan. Glenchree, Co. Wicklow. River Bann, near Coleraine, Co. Derry. River Erne, Crossdoney, Co. Cavan. Royal Canal, Enfield, Co. Meath. Lough Neagh, near Lurgan, Co. Armagh. Lough Mourne deposit. Lough Island-Reavy deposit, found also living in the same place.

Cyclotella operculata, var. Fresh water.
Margin of valve fringed with short rounded distinct costæ, over which there is a circle of very fine linear striæ, short; centre of the valve as in the former, but the moniliform striæ much finer and more obscure. (Pl. 26, fig. 12, b.)
On banks of the Liffey, near Ballymore Eustace, Co. Kildare. Lough Neagh, near Lurgan, Co. Armagh.

Cyclotella antiqua, (Wm. Sm.) Fresh water.
Marginal portion of the valve narrow, marked with short, broad, triangularly formed bars, over which there is a circlet of very fine short linear striæ; central portion occupied by about nine triangular bars which do not reach the centre. (Pl. 26, fig. 13.)

Smith does not figure the fine marginal striæ, and describes the marginal triangular bars as if they were moniliform; but with this exception his figure is in every respect accurate, so as to remove all doubt as to the identity of the species. Walker-Arnott considers that Smith's form is identical with C. minutula, Kütz., found by him in the Lüneburg deposit, and adds, "It is this which Smith obtained from the Lough Mourne deposit, but which he has unfortunately referred to C. antiqua, a species which does not occur in any of the Irish deposits which I have examined." On Cyclotella, Q. J. M. S., Oct., 1860, p. 246. The forms of Cyclotella found on the only slide I possess from the Lüneburg deposit are those of C. operculata. Walker-Arnott evidently had not seen any specimen of C. antiqua, for the distinctiveness of the species is too obvious to have escaped his keen observation, had even a single form of it come under his notice.

Wm. Sm., B. D., Vol. i., p. 28; Pl. v., fig. 49. Ralfs, in Pritch., p. 812. Rab. Fl. Eur., p. 33.

Lough Mourne deposit, in which I have occasionally noticed it. Sub-peat deposit, Dromore, Strangford Peat, Co. Down.

Cyclotella rotula, (Kütz.) Fresh water.

Valve with a slight depression towards the centre, striæ radiate, running from the margin to the centre; coarse at the margin, finer and finer as they approach the centre, where they appear confused. Striæ linear, but notched, so as to seem moniliform. (Pl. 26, fig. 14.)

In consequence of supposing that Discoplea rotula of Ehr., Mic., T. xxxv. A. xxii., fig. 67, was a species of Cyclotella, Kützing, in his Species Algarum, changed his original specific name to that of Cyclotella astræa, and this nomenclature has been adopted by Ralfs and Rabenhorst. It is not, however, certain that Ehrenberg's form properly belongs to Cyclotella, and therefore the original name ought to be retained.

Kütz. Bac., p. 50, T. ii., fig. 4. W. Sm., B. D., Vol. i. p. 28; Pl. v., fig. 50. Walker-Arnott, Q. J. M. S., Oct., 1860, p. 247.—Cyclotella astræa, Ralfs, in Pritch., p. 812. Rab. Fl. Eur., p. 34.—Orthosira rotula, Heiberg, De Danske Diat., p. 32. Cleve, Om Svenska och Norska, Diat., p. 217.

Lough Neagh, in several parts. Lucan, Feather-bed mountain, and Grand Canal, Co. Dublin. River Bann, near Coleraine, Co. Derry. Lough Mourne and Lough Island-Reavey deposits. Small forms of this species may be, at first view, readily mistaken for Cyclotella operculata, but on close inspection the difference will be obvious.

Cyclotella papillosa, (N. S.) Fresh water.

Marginal striæ of the valve linear, very fine, central portions unstriate and occupied by a circlet of papillæ, usually five or six in number. (Pl. 26, fig. 15.)

There is a form resembling the present, described by Ehrenberg as Discoplea atmospherica, from Nepal, Mic., T. xxxii. v., fig. 4; and also from Fayoom, Egypt, Mic., T. xxxii. i., fig. 3; but as the figures of Discoplea atmospherica differ so widely from one another, even if there were no doubt as to the identity, a different name is needful to mark the peculiarity of the present species.

Lough Neagh, near Lurgan, Co. Armagh. Lough Mask, near Tourmakeady, Co. Mayo. There is a form occurring in the Lough Mourne deposit, which may be the same as this, but the papillæ are usually injured, and, judging from the traces that remain, they seem to have been more numerous, more slender, and more scattered than in the living forms.

Cyclotella Scotica, (Kütz.) Marine.
Valve very small, finely striate on the margin; the centre unstriate. Kütz.
Bac., p. 50, T. i., figs. 2 and 3. Ralfs, in Pritch., p. 811. Pl. xiv., fig. 17. (Pl. 26, fig. 16.)
On sea-weeds at the Giants' Causeway, Co. Antrim. Kützing and Ralfs describe this species as adnate, but as my specimens had been treated with acid before observation, I cannot confirm this character.

Cyclotella dallasiana, (W. Sm.) Marine.
Margin of the valve coarsely striate; central part rugose, as if blistered. Smith represents the central part as " cellulate ;" but Walker-Arnott has more accurately described it as " puckered, or as if blistered."
Wm. Sm., B. D., Vol. ii., p. 87. Walker-Arnott, Q. J. M. S, Oct., 1860, p. 245. Ralfs, in Pritch., p. 813. Rab. Fl. Eur., p. 33.

Stomachs of Ascidians. Roundstone Bay, Co. Galway.

Cyclotella punctata, (Wm. Sm.) Fresh water.
Frustules undulate on front view; on side view, striæ close, radiate, very finely punctate, puncta smaller towards the margin, which latter is surrounded by a circlet of short, fine costæ. (Pl. 26; fig. 17.)
Wm. Sm., B. D., Vol. ii., p. 87. Ralfs, in Pritch., p. 813. Pl. viii., fig. 13. Rab. Fl. Eur., p. 33.

Lough Island-Reavey, Co. Down. Float bog, Co. Westmeath.

Genus VI. COSCINODISCUS, Ehr.

Frustules simple, free, lenticular; valve generally uniformly striate. Striæ areolate or moniliform. Without processes or undulations.

Kützing noticed the close affinity between Melosira and the present genus, but in his classification placed them very widely apart, simply because in the latter the striation was, as he describes it, areolate. But subsequent writers found this distinction untenable, inasmuch as in Creswellia, connected with Melosira by the filamentous character of its frustules, the striation is distinctly areolate, while in some of the species which are properly included in the genus Coscinodiscus the areolate character disappears.

Heiberg is dissatisfied with the diagnoses which preceding authors have given, but in consequence of the limited amount of material for observation at his command, declines to attempt a more satisfactory definition. It appears to me that if Coscinodiscus excentricus, which is described as having a spinous or dentate margin, be excluded, we shall then have a tolerably well-marked group, as above defined.

(a) *Disk with a central rosette.*

Coscinodiscus oculus iridis, (Ehr.) Marine.
Central rosette, consisting of from six to nine large oblong cellules. Cellules large, hexagonal, radiate, distinctly smaller as they approach the margin. (Pl. 26, fig. 18.)
Ehr. Mic., T. xviii., fig. 49. Ralfs, in Pritch., p. 828. Raben. Fl. Eur., p. 34. Heiberg, De Danske Diat., p. 35. Cleve, Om Svenska och Norska Diat., p. 217.

Tide pool, Monkstown; on sea-weeds, Ballybrack; tide pool, Dalkey; Oyster-shells, Dublin Bay, all in the County Dublin.

Coscinodiscus centralis, (Ehr.) Marine.
Central rosette consisting of about eight large rounded cellules surrounding a single central one. Cellules distinctly hexagonal, radiate, nearly equal, and smaller than in the former species. (Pl. 26, fig. 19.)
Ehr. Mic., T. xviii., fig. 39. Greg. Diat. of Clyde. p. 28, Pl. xi., fig. 49. Ralfs, in Pritch., p. 828. If Gregory describes and figures with accuracy the form so named, and found by him in Glenshira Sand, as well as in the Clyde, it can scarcely be identical with the present species. The only difference, however, is in the character of the cellules forming the central rosette, which, in his form, consists of "three large oblong cells meeting in a point, and between these, a little farther from the centre, three more cells, a little smaller." Ralfs, however, as above cited, describes this portion of the valve as consisting of "a few oblong cellules, round a circular one;" which description accurately represents the appearance of the rosette in the present form, and therefore I adopt the specific name.

On sea-weeds, Ballybrack, Dalkey, Co. Dublin. Stomachs of Ascidians, Belfast Lough.

Coscinodiscus stellaris, (Roper.) Marine.
Central rosette, consisting of five or six long and narrow cellules; striæ extremely minute, punctate, radiate.
Roper, Q. J. M. S., Vol. vi., p. 21, Pl. iii., fig. 3. Ralfs, in Pritch., 828, Pl. v., fig. 83.
Oyster Shells, Dublin Bay.

Coscinodiscus concinnus, (Wm. Sm.) Marine.
Central rosette, consisting of from three to eight large flattened cellules. Cellules small, radiate; valve divided into compartments by radiating lines, which do not reach the margin.
Wm. Sm., B. D., Vol. ii., p. 84. Roper, Q. J. M. S., Vol. vi., p. 20, Pl. iii., fig. 12. Ralfs, in Pritch., p. 828. Roper, as above cited, states that "the larger specimens show plainly a point that is not easily discernible in those under ·004″ in. diameter, namely a submarginal row of minute spines, varying from $\frac{1}{5000}$th to $\frac{1}{1000}$th of an inch apart, according to the size of the disk, and from each of which there is a radiating line almost to the centre of the valve." I have, in consequence, considerable hesitation in including the species under the genus Coscinodiscus; but, as the specimens that came under my notice were few in number, and in every case imperfect, I would not presume to make any change in the position to which it has been assigned.

It was found by Wm. Sm. in Kinsale Bay, and fragments have occurred on sea-weeds, Ballybrack, and on oyster-shells from Dublin Bay, both in the County Dublin.

(b). *Disk with a central hyaline space like a perforation.*

Coscinodiscus perforatus, (Ehr.) Marine.
Hyaline centre, small, surrounded by about five rounded cellules. Cellules large, indistinctly hexagonal, radiate, decreasing in size near the margin. (Pl. 26, fig 20.)
Smith describes the cellules as "equal," and Ralfs as "minute;" but in my specimens they differ as stated above.
Ehr. Mic., T. xviii., fig. 46. Wm. Sm., B. D., Vol. ii., p. 85. Ralfs, in Pritch., p. 829.

From stomachs of Howth Oysters, Tide-pool, Monkstown, Dalkey, Ballybrack; on Oyster shells, Dublin Bay. Stomachs of Ascidians, Belfast Bay.

(c). *Disk without a central rosette or vacant space. Cellules radiate.*

Coscinodiscus gigas, (Ehr.) Marine.
Disk very large, cellules not very large, hexagonal, radiate, smaller towards the centre. (Pl. 26, fig. 21).
Ehr. Mic., T. xviii., fig. 34. Kütz. Bac., p. 132, T. i., fig. 16.

Stomachs of Ascidians, dredged on the coast of County Clare.

Coscinodiscus radiatus, (Ehr.) Marine.

Cellules large, hexagonal, radiate, somewhat smaller near the margin.

Ehr. Mic., T. xx., fig. 1. Kütz. Bac., p. 132, T. i., fig. 18. Wm. Sm., B. D., Vol. i., p. 23, Pl. iii., fig. 37. Ralfs, in Pritch., p. 830, Pl. xi., figs. 39 and 40. Heiberg, De Danske Diat., p. 36. Cleve, Om Svenska och Norska Diat., p. 218. Rab. Fl. Eur., p. 34.

On sea-weeds, Bannow, County Wexford. Piles of wooden bridge, Dollymount; Malahide. Stomach of Pectens, Dalkey. On corallines, Howth. On sea weeds, Ballybrack, County Dublin. On sea weeds, Kilkee, County Clare. From stomachs of Ascidians, coast of County Clare.

Coscinodiscus radiolatus, (Ehr.) Marine.

Disk small, cellules minute, obscurely hexagonal, arranged partly in radiate bands, and partly in the intervals of these bands in converging lines. Cellules confused at the centre of the disk, smaller towards the margin. (Pl. 26, fig. 22.)

Kütz. Bac., p. 132, T. xxix., fig. 91. Ralfs, in Pritch., p. 830, who describes the form thus :—" Cellules punctiform, equal, radiating," whereas, in fact, they are minutely hexagonal, and diminish slightly near the margin.

Oyster shells, Dublin Bay. Tide-pool, Dalkey, County Dublin. Stomachs of Ascidians, Roundstone Bay, County Galway. Stomachs of Ascidians, County Clare.

Coscinodiscus cervinus, (Brightwell.) Marine.

Cellules very minute, radiate, close, dry valve fawn-coloured, frustule convex.

Brightwell has described and figured this form as Hyalodiscus cervinus, Q. J. M. S., Vol. viii., p. 95, Pl. vi., fig. 13. He describes the "puncta or dots" as "scattered over the whole surface;" but in his figure represents them as regularly radiate, which latter corresponds exactly with my specimens. Ralfs, in Pritch., p. 831, places the form among the doubtful species of Coscinodiscus, to which genus it properly belongs.

From stomachs of Ascidians, Roundstone Bay, County Galway. From stomachs of Ascidians, County Clare.

Coscinodiscus Smithii, (Wm. Sm.) Fresh water.

Disk small, punctate, puncta regularly radiate.

Wm. Sm., B. D., Vol. i., p. 23, Pl. iii., fig. 36.

Smith has unaccountably confounded this form with Coscinodiscus minor, Ehr., from which it is plainly distinguished, both by its habitat and the character of the striation; the latter being marine and areolate, the former a fresh water species, and punctate.

Ralfs, in Pritch., p. 818, considers this form may be identical with Melosira nivalis, but it plainly belongs to the genus Coscinodiscus.

Lough Neagh, near Lurgan, County Armagh. Lough Island-Rearey, County Down. River Blackwater, near Kells, County Meath.

Coscinodiscus Normanni, (Greg.) Marine.
Cellules on the the disk small, obscurely hexagonal, radiate, arranged in fascicles of about six lines, decreasing in size as they approach the margin ; valve very convex in the centre.
Greville, Q. J. M. S., Vol. vii., p. 81, Pl. vi. fig. 3. Ralfs, in Pritch., p. 830.—Coscinodiscus fasciculatus, O'M., Q. J. M. S., New Series, Vol. vii., p. 249, Pl. vii., fig. 1.

Arran Island, County Galway. Stomachs of Ascidians, Roundstone Bay, County Galway.

Coscinodiscus nitidus, (Greg.) Marine.
Margin of the disk striated, cellules distant, roundish, large, distinctly radiate, except near the centre, where they are slightly confused. Smaller at the margin, gradually increasing in size towards the centre.
Greg. Diat. of Clyde, p. 27, Pl. x., fig. 45. Ralfs, in Pritch., p. 833, Pl. viii., fig. 18.

Arran Island. Stomachs of Ascidians, Roundstone Bay, County Galway. Malahide, County Dublin. Rostrevor, County Down. Kilkee, County Clare.

Coscinodiscus Gregorii, N. S. Marine.
Margin of the disk striated, cellules sub-quadrangular, much smaller than in the former species, and more equal in size, radiate ; a small vacant angular space in the centre, from the angles of which so many lines of cellules run to the margin, the interspaces filled up by rows of cellules, gradually shortening. (Pl. 26, fig. 23.)
Gregory, Diat., from Glenshira Sand, Q. J. M. S., Vol. v., Pl. i., fig. 50. After describing Coscinodiscus nitidus, Gregory remarks, " this pretty disk was figured, without a name, in my last Paper on the Glenshira Sand (Trans. Mic. Soc., Vol. v., Pl. i., fig. 50). Having found it tolerably frequent in Lamlash Bay, I now figure a perfect example, which provisionally I refer to Coscinodiscus." Diat. of Clyde, p. 28. This form may easily be confounded with the preceding, as Gregory has done ; but a more careful comparison of the many specimens that have come under my observation convinces me the forms are distinct ; and accordingly I give to the present the name of Gregory, who first discovered it.

Arran Island. From stomachs of Ascidians, Roundstone Bay, County Galway. Stomachs of Ascidians, County Clare.

(d). *Cellules radiate at the margin, linear in the central portion.*

Coscinodiscus fimbriatus, (Ehr.) Marine.
Cellules hexagonal; small; in the central portion of the disk arranged in lines crossing in quincunx; towards the margin radiate; smaller towards the margin.
Ehr. Mic. Ralfs, in Pritch., p. 829.

Stomachs of Ascidians, County Clare.

(e.) *Cellules arranged variously.*

Coscinodiscus marginatus, (Ehr.) Marine.
Cellules large, hexagonal, arranged in irregularly curved lines, with a distinct narrow strongly costate margin.
Ehr. Mic. Ralfs, in Pritch., p. 829. Weisse, Recherches Microscopique sur le Guano, Bul. de l'Academie Imp. de St. Petersburg, T. xii., p. 122, Pl. i., fig. 21.

Stomachs of Ascidians, Roundstone Bay. Arran Islands. Stomachs of Ascidians, Broadhaven Bay, Co. Galway.

Coscinodiscus lineatus, (Ehr.) Marine.
Cellules rounded, arranged in oblique, parallel lines.
Ehrenberg, in his Microgeologie, gives several figures under this name. One of them, T. xxii., fig. 6 a. b., seems scarcely assignable to the genus Coscinodiscus, inasmuch as it is furnished with a marginal circlet of nodules. Besides this there are two other forms, quite distinct: one in which the striæ are linear, to be immediately described; the other, the present form, which is furnished with cellules as described above.
Ehr. Mic. Kütz. Bac., p. 131, T. i., fig. 10. Ralfs, in Pritch., p. 830.

Malahide. Monkstown. Dredgings in Bay, Co. Dublin. Seaweeds, Wicklow. Breaches near Newcastle, Co. Wicklow. Bannow, Co. Wexford. Stomachs of Ascidians, Co. Clare. Stomachs of Ascidians, Roundstone Bay, Arran Islands, Co. Galway.

Coscinodiscus Ehrenbergii, N. S. Marine.
Disk striate. Striæ linear, in two series, crossing each other obliquely. (Pl. 26, fig. 24.)
This is the form described by Ehrenberg as Cos. lineatus, Mic., T. xxxv., A. 17, fig. 7; T. xxxv., A. 16, fig. 3. Weisse, Bul. de l'Academie de St. Petersburg, Tom. xii., Pl. i., fig. 20 a.

Malahide. Piles of wooden bridge, Dollymount, Co. Dublin. Stomachs of Ascidians, Roundstone Bay, Co. Galway.

Coscinodiscus minor, (Ehr.) Marine.
Disk small. Cellules roundish, without any perceptible arrangement. (Pl. 26, fig. 25.)
Ehr. Mic., T. xviii., fig. 31; T. xx.-i., fig. 28; T. xxii., fig. 27; T. xix., fig. 3. Kütz. Bac., p. 131, T. i., figs. 12, 13. Ralfs, in Pritch., p. 831. Weisse, Recherches Microscopiques sur le Guano, Bul. de l'Academie Imperial de Science de St. Petersburg, T. xii., p. 121, Pl. i., fig. 22.

Tide-pool, Dalkey, Co. Dublin.

Coscinodiscus punctulatus, (Greg.) Marine.
Striæ indistinct. Disk covered with what appear to be fine puncta, irregularly scattered.
Gregory describes the disk in his specimens as " marked by very fine and obscure lines, which, near the margin, are traceable as rays, but which soon become fainter, and apparently wavy, at the same time as they proceed towards the centre."—Diat. of Clyde, p. 28.
Several specimens, from different localities, came under my notice, but all mounted in balsam. In consequence I could not trace the lines referred to; and, moreover, the puncta in such forms as were seen obliquely had the appearance of fine hairs. This circumstance increases the doubt which I entertain, in common with Gregory and Ralfs, as to whether the form is properly referred to the genus Coscinodiscus.
Gregory, Diat. of Clyde, p. 28, Pl. x., fig. 46. Ralfs, in Pritch., p. 831.

Arran Islands. From stomachs of Ascidians, Roundstone Bay, Co. Galway. On Fucus serratus, Ballybrack, Co. Dublin.

Genus VII. ARACHNOIDISCUS, Ehr. Deane.

Arachnoidiscus Ehrenbergii, (Bailey.) Marine.
" Disk with a central hyaline nodule or umbilicus, and numerous radiating lines, connected by concentric circles of large pearly granules; the circle next the umbilicus formed of short lines."—Ralfs.
Wm. Sm., B. D., Vol. i., p. 25; Supp. Pl. xxxi., fig. 256. Ralfs, in Pritch., p. 842, Pl. xv., figs. 18-21.
This truly splendid form has been discovered in the fossil earths of California, and in a living state it has been gathered in Japan, California, and South Africa. It is its habit in congenial climates to cover completely the plants to which it is attached. It admits of serious doubt, therefore, whether the few isolated specimens which have been discovered in this kingdom entitle it to be included among our British forms. Rabenhorst does not give it a place among the European species of Diatomaceæ; and perhaps he was right in excluding it. But it seems desirable to notice the fact of its having been found. Besides

the case mentioned by Smith, Captain Hutton found some two or three specimens in a gathering made by him at Malahide, Co. Dublin, as mentioned in the Proceedings of the Dublin Microscopical Club, 15th December, 1864; Q. J. M. S., April, 1865, p. 167. Had these forms been found in the proximity of a harbour resorted to by foreign vessels, it might be suspected they were imported from foreign seas, and deposited as the vessels unladed their freight; but such a supposition cannot be entertained regarding Malahide. I was present at the meeting when the specimens were exhibited, and remember that Captain Hutton informed me that he had not been working with any material likely to contain these forms, and that he was confident they were taken from the sea at Malahide, as the vessels used in the preparation were new, and had not been used before. I have myself to add, that a single frustule was recently found by me in a gathering made by Rev. M. H. Close, at a place called Drehidnamaud, on the coast of the Co. Kerry.

In the same gathering which yielded the specimens of Arachnoidiscus Ehrenbergii, Captain Hutton found some specimens of what he regarded as Arachnoidiscus ornatus; but considering it likely these latter were not specifically distinct, I only refer here to the circumstance as corroborative of the probability that Arachnoidiscus Ehrenbergii was found at Malahide.

Genus VIII. CRASPEDODISCUS, Ehr.

Disk not undulate, having a broad border, with areolation differing from that of centre.

Craspedodiscus coscinodiscus, (Ehr.) Marine.
Border broad, about the third of the entire diameter, areolate areoles hexagonal. Middle portion punctate. (Pl. 26, fig. 26.)
Ralfs, in Pritch., p. 832, Pl. v., fig. 80.—Craspedodiscus pyxidicula, Brightwell, Q. J. M. S., 1860, p. 95, Pl. v., fig. 4.

Stomachs of Ascidians, Broadhaven Bay, Co. Galway.

Genus IX. ACTINOPTYCHUS, Ehr.

Disk undulate, divided into strongly defined somewhat triangular compartments, with a distinct polygonal centre, the sides of the polygon being equal to the number of compartments into which the disk is divided.

The valves in this genus appear to consist of two distinct plates, with a striation somewhat different, hence the species have by some being unnecessarily multiplied.

Actinoptychus senarius, (Ehr.) Brackish or marine.
Valve divided into six compartments, areolate, areolæ more or less hexagonal. In this species the valves vary considerably in size. Ehr. Mic., T. xxi., fig. 18, a. b. Kütz. Bac., p. 134, T. i., fig. 21, T. xxi., fig. 26. The form there described does not differ from that which the same author has described and figured as Actinocyclus undulatus, Bac., p. 132, T. i., fig. 24. Ralfs, in Pritch., p. 839, Pl. ix., fig. 132.—Actinoptychus undulatus, Rab. Fl. Eur., sect. 1, p. 35.— Actinocyclus undulatus, Wm. Sm., B. D., Vol. i., p. 25; Plate v., fig. 43. Heib. De Danske Diat., p. 37. Cleve, Om Svenska och Norska Diat., p. 218.

Salt ditch near Wexford. Bannow, Co. Wexford. Rostrevor, Co. Down. Stomachs of Pectens, Dalkey. Dollymount. Portmarnock, Co. Dublin. Sea shore, near Ballysodare, Co. Sligo.

Var. denarius, (Ehr.) Marine.
Compartments ten in number. Ehr. Mic., T. xviii., fig. 23.
From stomachs of Ascidians, Roundstone Bay. Arran Islands, Westport Bay, Co. Galway.

Var. duodenarius, (Ehr.) Marine.
Compartments twelve in number. Ehr. Mic., T. xviii. f. 24. Ralfs, in Pritch., p. 840. Weisse, Bulletin de L'Academie Imp. de St. Petersbourg, Tome xii., p. 122, T. i., fig. 8.—Actinocyclus duodenarius, Wm. Sm., B. D., Vol. ii., p. 86.
From stomachs of Ascidians, Roundstone Bay. Arran Islands, Co. Galway.

Var. sedenarius, (Ehr.) Marine.
Compartments sixteen in number. Ehr. Mic., T. xviii., fig. 26. Weisse, Bulletin de L'Academie Imp. de St. Petersbourg, Tome xii., p. 122. T. i., fig. 9.—Actinocyclus sedenarius, Wm. Sm., B. D., Vol. ii., p. 86.
Sea-weeds, Bannow, Co. Wexford. Arran Islands. From stomachs of Ascidians, Roundstone Bay, Co. Galway.

Var. vicenarius, (Ehr.) Marine.
Compartments twenty in number. The only specimen of this variety found by me has marginal teeth obvious on some of the compartments, though not noticeable on others, owing perhaps to the circumstance of the valve not lying quite parallel to the side. These teeth disappeared altogether when the form was mounted in balsam. Ralfs, in Pritch., p. 840. Weisse, Bulletin de L'Academie Imp. de St. Petersbourg, Tome xii., p. 122.
Drehidnamaud, Co. Kerry.

Genus X. OMPHALOPELTA, Ehr.

Valves as in Actinoptychus, but having a marginal spine in each compartment.

Omphalopelta areolata, (Ehr.) Marine.
Valve having six compartments, areolate; submarginal spines small. Ehr. Mic., T. xxxv., A. Ralfs, in Pritch., p. 841, Pl. viii., fig. 15.—Actinocyclus areolatus, Brightwell. Q. J. M. S., 1860, p. 93, Pl. v., fig. 1.

Arran Islands, Co. Galway.

Genus XI. ACTINOCYCLUS, Ehr.

"Disk minutely and densely punctated, or cellulose, generally divided by radiating single or double dotted lines, and having a small circular hyaline intramarginal pseudo-nodule." "The disk is not undulated." Ralfs. To this description may be added, that the species of this genus usually exhibit a border in which the striæ are unlike those of the remainder of the disk; the striæ also almost or altogether reach the centre.

Actinocyclus Ralfsii, (Wm. Sm.) Marine.
Valve highly iridescent under a low power. Striæ radiate, moniliform; puncta nearly of uniform size throughout, the dividing radii equidistant, nearly reaching the centre; the next lines of puncta considerably shorter than the radii; the next again still shorter, exhibiting numerous subulate blank spaces; border tolerably wide, minutely punctate; submarginal nodule large, round; no central nodule, but the central portion marked by a few scattered puncta; diameter about ·0042. (Pl. 27, fig. 1.)
Ralfs, in Pritch., p. 835, Pl. v., fig. 84.—Eupodiscus Ralfsii, Wm. Sm., B. D., Vol. ii., p. 86.

Lough Kay, Co. Kerry. Stomachs of Pectens, Dalkey Sound, Co. Dublin. Stomachs of Ascidians, Belfast Lough, Co. Antrim.

Actinocyclus moniliformis, (Ralfs.) Marine.
Striæ moniliform, principal rays about twelve in number, running radiately from centre to border; intermediate rays becoming gradually shorter and parallel, except near the border, where a few short ones meet them at an angle. About four puncta, closely approximated in the centre, present the appearance of a nodule; border narrow, punctate; pseudo-nodule small, marginal. Diameter about ·0034. (Pl. 27, fig. 2.)

I have had considerable difficulty in identifying this species; in some respects it agrees with the description of Eupodiscus sparsus, Greg., Q. J. M. S., 1856, p. 81, Pl. i., fig. 47. But as it more nearly resembles specimens frequently to be met with in the Richmond deposit, which Ralfs seems to have had in view when he named the species, I have adopted his specific designation.
Ralfs, in Pritch., p. 834.

Salt ditch near Wexford. Sea-weeds, Ballybrack, Co. Dublin.

Actinocyclus crassus, (Wm. Sm.) Marine.
Striæ moniliform; principal rays strongly marked when viewed by a low power; arrangement of puncta somewhat confused; border narrow, punctate, puncta decussate; submarginal nodule small; diameter ·0020.
Ralfs, in Pritch., p. 835.—Eupodiscus crassus, Wm. Sm., B. D., Vol. i., p. 24, Pl. iv., fig. 41.

Sea-weeds, Ballybrack. Stomachs of Pectens, Dalkey Sound, Malahide, Howth, Co. Dublin. Stomachs of Ascidians, Co. Clare.

Actinocyclus fulvus, (Wm. Sm.) Marine.
Striæ moniliform, close, subradiate; border broad; striation indistinct; submarginal nodule small. Diameter about ·0025.
Ralfs, in Pritch., p. 835.—Eupodiscus fulvus, Wm. Sm., B. D., Vol. i., p. 24, Pl. iv., fig. 40.

Stomachs of Pectens, Dalkey Sound, Co. Dublin. Stomachs of Ascidians, Roundstone Bay, Co Galway.

Genus XII. EUPODISCUS, Ehr.

Valves having horn-like processes springing from the surface.

Eupodiscus argus, (Ehr.) Marine.
Disk large, areolate; areoles irregular, somewhat angular, radiately disposed; processes three or four, submarginal. Diameter from ·0065 to ·0120. (Pl. 27, fig. 3.)
Wm. Sm., B.D., Vol. i., p. 24, Pl. iv., fig. 39. Ralfs, in Pritch., p. 843, Pls. vi., fig: 2, and xi:, figs: 41, 42: Heiberg, De Danske Diat., p: 37: Rab. Fl. Eur., sect. i., p. 319.—Tripodiscus argus, Kütz. Bac., p. 136, T. i., fig. 6.

Dublin Bay.

Genus XIII. AULISCUS, Ehr.

Surface of the valve undulate, furnished with two large processes; striæ plumose, arranged in form of a quatrefoil.

Auliscus sculptus, (Wm. Sm.) Marine.
Striæ linear. (Pl. 27, fig. 4)
Ralfs, in Pritch., p. 845, Pl. vi., fig. 3. Greville, Q. J. M. S., 1863, p. 43, Pl. ii., figs. 1–3. Heiberg, De Danske Diat., p. 37. Cleve, Om Svenska och Norska Diat., p. 218.—Eupodiscus sculptus, Wm. Sm., B. D., Vol. i., p. 25, Pl. iv., fig. 42.—Aulacodiscus sculptus, Brightwell, Q. J. M. S., 1860, p. 94, Pl. v., fig. 3.

Malahide. Piles of wooden bridge, Dollymount, Co. Dublin. River Slaney, at Killurin, Co. Wexford. Sea-weeds, near town of Wicklow. Westport, Co. Galway.

Genus XIV. ODONTODISCUS, Ehr.

Disk furnished with marginal teeth.

In this genus I have united Ehrenberg's two genera, Odontodiscus and Systephania, deeming the distinction between them not of sufficient importance to justify their separation. The distinction, as expressed by Ralfs, is simply this, that in Odontodiscus "the dots are radiate, not parallel, as in Systephania."

Odontodiscus excentricus, (Ehr.) Marine.
Disk varying in size from ·0008 to ·0025; areolate; areoles round, arranged in curved excentric lines; teeth numerous, short. (Pl. 27, fig. 5.)
Ehr. Mic., T. xxxv., A. 18; fig. 11. Ralfs, in Pritch., p. 832. Pl. v., fig. 90.—Coscinodiscus excentricus, Kütz. Bac., p. 131, T. i., fig. 9, in which the teeth are not figured or described. Wm. Sm., B. D., Vol. i., p. 23, Pl. iii., fig. 38.—Eupodiscus excentricus, O'M., Q. J. M. S., 1867, p. 249, Pl. vii., fig. 2.

Sea-weeds, Bannow. Salt ditch near Wexford. Piles of wooden bridge, Dollymount, Malahide, Stomachs of Pectens, Dalkey, from Corallines, Howth, Sea-weeds, Ballybrack, Co. Dublin. Sea-weeds, Kilkee, Stomachs of Ascidians, Co. Clare. Stomachs of Ascidians, Roundstone Bay, Co. Galway.

Odontodiscus anglicus, (Donkin.) Marine.
Disk about ·0016 in diameter; teeth large and prominent, occupying a tolerably broad unstriate margin; striæ minutely punctate, decussately arranged. (Pl. 27, fig. 6).

Systephania anglica, Donkin, Q. J. M. S., 1861, p. 12, Pl. i., fig. 14.

Stomachs of Ascidians, Roundstone Bay, Co. Galway.

Odontodiscus hibernicus. N. S. Marine.

Disk about ·0018 in diameter; areolate; areoles round, decussately arranged, reaching the circumference; teeth more numerous than in former species, and shorter. (Pl. 27, fig. 7.)

Stomachs of Ascidians, Roundstone Bay, Co. Galway.

A. *Frustules symmetrical. Valves not circular.*

FAMILY II. BIDDULPHIEÆ, Kütz.

Valves lanceolate, in some cases nearly orbicular, furnished with distinct processes and spines; connecting zone largely developed in full-grown specimens. In such species as have been seen in a living state the frustules are united in filaments.

This group, established by Kützing without any very distinct definition, embraced the following genera, Isthmia, Odontella, Biddulphia, and Zygoceros. Ralfs, in Pritchard, adopts the same system of grouping, adding to those above named two other genera, Hemiaulus, and Hydrosera, but gives more distinct characteristics than the former author. His diagnosis rests mainly on the convexity of the frustules, in consequence of which the lateral valves "enter largely into the front view," and on the development of processes on the valves. Grunow adopts the group with no more distinct definition than the following. "Side view longish, or having three, four, or more angles," and includes in it four genera, namely, Isthmia, Biddulphia, Amphitetras, and Triceratium. Heiberg marks the group by the fact of the processes springing from the valve obliquely outwards, and places under it the genera Ceratulus, Biddulphia, Triceratium, Amphitetras; and in a sub-group named Biddulphieæ cuneatæ, the genus Eucampia also. Immediately connected with the Biddulphieæ, this Danish author places another group, the Hemiaulidæ, mainly distinguished from the former by this one feature, that the processes, instead of springing from the valve obliquely, are placed at right angles with the plane of the base.

The genus Isthmia which Kützing, Ralfs, and Grunow include in the Biddulphieæ, differs considerably in these respects, that the frustules on the front view are not symmetrical, and the valves are not furnished with processes, the structure which Ralfs regarded as such being only a mucous cushion or stipes, and on these grounds the genus Isthmia ought to be excluded. In the case of Hydrosera (Wallich), the frustules are not symmetrical, processes occurring on the one valve, and not on the opposite one. Wallich's description is "on one side only, with a remarkable series of aperture-like appendages." Wallich on Triceratium, Q. J. M. S., July, 1858, p. 251. For which reason I consider the genus Hydrosera is not properly comprehended in the group. The species marked by an angular outline of the valves as Triceratium, Amphitetras, &c., however closely related to the Biddulphieæ, seem however to possess such distinctive peculiarities of structure as to justify their being placed in a separate group; and if any forms of the genus Hemiaulus had occurred in Irish localities, I would have been disposed to include them with the Biddulphieæ as Rabenhorst has done in his Flora Europea Algarum.

Various generic names have from time to time been introduced by different writers to designate the forms of this group, in consequence of which much confusion has arisen, to obviate which a few remarks are here necessary.

The generic name Biddulphia was first adopted by Gray, and along with Biddulphia pulchella embraced some heterogeneous forms, which latter were afterwards removed to their proper places. Agardh then established the genus Odontella to receive the single species now known as Biddulphia aurita; Ehrenberg having applied the name Odontella to a species of Desmid, as Roper informs us, Q. J. M. S., Oct., 1858, p. 3, substituted for it the designation Denticella, which was thus equivalent to Agardh's Odontella. The forms included in these genera, Biddulphia and Denticella, were filamentous; and Ehrenberg having found kindred forms which, without sufficient examination, he considered to be simple, adopted the genera Zygoceros and Cerataulus, the former for those free forms, as he thought them allied to Biddulphia, the latter to Denticella. Some of these genera have been retained by succeeding writers, but Smith in his Synopsis has, as I think, wisely dispensed with these superfluous subdivisions, and included the forms contained in them under the one generic name.

Rabenhorst, in his Flora Europea Algarum, places the Biddulphieæ in close connexion with the septate forms, supposing, as I imagine, that the costæ on the valves of Bid. pulchella and other species with undulate surfaces are septa. On this subject the observations of Smith are worthy of notice: "The existence of septa in B. pulchella is by no means to be admitted, though the costæ may occasionally project into the interior of the cells." B. D., Vol. ii., p. 49.

Genus I. Biddulphia, Gray.

Processes projecting outwards at a more or less acute angle from the plane of the base.

(a.) *Surfaces of the valves not undulate.*

Biddulphia radiata, (Wm. Sm.) Marine.

Valve nearly circular; cellules distinct, roundish, radiate, larger at the margin than towards the centre, where they are small and more distant; processes two, large, alternating with two others smaller and spine-like.

It is with some difficulty that I have come to the conclusion that this form is identical with that described by Wm. Smith, first as Eupodiscus radiatus, B. D., Vol. i., p. 24, Pl. xxx., fig. 255; and subsequently as Biddulphia radiata, Vol. ii., p. 48, Pl. lxii., fig. 255. Neither as regards the outline of the valve, nor its areolation, can this form be regarded as obviously the same as that described in Smith's figure, which is perfectly orbicular, whereas in the present case the outline, though nearly circular, presents four distinct angles, the processes being placed at opposite ends of one diagonal line, the spines occupying the corresponding position on the other. Roper, Q. J. M. S., Oct., 1858, p. 19, Pl. ii., fig. 29, and Ralfs, in Pritch., p. 847, affirm the orbicular outline of the valve; but Smith, who was subsequently convinced that the form was wrongly placed in the genus Eupodiscus, and that its proper position was in Biddulphia, uses such language as to imply that the outline is not perfectly circular. Marking the distinctive peculiarities of Eupodiscus and Biddulphia, he says, the frustules of the former differ from those of the latter, "by the orbicular outline of their valves." B. D., Vol. ii., p. 48. The present form differs from Smith's figure not only in the outline, but in the character and arrangement of the cellules. In the latter, the cellules are minute, close, and not radiately disposed, and on this point Ralfs alleges, "the cellules are not radiant," Pritch., p. 847. The specific name given to the species by Smith is, however, suggestive of the thought that the figure is at fault in this respect. Roper's figure of the species exhibits the cellules as small and radiately arranged, but in his description he represents them just as they are in the form under consideration, "as distinctly reticulated, with small but rather irregular hexagons."

Cerataulus Smithii, Ralfs, in Pritchard, p. 847. Cleve, Om Svenska och Norska Diat., p. 218. Rab. Fl. Eur., sect. i., p. 313.

Salt marsh near Ballysodare, Co. Sligo.

Biddulphia turgida, (Ehr.) Marine.

Connecting zone transverse; valves nearly orbicular, having two large truncate processes, and two alternate spines both situated diagonally; a circlet of small marginal spines sometimes present, and numerous minute spines scattered irregularly over the surface; striation minutely punctate, the puncta arranged in close wavy lines.

This, as well as the former species, are by Ralfs, Heiberg, Rabenhorst, and Cleve, placed in a distinct genus named Cerataulus, the distinctive characteristic being the fact that the processes and spines are diagonally situated on the valve.

Wm. Sm., B. D., Vol. ii., p. 50, Pl. lxii., fig. 384. Roper, Q. J. M. S., Oct., 1858, p. 17, Pl. ii., fig. 23. Ralfs, in Pritch, p. 846, Pl. vi., fig. 8. Heiberg, De Danske Diat, p. 39. Rab. Fl. Eur., sect. 1, p. 313.

Saltmarsh, Ballysodare, Co. Sligo. Sea-weeds, Malahide, Co. Dublin.

Biddulphia aurita, (Lyngbye.) Marine.

Valves elliptical lanceolate, with the processes at the extremities of the longitudinal axis; processes large at the base, rounded off towards the fine extremity; the elevated centre of the valves bearing three fine and long spines; striation punctate, fine; puncta observed from front view, parallel; connecting zone finely punctate. (Pl. 27, fig. 8a).

Smith and Roper attribute this species to De Brébisson; but with Ralfs, Heiberg, and Rabenhorst, I consider it should be ascribed to Lyngbye, who first described it as Diatoma auritum.

Wm. Sm., B. D., Vol. ii., p. 49, Pl. xlv., fig. 319. Roper, Q. J. M. S., Oct., 1858, p. 10, Pl. i., fig. 3. Ralfs, in Pritch., p. 849. Heiberg, De Danske Diat., p. 41. Rab. Fl. Eur., sect. 1, p. 311. Cleve, Om Svenska och Norska Diat., p. 218.—Denticella aurita, Ehr. Mic., T. xxxv., A 23, fig. 7.—Odontella aurita, Kütz. Bac., p. 137, T. xxix., fig. 88.

Stomachs of Ascidians, Roundstone Bay, Co. Galway. Sea-weeds, Ballybrack, Malahide, Dollymount, Howth, Co. Dublin. Rostrevor, Co. Down. Tacumshane, Co. Wexford. Laytown, Co. Meath. Ballysodare, Co. Sligo. Dundalk, Co. Louth.

Biddulphia rhombus, (Ehr.) Marine.

Valves orbicular-lanceolate; processes at the extremity of the longitudinal axis; spines marginal; central elevation slight; striation finely punctate, seen on front view, parallel; connecting zone finely punctate.

Ehrenberg described this form as Zygoceros rhombus; to him, therefore, should it be ascribed, and not to Wm. Smith, as some authors have done.

Wm. Sm., B. D., Vol. ii., p. 49, Pl. lxi., fig. 320. Roper, Q. J. M. S., Oct., 1858, p. 11, Pl. i., fig. 4. Heiberg, De Danske Diat., p. 40. Rab. Fl. Eur., sect. 1, p. 311. Cleve, Om Svenska och Norska Diat., p. 218.—Zygoceros rhombus, Ehr., Berl. Acad., 1839, p. 156. Kütz. Bac., p. 138. T. xviii., fig. 9. Ralfs, in Pritch, p. 850.

Malahide, Baldoyle, Ballybrack, Dollymount, Co. Dublin.

Biddulphia baileyii, (Wm. Sm.) Marine.

Frustules, on front view, receding at the sides in a gentle slope; end surfaces nearly flat, with two slight elevations on which the spines are situated; processes long, and narrow towards the extremity, slightly curving inwards; striation very obscure; punctate; puncta parallel. On side view valves broadly elliptical; processes at extremities of the longitudinal axis; spines two, situated a little to the right and left of same, about one-third of the entire length from extremities; striæ very fine; lines of puncta appearing to cross each other, except upon a vacant, sigmoid, narrow space in the middle. (Pl. 27, fig. 8.)

Wm. Sm., B. D., Vol. ii., p. 50, Pls. xlv. and lxii., fig. 322. Rab. Fl. Eur., sect. 1, p. 311. Roper, Q. J. M. S., Oct., 1858, p. 12, Pl. i., figs. 5–9.—*Zygoceros mobilensis,* Ralfs, in Pritch, p. 850, Pl. vi., fig. 11.

Salt ditch near Wexford. Tacumshane, Co. Wexford. Dundalk, Co. Louth. Salt marsh, Drehidnamaud, Co. Kerry.

(b.) *Surfaces of the valves undulate.*

Biddulphia pulchella, (Gray.) Marine.

On front view the sides incline inwards towards the processes; the valves divided into compartments, from three to seven in number, the central being the largest and most elevated, from which, in perfect specimens, two or three spines are projected; compartments separated by what appear strong costæ; processes short, rounded at extremities; striation areolate; areoles roundish, and nearly parallel; connecting zone striate. On side view the valve is broadly elliptical; areoles ranged round the central point. (Pl. 27, fig. 9.)

Wm. Sm., B. D., Vol. ii., p. 48, Pls. xliv., xlv., xlvi., fig. 321. Roper, Q. J. M. S., Oct., 1858, p. 7. Ralfs, in Pritch, p. 848, Pl. ii., figs. 46–50.—Biddulphia trilocularis; B. quinqueocularis; B. septemlocularis, Kütz. Bac., p. 138, T. xxix., fig. 89, T. xix., fig. 1, T. xix., fig. 2.—Diatoma Biddulphianum, Agardh, Syst. Alg., p. 5.—Denticella Biddulphia, Ehr., Berl. Trans., 1843.

Malahide, Ireland's Eye, Baldoyle, Co. Dublin. Sea-weeds, Giants' Causeway, Co. Antrim. Stomachs of Ascidians, Roundstone Bay, Arran Islands, Co. Galway.

FAMILY III. TRICERATIEÆ.

Valves on side view presenting three or more angles, with a process springing from each angle.

This group includes the genera Amphitetras, Triceratium and Trinacria, which, in consequence of their obvious resemblance, are placed here, although differently arranged by other authors. Wm. Smith, recognising the affinity between Biddulphia and Amphitetras, placed them close together, but assigned to Triceratium a widely different position in his system of arrangement. Kützing distributes the included genera in two distinct groups—the Anguliferæ and Angulatæ, between which he interposed the Biddulphieæ and Tripodiscus argus = Eupodiscus argus. The Anguliferæ, he says, "are easily distinguished by means of their angular side view;" but of the Angulatæ, which embraces only the single genus Triceratium, he gives no other diagnosis than that contained in the description of that genus, "individuals free, with the bivalve lorica triangular, not concatenated," Ralfs omits Trinacria, a genus established by Heiberg subsequently to the publication of the "History of the Infusoria," and along with the other genera placed in the present group includes Euodia, and Hemidiscus. Of Hemidiscus I have never seen a specimen, and, therefore, can express no opinion regarding it; but as to Euodia, from the cuneate outline of its transverse section, it plainly should be excluded from this group, with which it has little, if any, affinity. Ralfs indicates two features by which the forms in this group may be distinguished from the Biddulphieæ: "The angles on the front view are usually less elongated, and the intervening margin less lobed." Of these characters the latter can scarcely be sustained in all cases; and as to the former, if Trinacria, in which the processes at the angles are very long, is to be admitted here, this, too, must be regarded as by no means a satisfactory diagnosis. Grunow does not refer to Trinacria, for the same reason as Ralfs, but includes the other forms of this group under the Biddulphieæ, which he thus defines: "Valves on side view longish, or three, four, or more angled," no reference being made to the processes springing from the angles which constitute so remarkable a feature of these forms. According to this author, the characteristic distinction between Amphitetras and Triceratium is the possession of four angles by the former, while the latter has but three. The fact that specimens of the former occur with five angles, and of the latter with four or more angles, evinces how untenable is this distinction as a generic diagnosis.

Heiberg includes Amphitetras and Triceratium in the Biddulphieæ, and his genus Trinacria in another group, namely, the Hemiaulidæ; the main distinction of which rests on the form and position of the processes, which are triangular, and spring at right angles from the basal plane of the valve. But these differences, though sufficient to establish generic distinction, seem scarcely to justify the establishment of a distinct group to receive the forms. It will thus appear that, in consequence of the projection of the processes from the angles of the valves, the relationship of this group to the Biddulphieæ is recognised by most authors: but no more satisfactory distinction between Amphitetras and Triceratium has been suggested than that in the former the frustules are concatenate, and in the other free. This distinction I adopt, not because I consider the supposed fact on which it rests in all cases substantiated by observation, but because it seems the most satisfactory. And not being in a position either to sustain or refute the assumption, I consider the proper course is to leave them as they stand.

Genus I. Amphitetras, Ehr.

Frustules concatenate; cubical; processes springing from each angle of the valve short.

Amphitetras antediluviana, (Ehr.) Marine.
Striation areolate; connecting zone more finely areolate than the valve. On side view, margins deeply concave; areoles radiate and concentric. (Pl. 27, fig. 10.)
Kütz. Bac., p. 135, T. xix. fig. 3; T. xxix. fig. 86. Ralfs, in Pritch., p. 858. Heiberg, De Danske Diat., p. 42. Rab. Fl. Eur., sect. 1, p. 318.—Amphitetras antediluviana, β. W. Sm., B. D.,Vol. ii. p. 47, Pl. lxiv., fig. 318 a'''.

Stomachs of Ascidians, Roundstone Bay, Arran Islands, Co. Galway.

Variety a.—On side view, sides parallel.—Amphitetras antediluviana, Wm. S., B. D., Vol. ii., p. 47, Pl. xliv., fig. 318. Ralfs, in Pritch., p. 858, Pl. xi., figs. 21 and 22.

Stomachs of Ascidians, Roundstone Bay. Arran Islands, Co. Galway. Malahide. Dublin Bay. Howth, Co. Dublin. Bundoran, Co. Donegal.

Variety b.—With five angles.
Stomachs of Ascidians, Roundstone Bay, Co. Galway.

Genus II. Triceratium, Ehr.

Frustules simple; normally triangular on side view; processes short, roundish, springing outwards, at an acute angle to the basal plane.

Triceratium favus, (Ehr.) Marine.
Striation areolate; areoles hexagonal, large; sides straight or slightly convex.
Kütz. Bac., p. 139, T. xvii., fig. 11. Wm. Sm., B. D., Vol. i., p. 26, Pl. v., fig. 44; Supp. Pl. xxx., fig. 44. Ralfs, in Pritch., p. 855. Pl. xi., fig. 43. Heiberg, De Danske Diat., p. 41. Rab. Fl. Eur., sect. 1, p. 315.

Stomachs of Ascidians, Roundstone Bay, Co. Galway.

Triceratium alternans, (Bailey.) Marine.
Sides nearly straight; striation areolate; areoles small, roundish; radiating towards the three angles; bases of the processes marked by what seem well defined costæ. (Pl. 27, fig. 11.)
Bailey, Mic. Observations made in Sth. Carolina, Smithsonian Contributions, Vol. ii., p. 40. Brightwell, Q. J. M. S., Vol. i., p. 251, Pl. vi., fig. 19. Wm. Sm., B. D., Vol. i., p. 26, Pl. v., fig. 45. Supp. Pl. xxx., fig. 45. Ralfs, in Pritch., p. 854, Pl. vi., fig. 21. Rab. Fl. Eur. sect. 1, p. 316.

Mud of River Liffey, Co. Dublin.

Triceratium amblyoceros, (Ehr.) Marine.
Sides convex; angles broadly rounded off; cellules radiate, distant, roundish; more deeply shaded at the borders. (Pl. 27, fig. 12.)
Ehr. Mic., T. xviii., fig. 51. Brightwell. Q. J. M. S., Vol. i., p. 250, Pl. iv., fig. 14. Ralfs, in Pritch., p. 857.

Stomachs of Poolbeg oysters. Dublin Bay.

Triceratium exiguum, (Wm. Sm.) Fresh water.
Valve very minute; areoles minute; angles elongated; sides inflexed. (Pl. 27, fig. 13.)
Wm. Sm., B. D., Vol. ii., p. 87. Brightwell, Q. J. M. S., 1856, p. 274, Pl. xvii., fig. 1. Ralfs, in Pritch., p. 857, Pl. vi., fig. 16.

River Liffey, Co. Dublin.

Genus III. TRINACRIA, Heiberg.

Frustules normally triangular; processes springing from the surface at a right angle, and surmounted by two curved spines; transverse section of the processes triangular.

Trinacria regina, (Heiberg.) Marine.
As but one specimen of this species has been met with by me, and that mounted in balsam, instead of giving my own diagnosis I consider it better to transcribe the exhaustive description of Heiberg.
"Outline of the basal-surface triangular, with an extended depression towards the centre and the short pointed angles. The outline of the side view less than that of the basal-surface, its sides bulged in the middle, and evenly depressed on both sides of the same. The side-surface separated from the front surface by a thick projecting border. The end-processes of varying height, with a prominent keel on the outer margin; spines slightly crescentic. The portion of the side-surface lying between the processes at the angles forms a gently elevated ridge, which again has a slight depression towards the middle

point. The striation of the valves formed of moderately scattered granules, arranged in curved radiating lines, slight or absent; about the middle point, more robust, and consisting of angular granules arranged in three or four longitudinal lines, and in short transverse lines diverging towards the suture, or that portion of the side-surface of the valve which lies between each pair of end-processes. Granules about 22 in 0.05^{mm} along the suture; striation of the connecting-zone unknown; length of the side of the basal surface = 0·055^{mm} – 0·175^{mm}." This beautiful form I considered to be an undescribed species of Triceratium, until I saw Heiberg's figure of Trinacria regina, when I at once recognised its identity. (Pl. 27, fig. 14).

Heiberg, De Danske Diat., p. 50, T. iii., fig. 7.

Arran Islands, Co. Galway.

In reference to the locality of this form, Heiberg says:—"It occurs abundantly in the brown Moleer from Fuur, in which it is one of the most common forms. In the white Moleer I have found only a few single specimens." It is then a matter of interest to discover it on our own coasts.

FAMILY IV. ISTHMIEÆ, Agardh.

Frustules trapezoidal on front view, on the side view broadly elliptical, without processes; one valve having the extreme corner produced, at the end of which is secreted the mucous cushion by which frustule is united to frustule, so as to form an irregularly branched filament.

In a classification founded on the symmetrical or unsymmetrical shape of the frustule, this family should in strictness be assigned to a different position; but I place it here not only in deference to the views of all authors known to me, but because in point of fact it presents considerable analogy to the Biddulphieæ, and without violence could not be suitably placed at a distance from that group.

Genus 1. ISTHMIA, Agardh.

Characters of the Genus those of the Family.

Isthmia nervosa, (Kütz.) Marine.

Striation of valves areolate; areoles large, close, somewhat hexagonal, with numerous strong anastomosing costæ springing from the margin, and disappearing towards the middle of the valve; connecting membrane areolate, areoles much smaller than those on the valve (Pl. 27, fig. 15.)

Kütz. Bac., p. 137, T. xix., fig. 5. Wm. Sm., B. D., Vol. ii.,

p. 52, Pl. xlvii. Ralfs, in Pritch., p. 581. Rab. Fl. Eur., sect. 1, p. 309.

This and the following species have been described by different authors under different generic and specific names, *e. g.*, Isthmia obliquata, Ag.; Diatoma obliquatum, Lyng.; Isthmia obliquata tenuior, Ag.; Conferva obliquata, Engl. Bot., tab. 1869; but as it is not certain in all cases which of the two species was intended, it seems better not to attempt further identification.

Collected in great abundance by Dr. D. Moore on Polysiphonia in Camlough Bay, Co. Antrim; and found by me in almost every marine gathering from that place northwards, but not at all in the same profusion. Malahide, Co. Dublin.

Isthmia enervis, (Ehr.) Marine.
Striation of valves areolate, areoles quadrangular; without costæ; areoles on connecting membrane much smaller, and roundish.

The frustules are generally slighter than in the former species, but the distinctive characters are, first, the absence of the costæ, and secondly, the want of a distinct border on the valve in side view, so conspicuous in Isthmia nervosa.

Kütz. Bac., p. 137, T. xix., fig. 4. Wm. Sm., B. D., Vol. ii., p. 52, Pl. xlviii. Ralfs, in Pritch., p. 851, Pl. x., fig. 183. Rab. Fl. Eur., sect. 1, p. 309.

Stomachs of Ascidians, Roundstone Bay. Arran Islands, Co. Galway. Malahide, Co. Dublin.

FAMILY V. FRAGILARIEÆ, Kütz.

Frustules in front view rectangular, without median line, central nodule, or internal diaphragms. The frustules are usually attached by a stipes, or united together in parallel or zig-zag filaments.

The group thus limited embraces the following genera:—Fragilaria, Denticula, Odontidium, Plagiogramma, Dimerogramma, Diatoma, Synedra, Raphoneis, and is tolerably well defined by the common characteristics above specified. In the case of Raphoneis indeed it is doubtful whether the frustules are free or stipitate. I have never seen them in a growing state, but in other respects they exhibit the common character of the Fragilarieæ.

The above genera have been distributed by different authors very differently from their present arrangement. Kützing grouped such of the above genera as were known to him under the Fragilarieæ, with the exception of Synedra, which he and others have unaccountably, as it appears to me, placed under the Surirelleæ. William Smith, who attaches great importance to what others have regarded as a subordinate feature—namely, the attachment of the frustules in filaments—has accordingly placed together such of the above-mentioned genera as seem to have been known to him, with the exception of Synedra, which he has ranged immediately after Pleurosigma. The position thus assigned to Synedra may possibly be owing to his supposing that the median, longitudinal, narrow, unstriated space, and the unstriated central space, which some of the forms present, are analogous to the median line and central nodule of the Naviculaceæ. Grunow has adopted a group, which he has named Diatomeæ, distributed into two sub-groups, distinguished by the absence of diaphragms in the one, and the presence of this structure in the other. The former very nearly corresponds with Fragilarieæ as here defined. The genera which Grunow includes in the first sub-group of Diatomeæ are Odontidium, Diatoma, Plagiogramma, Fragilaria, Dimeregramma, his new genus Cymatosira, Grammonema, Raphoneis, Doryphora, Synedra, Asterionella, and Desmogonium. Of these, Grammonema is considered by Ralfs, Kützing, Ehrenberg, and Meneghini, as not diatomaceous. If, however, it belong to the Diatomaceæ, as I think it does, its proper position is with the Fragilarieæ. Doryphora, Grunow describes as a stipitate Raphoneis, while in reality it is a stipitate Navicula, and should therefore be ranked with the Naviculaceæ. Asterionella should be excluded from this group, in consequence of its unsymmetrical outline, both on the front and side views; while the general characters of Desmogonium are those of the Fragilarieæ. Ralfs adopts Fragilarieæ as the designation of a group in which he includes Denticula, Plagiogramma, Odontidium, Fragilaria, Grammonema, Diatoma, all of which are placed by me in the present group; but he adds also the following very heterogeneous genera:—Asterionella, Nitzschia, Ceratoneis, and Amphipleura; while Synedra, Desmogonium, Dimeregramma, Staurosira, Raphoneis, under which he includes Doryphora, are ranged under the Surirelleæ. These latter genera seem to have little in common with the Surirelleæ, while, with the exception of Doryphora, already referred to, they exhibit the general features of the Fragilarieæ; Asterionella, Nitzschia, and Ceratoneis, which is unnecessarily separated from Nitzschia, on account of having unsymmetrical frustules, are incongruously forced into this group; and Amphipleura, by its conspicuous median line, is more analogous to the Naviculaceæ. Lastly, Heiberg adopts Kützing's group of Fragilarieæ, which he divides into two sub-groups—Fragilarieæ genuinæ, and Fragilarieæ cuneatæ. The former, so far as it extends, corresponds with the present group, while the genera contained in the latter, Meridion and Asterionella, seem so incongruous that they should be placed in a widely different position.

Genus I. FRAGILARIA, Lyngb..

Frustules on front view more or less perfectly quadrangular, united in filaments, in which they are parallel; connecting zone usually very narrow; striæ on the side view very fine, usually persistent, and appearing on the front view, where they form a narrow margin.

Fragilaria capucina, (Desmazieres.)   Fresh water.
Frustules flat, so that the band of striæ appearing on the front view is very narrow. On side view the valves are narrow, linear, with either acute or slightly rounded apices; striæ very fine, persistent.

This species includes Fragilaria acuta, which is scarcely distinguishable from it.

Kütz. Bac., p. 45, T. xvi., fig. 3. Rab. Süssw. Diat., p. 33; T. i., fig. 2. Wm. Sm., B. D., Vol. ii, p. 22, Pl. xxxv., fig. 296. Ralfs, in Pritch., p. 776. Grunow, Verhand der K. K. Zool. Bot. Gesel., Band xii., 1862, p. 372. Castracane, Catalogo di Diat. raccolte nella Val. Intrasca, p. 15.

This species is of almost universal occurrence.

Fragilaria virescens, (Ralfs.)   Fresh water.
Frustules more arched than in the preceding species, and the marginal line of striæ, as seen on the front view, therefore wider. On side view linear, or slightly elliptical; narrowed at the ends, but not constricted; striæ fine, persistent.

Ralfs, A. N. H., Vol. xii., Pl. ii., fig. 6. Kütz. Bac., p. 46, T. xvi,, fig. 4. Rab. Süssw. Diat., p. 33, T. i., fig. 1. Wm. Sm. B. D., Vol. ii, p. 22, Pl. xxxv., fig. 297. Ralfs, in Pritch., p. 777. Grunow, Verhand der K. K. Zool. Bot. Gesel., Band xii., 1862, p. 373, T. iv., fig. 15. Heiberg, De Danske Diat., p. 60. Castracane, Catalogo di Diat. raccolte nella Val. Intrasca, p. 15. Cleve, Om Svenska och Norska Diat., p. 219.

Friarstown, Piperstown, Killikee, Co. Dublin. Glenchree, Greenane, Co. Wicklow. Feighcullen, Co. Kildare. (Moanarone, Co. Cork; Wm. Sm.)

Fragilaria æqualis, (Heiberg.)   Fresh or Brackish water.
Frustules considerably longer than in the last species; on side view linear; ends attenuated and rounded; striæ fine, persistent. Heiberg's figure represents the striæ as interrupted by a narrow median space, but in the forms that came under my inspection the striæ, although at first they seemed interrupted, as described by Heiberg, on closer examination were obviously persistent.

Heiberg, De Danske Diat., p. 61, T. iv., fig. 12. Cleve, Om Svenska och Norska Diat., p. 219.

Oyster beds, Malahide, Co. Dublin.

Fragilaria maxima, N. S. Fresh water.
Frustules very large; on side view, considerably expanded in the middle, and gradually tapering towards the rounded ends; striæ fine, persistent. (Pl. 27, fig. 16.)

Aghold, Co. Wicklow.

Fragilaria crotonensis, (Kitton.) Fresh water.
Frustules long; margins on front view slightly waved; on the side view narrow; very slightly expanded in the middle, and gently attenuated towards the slightly capitate ends; striæ fine, persistent.
This species seems widely diffused, having been found by me in gatherings made by Mr. Mozeley, of H.M.S. Challenger, at Kerguelin's Land.

Pond, Newcastle Lyons, Co. Dublin. Mill-pond, Greenane, near Rathdrum, Co. Wicklow. Lough Derg, Co. Galway. Bundoran, Co. Donegal.

Fragilaria tenuicollis, (Heib.) Fresh water.
Frustules small; on front view slightly attenuated at the ends; on side view narrow, considerably expanded in the middle, and gently attenuated towards the capitate, rounded ends; striæ fine, persistent.
Heiberg, De Danske Diat., p. 62, T. v., fig. 13.

Mill-pond, Greenane, near Rathdrum, Co. Wicklow. Malahide, Co. Dublin.

Fragilaria striatula, (Lyngb.) Marine.
Frustules short; on side view linear, rounded at the ends; striæ extremely fine, persistent.
Lyngbye, Tent. Hydr. Dan., p. 183, T. lxiii. Wm. Sm., B. D., Vol. ii., p. 23. Cleve, Om Svenska och Norska Diat., p. 219.—Fragilaria aurea, Grev. Brit. Flora, p. 403. Harvey's Manual, p. 197.—Grammonema jurgensii, Agardh, Consp., p. 63. Ralfs, in Pritch., p. 778, Pl. xv., figs. 24, 25. Rab., Fl. Eur., sect. 1, p. 124.—Grammatonema stratulum, Kütz. Sp. Alg., p. 187.

Salt ditch, Arklow, Co. Wicklow. Ballybrack, Monkstown, Kingstown, Co. Dublin. Larne, Rathlin Island, Co. Antrim.

Fragilaria construens, (Ehr.) Fresh water.
Frustules short; on side view greatly expanded; ends short and attenuated; striæ fine, persistent.
Grunow, Verhand der K. K. Zool. Bot. Gesel., Band xii., 1862, p. 371. Rab., Fl. Eur., sect. 1, p. 120.—Staurosira construens, Ehr. Mic., T. iii. 3, fig. 8; T. iii. 1, fig. 15; T. xxxix. 2, fig. 10. Ralfs, in Pritch., p. 791. Pl. xv., fig. 5.—Odontidium tabellaria, Wm. Sm.,

B. D., Vol. ii., p. 17. Pl. xxxiv., fig. 291 *a*., and Fragilaria undata, Supp. Pl. lx., fig. 377 *a*.

Piperstown, Killikee, Co. Dublin. Verner's Bridge, Co. Armagh, Float bog, Co. Westmeath.

Wm. Smith has described a form as Odontidium parasiticum, sometimes expanded in the middle, sometimes constricted, B. D., Vol. ii., p. 19, Supp. Pl. lx., fig. 375. The separate valves of the latter would seem to be a variety of the following species, those of the former to belong to the present; the habit of growth, however, is much more that of Synedra than of Fragilaria. Some few specimens have occasionally come under my notice, parasitic on Nitzschia sigmoidea, and in no way differing from the representation in Smith's figure. So seldom, however, did they occur, and in such small quantity, I never could make any satisfactory examination of them, and therefore refer to the subject here in deference to the opinions of the best authors, who have placed them in the genus Fragilaria—not because I agree with them in considering such is their proper place, but because I consider it inexpedient to make any change until an opportunity for more thorough examination shall have been afforded.

The forms have occurred in gatherings from Bohernabreena and Killikee, Co. Dublin.

Fragilaria undata, (Wm. Sm.) Fresh water.

Valves broad on side view; constricted in the middle; ends attenuated; striæ strong, persistent.

Wm. Sm., B. D., Vol. ii., p. 24, Supp. Pl. lx., fig. 377.—Odontidium tabellaria, Wm. Sm., B. D., Vol. ii., p. 17; Pl. xxxiv., fig. 291 *a*.— Fragilaria constricta in part, Ralfs, in Pritch., p. 777.—Fragilaria virescens var. undata, Grunow, Verhand der K. K. Zool. Bot. Gesel., Band xii., 1862, p. 374. Grunow regards this form as likely identical with Fragilaria constricta, Ehr. Mic., T. xvi., 2, figs. 34, 35; as also with F. binodis, Ehr. Mic., T. vi. 1, fig. 43; but as there is some doubt on this point, and as some of the figures of the forms so named appear to be incorrectly attributed to this species, it is better to refer the species to Wm. Smith, whose figure admits of no doubt.

Bohernabreena, Killikee, Co. Dublin.

Fragilaria mesolepta, (Rab.) Fresh or brackish water.

Frustules on front view regularly quadrangular; on side view narrow, constricted at the middle, and more slightly constricted towards the apices, which are narrowed, produced, and sub-capitate; striæ fine, persistent.

Heiberg, De Danske Diat., p. 61, T. iv., fig. 11.—Fragilaria capucina var. mesolepta, Rab., Fl. Eur., sect. 1, p. 118.

Rock pool on sea-shore, Carrickfergus, Co. Antrim. Malahide; Basin, Ringsend, Co. Dublin.

Genus II. DENTICULA, Kütz.

Frustules united in parallel filaments; on front view regularly quadrangular, on side view narrow, elliptical, costate, costæ not pervious.

Kützing's distinction between this genus and Odontidium is not very obvious. Smith entertains considerable doubt as to the propriety of separating them, but distinguishes them by the relative length of the filaments. Those whose frustules form short filaments, he attributes to Denticula, while those forming filaments of considerable length constitute the genus Odontidium. Ralfs retains the two genera, interposing that of Plagiogramma between them, and remarks that, in the valves of Denticula, fine striæ are interposed between the costæ, this peculiarity not being noticeable in the valves of the several species of Odontidium. Rabenhorst also retains the two genera, and interposes the genus Gomphogramma between them, his distinguishing character being the same as that on which Smith relies. Grunow relegates the genus Denticula to the group Nitzschieæ, separating from it Denticula obtusa, Kütz., which he includes under Fragilarieæ; while Heiberg, who appears to be followed by Cleve, drops both genera, referring Odontidium parasiticum, Wm. Sm., to the genus Fragilaria, and Odontidium mutabile, Wm. Sm., to the genus Diatoma.

The distinctive characters of the genera, as here defined, rest on the fact that, in Denticula, the costæ are interrupted by a broader or narrower intermediate space, while the costæ in Odontidium are pervious.

Denticula obtusa, (Kütz.) Fresh water.

Filaments short; on side view narrow; elliptical, costæ marginal, with fine pervious striæ interposed.

Kütz. Bac., p. 44, T. xvii., fig. 14. Rab. Süssw. Diat., p. 33, T. i., fig. 8. Wm. Sm., B. D., Vol. ii., p. 19, Pl. xxxiv., fig. 292. Ralfs, in Pritch., p. 773.

River Dodder, Basin of Grand Canal, Co. Dublin.

Denticula mutabilis, (Wm. Sm.) Fresh water.

Frustules varying greatly in size, generally forming long filaments; on side view nearly oval, and sometimes narrow, elliptical; costæ broadly marginal, without interstitial striæ. (Pl. 27, fig. 17.)

Odontidium mutabile, Wm. Sm., B. D., Vol. ii., p. 17, Pl. xxxiv., fig. 290. Grunow, Verhand der K. K. Zool. Bot. Gesel., Band xii., 1862, p. 369.—Fragilaria mutabilis, Rab. Fl. Eur., sect. 1, p. 118. Diatoma mutabile, Heiberg, De Danske Diat., p. 58. Cleve, Om Svenska och Norska Diat., p. 219.—Dimeregramma mutabile, Ralfs, in Pritch., p. 790.

Smith, with doubtfulness, refers Diatoma tenue, Kütz. Bac., p. 48, T. xviii., figs. 9, 10, and Odontidium striolatum, Kütz. Bac., p. 45, T. xxi., fig. 20, to this species; and Grunow, under Diatoma tenue, Kütz., remarks, "I do not find this variety described in Wm. Smith's Brit. Diat.," Verhand der K. K. Zool. Bot., Gesel., Band xii., 1862, p. 362. As so much doubt rests upon the forms described by Kützing, I have referred the species to Wm. Sm., whose accurate figure removes all doubt as to the identification of it.

Lough Mourne deposit. Ditch near Giants' Causeway, Ballyleg, Co. Antrim. Derrylane Lough, Stream near Crossdoney, Co. Cavan. Lucan, Bohernabreena, Co. Dublin. Connemara, Co. Galway. Black Castle, Glenchree, Co. Wicklow. Feighcullen, Royal Canal, near Enfield, Co. Kildare. Tacumshane, Co. Wexford. Killeshin, Queen's County.

Genus III. ODONTIDIUM, Kütz.

Frustules united in longer or shorter parallel filaments; on front view regularly rectangular, on side view elliptical, costate; costæ pervious; their ends very conspicuous on front view.

Odontidium sinuatum, (Wm. Sm.) Fresh water.

Frustules united in short filaments; on side view somewhat lanceolate; outline sinuous; expanded and angular in the middle; costæ relatively fine.

In consequence of the supposed excentric structure of the frustule of this species, Grunow has transferred the genus Denticula, as before stated, to the group Nitzschieæ; and Rabenhorst, taking the same view of the structure of the frustule, adopts his suggestion, but establishes a special genus, Grunowia, for its reception, a course in which he is followed by Cleve. This treatment appears to me inadmissible, inasmuch as the frustules are, in general structure, perfectly symmetrical. In some specimens the striation appears on one side, while the opposite side seems destitute of costæ. This may be an illusory appearance, arising from the convexity of the valve when viewed at an angle to the plane of the field; but, certainly, it is by no means universal. By accurate adjustment I have traced the costæ from one side to the other, and at the extremities, where the convexity appears less than in the middle, the persistent character of the costæ is easily traced.

Denticula sinuata, Wm. Sm., B. D., Vol. ii., p. 21, Pl. xxxiv., fig. 295. Castracane, Catalogo di Diat. raccolte nell Val Intrasca, p. 14. —Dimeregramma sinuatum, Ralfs, in Pritch., p. 730, Pl. iv., fig. 12.

River Dodder, Co. Dublin. Slate quarry, Glanmore, Co. Wicklow. Lough Gill, Co. Kerry.

Odontidium hyemale, (Lyngb.) Fresh water.

Frustules in long filaments; valve on side view narrow, elliptical; costæ strong, about ten in number, with distinct linear striæ between the costæ; ends of costæ on front view forming a narrow margin.

Kütz. Bac., p. 44, T. xviii., fig. 4. Rab. Süssw. Diat., p. 34, T. ii., fig. 4. Wm. Sm., B.D., Vol. ii., p. 15, Pl. xxxiv., fig. 289. Ralfs, in Pritch., p. 775, Pl. xiii., fig. 25. Grunow, Verhand der K. K. Zool. Bot. Gesel., Band xii., 1862, p. 356.—Diatoma hyemale, Heiberg, De Danske Diat., p. 58. Cleve, Om Svenska och Norska Diat., p. 219. —Fragilaria hyemalis, Lyngb., Tent. Hydr. Dan., p. 63.

Wet rock, Black Castle, Co. Wicklow. Streamlet near Belfast, Co. Antrim.

Odontidium mesodon, (Ehr.) Fresh water.

Frustules united in long filaments, shorter, wider, and broader than in the preceding species; on side view broadly elliptical, with three to five strongly developed costæ, which, in consequence of the greater convexity of the valve, appear longer on the front than in the foregoing species; fine striæ may be discovered between the costæ without much difficulty. (Pl. 27, fig. 18.)

Heiberg attributes the species to Lyngbye, Smith to Kützing; but as Kützing himself identifies it with Fragilaria mesodon of Ehr, and the Fragilaria hyemalis of Lyngbye is regarded by the same writer as identical with both Odontidium hyemale and O. mesodon, the species may properly be referred to Ehrenberg.

Kütz. Bac., p. 44, T. xvii., fig. 1. Rab. Süssw. Diat., p. 34, T. ii., fig. 2. Wm. Sm., B.D., Vol. ii., p. 16, Pl. xxxiv., fig. 288. Ralfs, in Pritch., p. 75.—Odontidium hyemale var. mesodon, Grunow, Verhand der K. K. Zool. Bot. Gesel., Band xii., 1862, p. 357.—Fragilaria mesodon, Ehr. Mic., T. ii., fig. 9.—Diatoma hyemale, Heib., De Danske Diat., p. 58. Cleve, Om Svenska och Norska Diat., p. 219. Both these last named authors regard this and the preceding species merely as varieties.

Friarstown, Piperstown, Co. Dublin. Glenchree, Powerscourt, Co. Wicklow. Well at Farraghy, River Dour, Co. Cork.

Odontidium anomalum, (Wm. Sm.) Fresh water.

Filaments short; frustules on front view usually exhibiting internal cells, likely the result of imperfect self-division; on side view narrow, linear, slightly constricted at the ends. Costæ strong, about eight or ten in number.

Wm. Sm., B.D., Vol. ii., p. 16, Supp. Pl. lxi., fig. 376. Ralfs, in Pritch., p. 776. Grunow, Verhand der K. K. Zool. Bot. Gesel., Band xii., 1862, p. 357, T. iv., fig. 4. Rab. Fl. Eur., sect. 1, p. 116.

Ditch near Newcastle, Co. Wicklow. This form is usually found in Alpine districts.

Odontidium tenue, (Kütz.) Fresh water.

Frustules united in short filaments; on side view narrow, elliptical, with sharp ends; costæ numerous, with interrupted linear striæ interposed.

Denticula tenuis, Kütz. Bac., p. 43, T. xvii., fig. 8. Wm. Sm., B. D., Vol. ii., p. 20, Pl. xxxiv., fig. 293. Ralfs, in Pritch., p. 773. Rab. Fl. Eur., sect. 1, p. 114.

Powerscourt, Co. Wicklow. River Dour, Co. Cork.

Odontidium inflatum, (Wm. Sm.) Fresh water.

Frustules united in short filaments; on side view short, broadly elliptical, costæ close.

Denticula inflata, Wm. Sm., B. D., Vol. ii., p. 20, Pl. xxxiv., fig. 294. According to Ralfs, = Denticula crassula, Nägeli. Ralfs, in Pritch., p. 773. Rab. Fl. Eur., sect. 1, p. 115.

River Dour, Co. Cork.

Odontidium elegans, (Kutz.) Fresh water.

Frustules united in short filaments, on front view slightly elliptical; truncate, with large glandular expansions at the ends of the costæ; on side view, narrow, elliptical, pointed at the ends; costæ close.

Denticula elegans, Kütz., p. 44, T. xvii., fig. 5. Rab. Süssw. Diat., p. 33, T. i., fig. 4. Ralfs, in Pritch., p. 773, Pl. xiii., fig. 4. Grunow, Verhand der K. K. Zool. Bot. Gesel., Band xii., 1862, p. 549. Rab. Fl. Eur., sect. 1, p. 115.—Denticula ocellata, Wm. Sm., B. D., Vol. ii., p. 20.

Rocks, Bundoran, Co. Donegal. Powerscourt, Rathdrum, Co. Wicklow. Rocks near the sea at Black Castle, and the Silver sands in the neighbourhood of Wicklow. Rocks, Portrush, Co. Antrim. This species has usually been found by me on moist rocks.

Genus IV. DIMEREGRAMMA, Ralfs.

Frustules in short filaments, parallel to each other. On the front view slightly constricted near the ends; on side view elliptical, striate; the striæ marginal.

This genus, in the general appearance of its frustules, bears a strong resemblance to some of the forms included in Odontidium and Denticula, to which latter Gregory assigned the numerous forms described by him, but may be distinguished by the fact that the margin on front view presents a slight constriction at the ends.

O'MEARA—*Report on the Irish Diatomaceæ.* 289

Dimeregramma nanum, (Greg.) Marine.
Frustules on front view slightly arched, short, but broad; end of striæ appearing at the margin; on side view broadly elliptical, lanceolate; marginal striæ long, leaving but a narrow unstriated median space.
Ralfs, in Pritch., p. 790, Plate iv., fig. 33.—Dimeregramma Gregorianum, Grunow, Verhand der K. K. Zool. Bot. Gesel., Band xii., 1862, p. 346. This last named author changes the specific name given by the discoverer, on the ground that the original designation answers only for the smaller forms, the species varying greatly as regards size. Rabenhorst retains the original specific name imposed by Gregory, and adopts the generic name Dimeregramma, but erroneously ascribes the species to Pritchard. Fl. Eur., sect. 1, p. 123.—Denticula nana, Gregory, Diat. of the Clyde, p. 23, Pl. x., fig. 34.

Stomachs of Ascidians, Belfast Lough, Co. Antrim.

Dimeregramma minus, (Greg.) Marine.
Frustules on front view as in the preceding species, only narrower for the length; on side view narrow, elliptical, and pointed at the ends; marginal striæ long, leaving the central unstriate band very narrow.
Ralfs, in Pritch., p. 790. Grunow, Verhand der K. K. Zool. Bot., Gesel., Band xii., 1862, p. 376, T. iv., fig. 29. Rab. Fl. Eur., sect. 1, p. 123, who attributes this species as well as the preceding to Pritchard.—Denticula minor, Gregory, Diat. of Clyde, p. 23, Pl. x., fig. 35.

On piles of wooden bridge, Dollymount. On sea-weeds, Ireland's Eye, Co. Dublin.

Dimeregramma distans, (Greg.) Marine.
Frustules on front view similar in outline to the preceding species; on side view broadly elliptical, and somewhat lanceolate at the ends; marginal striæ costate,'short, leaving a broad, unstriate, median space. (Pl. 27, fig. 19.)
Ralfs, in Pritch., p. 790, Pl. iv., fig. 34. Grunow, Verhand der K. K. Zool. Bot. Gesel., Band xii., 1862, p. 376. Rab. Fl. Eur., sect. 1, p. 123.—Denticula distans, Gregory, Diat. of Clyde, p. 23, Pl. x., fig. 36.

Stomachs of Ascidians, Belfast Lough, Co. Antrim.

Dimeregramma marinum, (Greg.) Marine.
Frustules on front view linear, slightly constricted at the ends; on side view linear, with cuneate ends, and slightly expanded in the middle; striæ moniliform, long, leaving the median unstriate band

very narrow. This species is very much larger than the species heretofore described.

Ralfs, in Pritch., p. 790. Rab. Fl. Eur., sect. 1, p. 124.—Denticula marina, Gregory, Diat. of Clyde, p. 24, Pl. x., fig. 39.

From stomachs of Ascidians, Roundstone Bay, Co. Galway. Seaweeds, near the Newtownlimavady junction, Co. Derry.

Genus V. PLAGIOGRAMMA, Grev.

Frustules similar to those of the preceding genus, from which they are distinguished by the presence of a pair of strong, transverse costæ, including a central unstriate band. Some of the species have also, besides, a similar terminal costa at either end, the space between which and the apex is unstriate; valves striate, except at the central and terminal portions referred to; striæ sometimes interrupted in the middle, sometimes persistent; filaments short.

Plagiogramma staurophorum, (Greg.) Marine.
Valves furnished with a central pair of transverse, pervious costæ; on front view margin slightly dilated; on side view elliptical, obtuse; striæ fine, moniliform, persistent; central costæ inflexed; the unstriate band bounded by the same, narrow, and extending across the valve, from margin to margin.

Heiberg, De Danske Diat., p. 165. Cleve, Om Svenska och Norska Diat., p. 219.—Denticula staurophora, Gregory, Diat. of Clyde, p. 24, Pl. x., fig. 37. Plagiogramma Gregorianum, Grev., Q. J. M. S., July, 1859, p. 208, Pl. x., figs. 1 and 2. Ralfs, in Pritch., p. 774. Rab. Fl. Eur., sect. 1, p. 117.

On piles of wooden bridge, Dollymount, Oyster beds, Malahide, Co. Dublin. Sea-weeds, near Newtownlimavady junction, Co. Derry. Sea-weeds, Bannow, Co. Wexford. From stomachs of Ascidians, Roundstone Bay, Co. Galway.

Plagiogramma costatum, (O'M.) Marine.
Valves furnished with both a central pair of costæ and a single costa at either end; frustules in front view quadrangular; terminal constriction slight; on side view central and terminal costæ inflexed; valve broadly elliptical, with slightly-cuneate ends; central unstriate band extending across the valve; striæ costate; costæ pervious. (Pl. 27, fig. 20.)

O'Meara, Q. J. M. S., April, 1869, p. 150, Pl. xii., fig. 2.

Arran Islands, Co. Galway.

Genus VI. DIATOMA, De Candolle.

Frustules united in zig-zag filaments; strongly costate; costæ pervious.

Grunow states that the various species of this genus, as well as those of Odontidium, possess fine striæ interposed between the costæ, although in the former they are more difficult to be discovered than in the latter. The most careful examination of the valves of Diatoma, on my part, has, as yet, failed to bring them out.

Diatoma vulgare, (Bory.) Fresh water.
Valves much arched, so that the costæ present a deep margin on the front view; on side view the outline is elliptical, sometimes narrowed towards the ends; costæ strong and close.
Kütz. Bac., p. 47, T. xvii., fig. 15, 1–4. Rab. Süssw. Diat., p. 35, T. ii., fig. 6. Wm. Sm., B. D., Vol. ii., p. 39, Pl. xl., fig. 309. Ralfs, in Pritch., p. 778, Pl. iv., fig. 13, Pl. ix., fig. 168. Grunow, Verhand der K. K. Zool. Bot. Gesel., Band xii., 1862, p. 363. Heiberg, De Danske Diat., p. 57. Cleve, Om Svenska och Norska Diat., p. 219. Castracane, Catalogo di Diat. raccolte nell Val Intrasca, p. 15.

River Dodder, Grand Canal at Portobello, Co. Dublin. Well, Strokestown, Co. Roscommon. Stream in Glebe, Delgany, Co. Wicklow. River Moy, Foxford, Co. Mayo. Stream, Killeshin, Queen's County. River Lee, Co. Cork.

Diatoma grande, (Wm. Sm.) Fresh water.
Frustules on front view slightly inflexed; on side view linear, slightly constricted towards the capitate ends; costæ fine, close. (Pl. 28, fig. 1.)
Wm. Sm., B. D., Vol. ii., p. 39, Pl. xl., fig. 310. Ralfs, in Pritch., p. 779. Heiberg, De Danske Diat., p. 57. Castracane, Catalogo di Diat. raccolte nell Val Intrasca, p. 15.—Diatoma vulgare var. grande. Grunow, Verhand der K. K. Zool. Bot. Gesel., xii., Band 1862, p. 364.—Diatoma Ehrenbergii forma grandis, Rab. Fl. Eur., sect. 1, p. 122. Grunow stands alone in subordinating this form to Diatoma vulgare, from which it stands distinguished by numerous characters: so distinct is it from that species in the outline of the valve, both in front and side view, that it seems deserving of occupying the place of a separate species.

River at Belleek, Co. Fermanagh. Tacumshane, River Slaney, near Killurin, Co. Wexford. River Shannon, near Athlone, Co. Roscommon. Lough Corrib, Co. Mayo. Lough Derg, Co. Galway. Lough Neagh, Co. Armagh. Killikee, River Liffey, Co. Dublin.

Diatoma elongatum, (Agardh.) Fresh water.

Frustules on front view greatly inflexed; on side view linear, narrow, with capitate and expanded ends; valves not so much arched as in the preceding species, so that the costæ appear, on front view, as a row of puncta.

There is considerable diversity in the outline of various forms of this species; in some the capitate ends are not so much expanded as in others. In some the margin on side view, instead of being perfectly straight, is slightly expanded towards the middle. The species might, in some cases, be confounded with the preceding; but the characters above given will serve to distinguish between them.

Agardh, Syst., p. 4. Kütz. Bac., p. 48, T. xviii., fig. 18. Rab. Süssw. Diat., p. 35, T. ii., fig. 1. Wm. Sm., B. D., Vol. ii., p. 40, Pl. xl., fig. 311. Ralfs, in Pritch., p. 779, Pl. iv., fig. 14, Pl. ix., fig. 169. Heiberg, De Danske Diat., p. 57. Castracane, Catalogo di Diat., raccolte nell Val. Intrasca, p. 15. Cleve, Om Svenska och Norska Diat., p. 219.—Diatoma tenue var. elongatum, Grunow, Verhand der K. K. Zool. Bot. Gesel., Band xii., 1862, p. 363.

Dundrum, Co. Dublin. Newcastle, Co. Wicklow. (Cork harbour. Belfast, Wm. Sm.)

Diatoma tenue, (Kütz.) Fresh water.

Frustules small; on front view regularly quadrangular; ends of the costæ appearing like a fine line of puncta; on side view broadly elliptical; ends rounded; costæ fine.

Smith makes this species a variety of Diatoma elongatum. Grunow regards it as the representative of a species of which Diatoma elongatum is a variety. A careful examination of the form, I think, will lead to the conclusion that it deserves to rank as a distinct species. In general appearance, in outline, both on front and side view, it differs from Diatoma elongatum; on front view D. elongatum is not regularly quadrangular, but somewhat inflexed at the sides, the ends being broader than the middle; whereas in D. tenue, the front view normally is perfectly quadrangular; on the side view, D. elongatum is more or less distinctly capitate, the ends being broader than the middle; the sides are usually straight and parallel; in D. tenue the side view in outline is broadly elliptical; the ends narrowed and rounded. For these reasons I consider D. tenue is obviously distinct from D. elongatum. It might more likely be considered a variety of Diatoma vulgare, but its features are perfectly distinctive. The valve of D. vulgare is greatly arched, so that the ends of the costæ occupy a large portion of the front view; whereas in D. tenue, the valve is flat, and the ends of the costæ, on the front view, are barely noticeable.

Kütz. Bac., p. 48, T. xvii., fig. 9, 10. Rab. Süssw. Diat., p. 35, T. ii., fig. 5. Ralfs, in Pritch., p. 779. Grunow, Verhand der K. K. Zool. Bot. Gesel., Band xii., 1862, p. 362.—Diatoma elongatum, variety γ. Wm. Sm., B. D., Vol. ii., p. 40, Pl. xli. fig. 311 γ.

Found abundantly in a gathering from salt water at Howth, in which fresh and marine forms were mingled, the latter greatly predominating. Some cuneate forms occurred along with those in a normal state, just as described in Smith's figure; but the former are obviously to be regarded as monstrosities.

Genus VII. RALFSIA, N. G.

As Diatoma, differing only in this respect, that the valves are hyaline, and without costæ.

Ralfsia hyalina, (Kutz.) Marine.
Valves on front view quadrangular; on side view narrow, nearly linear, narrowed at ends.
Diatoma hyalinum, Kütz. Bac., p. 47, T. xvii., fig. 20. Wm. Sm., B. D., Vol. ii., p. 41, Pl. xli., fig. 312. Ralfs, in Pritch., p. 778, Pl. iv., fig. 16. Rab. Fl. Eur., sect. 1, p. 122.—Fragilaria hyalina major, Grunow, Verhand der K. K. Zool. Bot. Gesel., Band xii., p. 374.— Fragilaria tenerrima, Heiberg, De Danske Diat., p. 63. Cleve, Om Svenska och Norska Diat., p. 220.

Salt ditch, Breaches near Newcastle, Co. Wicklow. Sea-weeds, Tramore, Co. Waterford.

Ralfsia minima, (Ralfs.) Marine.
Frustules very small; on front view quadrangular; on side view broadly elliptical.
Diatoma minimum, Wm. Sm., B. D., Vol. ii., p. 41, Pl. xli., fig. 313. Ralfs, in Pritch., p. 778.—Diatoma hyalinum, var. minimum, Rab. Fl. Eur., sect. 1, p. 123.,—Fragilaria minima, Grunow, Verhand der K. K. Zool. Bot. Gesel., Band xii., 1862, p. 347.—Fragilaria tenerrima, Heiberg, De Danske Diat., p. 63. Cleve, Om Svenska och Norska Diat., p. 220.

Found by Ralfs attached to Surirella gemma, but found by me in a brackish ditch, Kilkee, Co. Clare, in which no specimen of Surirella gemma appeared.

Ralfsia tabellaria, N. S. Marine.
Frustules very long, ·0038; on front view regularly quadrangular; on side view capitate at the ends; gently decreasing in breadth, and then gradually expanding towards the middle. (Pl. 28, fig. 2.)

Sea-weeds, Tramore, Co. Waterford. Lough Strangford, Co. Down.

Genus VIII. Rhaphoneis, Ehr.

The characters on which this genus is grounded are:—First. The symmetry of the frustules by which they are separated from Cocconeis, which some of the species in other respects closely resemble. Secondly. They do not form parallel filaments, by which circumstance they are distinguished from those of Denticula and Dimeregramma. Thirdly. The striæ are interrupted by the interposition of an unstriate longitudinal band, more or less broad—a feature by which the forms of the genus may be discriminated from those of Diatoma and Odontidium.

While adopting this genus, I do so with somewhat of the feeling which Grunow has so well expressed in the following remarks:— "The genus Rhaphoneis, which here I represent in Ehrenberg's sense of it, is widely separated therefrom, for the purpose of receiving forms which, in point of fact, have but little generic relationship to each other. Meanwhile, it is nevertheless a sort of refuge for various Diatoms which have not been thoroughly investigated, and which, in some cases, are known only so far as their side view is concerned. A portion of these, upon more mature knowledge, may be transferred to Dimeregramma, while others, from their Cocconeis-like habit, must certainly be constituted as a special genus. Very numerous instances of forms belonging to the latter class have come under my notice; and I am convinced that they do not underlie the upper valves of Cocconeis—and for this reason, that I have never found associated with them valves of Cocconeis with a central nodule, or valves which in other details of structure would be supposed to correspond with them." Verhand der K. K. Zool. Bot. Gesel., Band xii., 1862, p. 378. Two of the forms herein included—namely, Rhaphoneis amphiceros and Rhaphoneis rhombus, Smith has placed side by side, under the same generic name, with Doryphora Boeckii, with which, beyond the fact of being stipitate, they have little in common. Rhaphoneis amphiceros was observed by Kützing *in situ*, and described and figured by him as stipitate. I am not aware whether, in the case of the other forms included, a similar fact has been noticed. Whatever presumption there may be in favour of the supposition, this feature cannot be as yet admitted as a general characteristic of the group. Odontidium Harrisoni, Wm. Sm., the frustules of which in general structure are similar to those of Denticula, as I have defined that genus, exhibits nevertheless a different habit of growth, the frustules being attached by a cushion or short stipes, and forming a filament, the several frustules adhering by their ends to one another. It seems then in this respect, as well as in the interrupted striation, to stand in close relationship with Rhaphoneis amphiceros, and on this account I include it in the same genus; not indeed because I feel quite satisfied on this point, but because, all things considered, I regard this most suitable as a provisional arrangement.

Rhaphoneis amphiceros, (Ehr.) Marine.

On side view valves short, broadly rhomboid; very slightly produced at the apices; striæ large, moniliform, radiate; median free space linear, and very narrow, so much so as to be sometimes scarcely discernible; frustules stipitate. (Pl. 28, fig. 3.)

Ralfs. in Pritch., p. 791, Pl. xiv., fig. 21. Rab. Fl. Eur., sect. 1, p. 126.—Doryphora amphiceros, Kütz. Bac., p. 74., T. xxi., fig. 2. Wm. Sm., B. D., Vol. i., Pl. xxiv., fig. 224. Grunow, Verhand der K. K. Zool. Bot. Gesel., Band xii., 1862, p. 384.

From mud on sea-shore, Co. Clare, supplied by Professor Sullivan. On Sea-weeds, Co. Clare. On Sea-weeds, Co. Donegal.

Var. leptoceros, (Ehr.) Marine.

Similar in all respects to Rhaphoneis amphiceros, but longer, narrower, and the ends produced into long beaks.

Rhaphoneis leptoceros, Ralfs, in Pritch., p. 791.

Sea-weeds, Co. Donegal; sea-weeds, Co. Clare.

Rhaphoneis rhombus, (Ehr.) Marine.

Valves narrow, elliptical; ends rounded, striæ fine; moniliform; parallel in the middle, and slightly radiate towards the ends; median unstriate space narrow, linear in the middle, and expanding towards the ends.

Ralfs, in Pritch, p. 792. Grunow, Verhand der K. K. Zool. Bot. Gesel., Band xii., 1862, p. 379, T. iv., fig. 36. Roper, Q. J. M. S., Trans., Vol. ii., 1854, Pl. vi., figs. 7–10.

Concerning this form, Grunow, as above cited, makes the following noteworthy remarks :—" Rhaphoneis rhombus ought to be considered as the type of the genus Rhaphoneis, which must ever stand, though other species be separated as not belonging to it. The frustules in contradistinction to Doryphora occur free, as I consider I have satisfied myself to be the case."

Sea-weeds, Dundalk, Co. Louth. Piles of the wooden bridge, Dollymount, Co. Dublin. Sea-weeds, Co. Donegal.

A smaller variety occurs frequently in the last named gathering, much broader for the length than the ordinary specimens, but in other respects so similar that it cannot be considered even a variety.

Rhaphoneis scutelloides, (Grunow.) Marine.

Valves small, on front view broadly elliptical, rounded at the ends, stiræ obscurely moniliform, nearly parallel at the middle, and slightly radiate towards the ends; median free space, narrow, elliptical. (Pl. 28, fig. 4.)

Grunow, Verhand der K. K. Zool. Bot. Gesel., Band xii., 1862, p. 383, T. iv., fig. 34.

Sea-weeds, Co. Donegal.

Rhaphoneis lorenziana, (Grunow.) Marine.
Valves considerably larger than the last named, and in all respects similar, except that in outline the valves are rhomboid.
Grunow, Verhand, der K. K. Zool. Bot. Gesel., Band xii., 1862, p. 381, T. iv., fig. 5.

Piles of wooden bridge, Dollymount, Co. Dublin.

Rhaphoneis liburnica, (Grunow.) Marine.
Valves broadly elliptical, almost circular; striæ large, moniliform, squarish, distinct, larger at the middle, and decreasing in size as they approach the margin, radiate; median unstriate, space narrow, elliptical. (Pl. 28, fig. 5.)
This form presents very much the appearance of a Cocconeis, in which genus I would have provisionally placed it, were it not that Grunow, who first discovered it, placed it here.
Grunow, Verhand der Zool. Bot. Gesel., Band xii., 1862, p. 383, T. iv., fig. 6.

Arran Islands, Co. Galway.

Rhaphoneis Harrisonii, (Wm. Sm.) Fresh water.
Frustules attached, filamentous, connected by their ends; on front view quadrangular; on side view somewhat cruciform; angles rounded; striæ costate, slightly radiate; median unstriate space narrow, linear.
Odontidium Harrisonii, Wm. Sm., B. D., Vol. ii., p. 18, Supp. Pl. lx., fig. 373.—Dimeregramma Harrisonii, Ralfs, in Pritch., p. 290, Pl. viii., fig. 6.—Fragilaria Harrisonii, Rab. Fl. Eur., sect. 1, p. 119.—Diatoma Harrisonii, Cleve, Om Svenska och Norska Diat., p. 219.

Friarstown, Killikee, River Dodder, Bohernabreena, Co. Dublin. Royal Canal, near Enfield, Co. Kildare. Portadown. Verner's Bridge, Co. Armagh.

Genus IX. SYNEDRA, Ehr.

Frustules long and narrow, both on side and front view; attached by a gelatinous cushion, or by a longer or shorter stipes.

The characteristics of this genus are so well marked, that very little difference of opinion has existed from the first as to the grouping of the several species, although the relation of the genus to other genera has been very differently represented. Kützing includes Synedra in his group of Surirelleæ, in which besides he ranges the genera Campylodiscus, Surirella, and Bacillaria. The last named has, indeed, a superficial resemblance to the frustules of Synedra, but, in consequence of its unsymmetrical character, has, by more recent authors, been transferred to the Nitzschieæ; but with Campylodiscus and Surirella, Synedra has few common characteristics. Ralfs, while he adopts this grouping of Kützing, expresses dissatisfaction with an arrangement so heterogeneous, and suggests that, with more propriety, Synedra should be ranked under the Fragilarieæ. It is not very easy to ascertain precisely what Smith's views were as to the relations of Synedra; for while in the plates the Synedræ are ranged next to the Nitzschiæ, in the text they are interposed between Pleurosigma and Cocconema. For the reason already specified, the Synedræ and Nitzschiæ stand very remote from one another, in a classification based on the symmetrical or unsymmetrical structure of the frustule. And on the same ground, as well as for other reasons, I cannot consider that the right position of Synedra is in close relation either with Cocconema or Pleurosigma. Grunow, either led by the suggestion of Ralfs, or by his own sagacity, included the genus in the first sub-group of his group Diatomeæ; and although some genera which, for reasons specified before, ought not to be placed in this connexion, are included in the sub-group, still, by this arragement, the genus was associated with its natural allies. Heiberg's group of Fragilarieæ is nearly identical with Grunow's sub-group of Diatomeæ, the only difference being, that he includes in it the genus Meridion, which, in consequence of the unsymmetrical structure of its frustules, requires a different collocation. With the exceptions mentioned, I agree with Grunow and Heiberg as to the true relationship of Synedra; and in this view am sustained by the judgment of Rabenhorst also, who, though in his Süssw. Diat. he places the Synedræ between the Naviculeæ and Cuneatæ, in his more recent work, "Flora Europaea Algarum," follows the more natural grouping of Grunow and Heiberg. The frustules of Ralfsia tabellaria, regarded separately, might be considered to belong to the Synedræ, and were, indeed, regarded by me as identical with Synedra gracilis vera, not of W. Smith, but of Grunow, Verhand der K. K. Zool. Bot. Gesel., Band xii., 1862, p. 401, T. v., fig. 17, which it strongly resembles, until I had seen the frustules *in situ*, and so became convinced of my mistake. And in some cases it is difficult to distinguish between the separate frustules of some of the larger forms of Fragilaria, and some species of Synedra. I would specially refer to Fragilaria ungeraria, Grunow, the frustules of which, when detached, are scarcely, if at all, distinguishable from those of the form described by Kützing as Synedra amphirhynchus. But whatever slight confusion may arise in such cases, attention to the distinctive characteristics of the genus will readily remove it.

(a.) *Striæ pervious ; frustules not arcuate on side view.*

Synedra chrystallina, (Lyngb.) Marine.
Valve very long ; slightly expanded at the centre and extremities ; striæ costate ; costæ coarse ; an intramarginal longitudinal line appears on both sides throughout the entire length. (Pl. 28, fig. 6.)

Grunow describes the stipes as short, and occasionally slightly branched. Kützing regards this species as identical with Diatoma crystallinum of Agardh, and suggests, with a note of doubtfulness, that it may be the same as Echinella fasciculata of Lyngbye. Smith confirms the former opinion, and that on the inspection of authentic specimens. Heiberg, who seems to have had the opportunity of inspecting authentic specimens of Lyngbye's species, considers it the same as the present. The species I attribute to Lyngbye, and adopt Agardh's name to obviate confusion with other species named S. fasciculata.

Kütz. Bac., p. 69, T. xvi., fig. 1. Wm. Sm., B. D., Vol. i., p. 74, Pl. xii., fig. 101. Ralfs, in Pritch., p. 789. Grunow, Verhand der K. K. Zool. Bot. Gesel., Band xii., 1862, p. 407. Heiberg, De Danske Diat., p. 64. Rab. Fl. Eur., sect. 1, p. 139.—Diatoma chrystallinum, Agardh Consp., p. 52.—Echinella fasciculata, Lyngb. Tent. Hydrophyt. Dan., p. 210.

On sea-weeds, Salthill, Co. Dublin. From stomachs of Ascidians, Roundstone Bay, Co. Galway. On sea-weeds, near Dundalk, Co. Louth. On sea-weeds, Belfast Lough, Co. Antrim.

Synedra fulgens, (Greville.) Marine.
Similar to the preceding species, with which it is often associated, but may be distinguished by the greater delicacy of the striæ. The stipes as described by Kützing is long and branched. (Pl. 28, fig. 7.)

Wm. Sm., B. D., Vol. i., p. 74, Pl. xii., fig. 103. Ralfs, in Pritch., p. 789. Grunow, Verhand der K. K. Zool. Bot. Gesel., Band xii., 1862, p. 408. Raben. Fl. Eur., sect. 1, p. 140. Cleve, Om Svenska och Norska Diat., p. 220.—Lichmophora fulgens, Kütz. Bac., p. 123, T. xiii., fig. 5. Kützing and Smith concur in the identification of this species with Exilaria fulgens, Greville, who has a prior claim to the authorship of this species.

Salt ditch near Wexford. Bannow, Co. Wexford. Sea-weeds, Malahide. Stomachs of Pectens, Dublin Bay. Dollymount, Co. Dublin. Stomachs of Ascidians, Co. Clare. Sea-weeds, Dundalk, Co. Louth. Sea-weeds, Belfast Lough, Co. Antrim.

Synedra baculus, (Greg.) Marine.
Similar to preceding species, but not expanded at the middle or ends as it is; striæ somewhat coarser, and without the submarginal longitudinal lines. (Pl. 28, fig. 8.)

Gregory, Q. J. M. S. Trans., Vol. v., 1857, p. 88, Pl. i., fig. 54.

Sea-weeds, Co. Clare. Stomachs of Ascidians, Roundstone Bay, Co. Galway.

Synedra superba, (Kütz.) Marine.

Frustules long on front view, quadrangular, slightly tapering at the ends; on side view tapering slightly from the middle to the broadly rounded ends; submarginal longitudinal lines strongly developed; striæ linear, coarse, and slightly waved; stipes short. (Pl. 28, fig. 9.)

Kütz. Bac., p. 69, T. xv., fig. 13. Wm. Sm., B. D., Vol. i., p. 74, Pl. xii., fig. 102. Ralfs, in Pritch., p. 789. Grunow, Verhand. der K. K. Zool. Bot. Gesel., Band xii. p. 406. Ralfs, in Pritch., p. 789. Cleve, Om Svenska och Norska Diat., p. 220. Rab. Fl. Eur., sect. 1, p. 139.

From stomachs of Ascidians, as well as from seaweeds, Belfast Lough, Co. Antrim. Seaweeds, Rostrevor, Co. Down. Seaweeds, near Wexford. Seaweeds, Malahide, Co. Dublin. Arran Islands, Stomachs of Ascidians, Roundstone Bay, Co. Galway.

Synedra amphicephala, (Kütz.) Fresh water.

Frustule small and narrow, length ·0018, breadth in middle, on side view ·00015. On front view linear; on side view nearly linear in the middle, and gradually attenuated towards the slightly dilated apices; striæ very fine. (Pl. 28, fig. 10.)

Grunow places this species in association with those in which the striæ are interrupted in the middle by a longitudinal sulcus, but in the specimens which have come under my notice the striæ are obviously pervious.

Kütz. Bac., p. 64, T. iii., fig. 12. Rab. Süssw. Diat., p. 53, T. iv., fig. 28. Ralfs, in Pritch., p. 787. Grunow, Verhand. der K. K. Zool. Bot. Gesel., Band xii., 1862, p. 400, T. v., fig. 11. Rab. Fl. Eur., sect. 1, p. 136.

Feighcullen, Co. Kildare. Kilcool, Powerscourt, Co. Wicklow. Bantry, Well at Farraghy, Co. Cork. Tarbert, Co. Kerry.

Synedra investiens, (Wm. Sm.) Marine.

Frustules minute, length varying from ·0005 to 0020; on front view quadrangular, on side view narrow, linear, tapering towards the rounded extremities; striæ coarse and very close. (Pl. 28, fig. 11.)

Wm. Sm., B. D., Vol. ii., p. 98. Ralfs, in Pritch, p. 787. Rab. Fl. Eur., sect. 1, p. 135. The last named author places this species in a group distinguished by the fact of the striæ being interrupted by a median free space; but in a slide kindly supplied to me by Major Crozier, R. E., and described as part of the original gathering of Smith's Synopsis, the forms answering Smith's description have strong pervious costæ.

Malahide. Kingstown Harbour. Salthill, Co. Dublin.

Synedra acula, (Kütz.)   Fresh water.

Frustules long and very narrow; on front view attenuated at the ends; on side view narrow, attenuated towards the ends, which are usually expanded very slightly, but frequently acute. (Pl. 28, fig. 12.)

Kütz. Bac., p. 65, T. xiv., fig. 20.—Synedra delicatissima, Wm. Sm., B. D., Vol. i., p. 72, Pl. xii., fig. 94, who represents the striæ as interrupted in the middle by a distinct median line with small central nodule, features which do not exist. Ralfs, in Pritch, p. 787. Castracane, Catalogo di Diat. raccolte nell Val. Intrasca, p. 10.—Synedra acus, var. elongata, Grunow, Verhand. der K. K. Zool. Bot. Gesel., Band xii. 1862, p. 399.

Tacumshane, Co. Wexford.   Stream, Crossdoney, Co. Cavan. Friarstown, Malahide, Well St. Fenton's, Sutton, Co. Dublin. Henderson's Well, Aughnacloy, Co. Tyrone.

Var. tenuissima, (Kütz.)   Fresh water.

In all respects like the typical species, except that it is smaller, and much less attenuated at the ends on side view.

Synedra tenera, Wm. Sm., B. D., Vol. ii., p. 98. Ralfs, in Pritch., p. 717, who makes the form described by Smith under this name distinct from Synedra tenuissima, with which I consider it is identical.—Synedra acus, Grunow, Verhand. der K. K. Zool. Bot. Gesel., Band xii., 1862, p. 398.

"Lough Alloa, near Blarney, and near Killaloe, Co. Cork," Wm. Sm., Bohernabreena, Dundrum, Boat harbour, Dolphin's barn. River Dodder, St. Fenton's Well, Sutton, Stream, Blackrock, Co. Dublin. Killeshin, Queen's County, Donoghmore, Co. Tyrone.

Synedra gracilis, (Kütz.)   Marine.

Frustules small, ·0012 in length; on front view attenuated towards the ends; on side view narrow, elliptical, broader in the middle, gradually attenuated towards the rounded and slightly-expanded ends; stipes short, nearly sessile; the frustules being few and radiating slightly. (Pl. 28, fig. 13.)

Kütz. Bac., p. 64, T. iii., fig. 14, T. xiv., fig. 2 *b*, T. xv., fig. 8, 1, 2, 5. Ralfs, in Pritch., p. 786, regards this form of Kützing as identical with that so named by Wm. Smith, B. D., Vol. i., p. 70, Pl. xi., fig. 85. The forms, however, are quite distinct. Grunow, Verhand. der K. K. Zool. Bot. Gesel., Band xii., 1862, p. 401. It is to be remarked that the last-named author regards this species and Synedra barbatula, Kütz. Bac., p. 68, T. xv., fig. 10, as so nearly allied that the latter is to be regarded merely as a variety of the former. I cannot adopt this view, and for these reasons: first, the growth of the two is quite distinct; the frustules in Synedra barbatula are attached in tablets, while those of Synedra gracilis are fewer in number, and somewhat radiately arranged. They differ as respects the character of the striation. In Synedra barbatula the striæ are easily detected, and are divided by a narrow, longitudinal sulcus; in the smaller specimens of Synedra gracilis the striation is obscure, but in the larger forms the striæ are apparent and pervious.

From stomachs of Ascidians, Roundstone Bay, Co. Galway. From seaweeds, Drehidnamaud, Co. Kerry. Seaweeds, Salthill, Co. Dublin. Seaweeds, Tramore, Co. Waterford. Seaweeds, Greenore, Co. Louth.

(b.) *Frustules arcuate on side view, striæ pervious.*

Synedra undulata, (Bail.) Marine.
Frustules very long and narrow, with undulate margins; expanded in the middle and towards the ends; striæ moniliform. (Pl. 28, fig. 14.)

Gregory, Diat. of Clyde, p. 59, Pl. xiv., fig. 107. Wm. Sm., B.D., Vol. ii., p. 97. Ralfs, in Pritch., p. 786. Grunow, Verhand. der K. K. Zool. Bot. Gesel., Band xii., p. 405, T. vi., fig. 1. Cleve, Om Svenska och Norska Diat., p. 220. Rab. Fl. Eur., sect. 1, p. 130.—Toxarium undulatum, Bailey, Mic. Obs., p. 15, figs. 24, 25.

Grunow associates this species with forms characterised by the fact of the striæ being interrupted in the middle, and it is so represented in the figure above referred to; but I have ever found the striæ pervious, as in Gregory's figure.

Stomachs of Ascidians, Co. Clare. Stomachs of Ascidians, Roundstone Bay, Co. Galway. Stomachs of Ascidians, and also from seaweeds, in great abundance, Belfast Lough, Co. Antrim.

Synedra lunaris, (Ehr.) Fresh water.
Frustules on front view quadrangular; on side view arcuate, attenuated towards the extremities; striæ linear, fine, but distinct; stipes short. (Pl. 28, fig. 15.)

Ehr. Infus., T. xviii., fig. 4. Kütz. Bac., p. 65, T. iii., fig. 11. Wm. Sm., B. D., Vol. i., p. 69, Pl. xi., fig. 82. Rab. Süssw. Diat., p. 54, T. v., fig. 6. Ralfs, in Pritch., p. 185. Grunow, Verhand. der K. K. Zool. Bot. Gesel., Band xii., 1862, p. 389. Heiberg, De Danske Diat., p. 65. Rab. Fl. Eur., sect. 1, p. 128. Cleve, Om Svenska och Norska Diat., p. 220. Castracane, Catalogo di Diat. raccolte nell Val Intrasca, p. 10.

Lucan, Co. Dublin. Glenchree, Glenmalure, Co. Wicklow. Derrylane Lough, Co. Cavan. Bellarena, Co. Londonderry. Fivemiletown, Lisnaskea, Co. Fermanagh. Pool, Glencar, Drumoughty Lough, near Kenmare, Co. Kerry. Bantry, Co. Cork. Connemara, Co. Galway.

Synedra biceps, (Kütz.) Fresh water.

Frustules considerably larger than those of the last species; on front view quadrangular; on side view arcuate; extremities capitate. (Pl. 28, fig. 16.)

Kütz. Bac., p. 66, T. xiv., figs. 18 and 21. Wm. Sm., B. D., Vol. i., p. 69, Pl. xi., fig. 83. Rab. Süssw. Diat., p. 55, T. v., fig. 9. Ralfs, in Pritch., p. 786. Heiberg, De Dansko Diat., p. 65.— Synedra flexuosa? Castracane, Catalogo di Diat. raccolte nell Val Intrasca, p. 10. Rab. Fl. Eur., sect. 1, p. 129.—Synedra flexuosa, var. biceps, Grunow, Verhand. der K. K. Zool. Bot., Gesel. Band xii., 1862, p. 390.

Killikee, Co. Dublin. Carrickmacrilly, Co. Wicklow. Glencar, Co. Kerry. Connemara, Co. Galway. Bantry, Co. Cork.

(c.) *Striæ pervious, except in the middle, where there is a free space, bounded by a more or less perfectly developed ring.*

The number of forms legitimately included in this sub-division is very limited, and still there is none, perhaps, in which greater confusion reigns. Smith includes the four following species: Synedra pulchella, Kütz., fresh water; S. gracilis, Kütz., brackish water; S. acicularis, Wm. Sm., which he makes = S. lævis, Kütz., brackish water; and S. minutissima, Kutz., fresh water. The same author excludes from this sub-division S. fasciculata, which seems really to belong to it, judging from the description given, as well as from the figure.

To look at the figures of these several species, it might be imagined there would no difficulty in distinguishing the one from the other; but, practically, the difficulty of determining is found to be considerable. Kützing's figures of them are too vague, and his descriptions too indefinite, to help the student out of the difficulty.

Grunow regards Syn. fasciculata, Kütz., as = Syn. Saxonica of the same author and Syn. gracilis, Kütz., in Wm. Sm., B. D. Syn. parvula, Kütz., he regards as = Syn. fasciculata, Kütz., Wm. Sm., B. D.; and Syn. vaucheriæ, Kütz., as = Syn. minutissima, Kütz., in Wm. Sm., B. D., as well as to Syn. vaucheriæ, Kütz., in Wm. Sm., B. D. The habitat to which these forms have been respectively assigned will furnish no satisfactory distinction. Some are attributed to fresh water, some to brackish; but when forms are ascribed to the latter, it is difficult to ascertain whether they are fresh water forms which have been carried down, or marine forms which have been carried up, or forms incidental to brackish water. Grunow has found Syn. fasciculata in salt water as well as in brackish, and likewise in the Franzensbad deposit, which is a fresh water deposit, and in which I have also found the form so named by that author; from this last fact, I conclude that the form is essentially a fresh water one, and not therefore to be discriminated on the ground of habitat from Syn. pulchella. Speaking of this last named form, Grunow sagaciously remarks, " Whether this species is actually distinct from the preceding (Syn. fasciculata, Grun. = to Syn. gracilis, Wm. Sm.), admits of considerable doubt. Single frustules are not distinguishable. The separation is founded only on the union in larger fans upon a stipes often tolerably thick, which is by no means constant, and the occurrence in fresh water." Verhand der K. K. Zool. Bot. Gesel., Band xii., 1862, p. 392. I am disposed to regard all these various forms as merely varieties of Syn. pulchella—and for this reason, that I have noticed them more or less mixed together in gatherings from fresh water localities, as well as in places where the water was slightly brackish, and almost always exhibiting features of mutual relationship.

Synedra pulchella, (Kütz.) Fresh water.
On front view linear, slightly attenuated towards the ends; on side view narrow, lanceolate, slightly capitate; the median ring strongly marked. (Pl. 28, fig. 17.)

I have never seen the median ring so round or so decided in its character as appears in Smith's figure of the species.

Kütz. Bac., p. 68, T. xxix., fig. 87. Wm. Sm., B. D., Vol. i., p. 70, Pl. xi., fig. 84, Supp., Pl. xxx., fig. 84. Rab. Süssw. Diat., p. 56, T. iv., fig. 17. Ralfs, in Pritch., p. 786. Grunow, Verhand. der K. K. Zool. Bot. Gesel., Band xii., 1872, p. 392. Heiberg, De Danske Diat., p. 65, who considers it a brackish water form.

River Erne, Crossdoney, Co. Cavan. Caum Lough, near Tralee. Pedler's Lake, Dingle, Co. Kerry. Kilcool, Co. Wicklow. Stream, Fintragh, Co. Donegal.

Var. gracilis, (Wm. Sm.) Fresh water.
This variety differs from the preceding only in not being constricted at the ends, and the stipes being short, the frustules scattered and not arranged in the form of a fan. In identifying this species we can go no further back than the date of Smith's work, in which it is faithfully delineated. Kützing's figures of the species named Syn. gracilis are so indistinct that it would be impossible to identify them with certainty. (Pl. 28, fig. 18.)

Synedra gracilis, Wm. Sm., B. D., Vol. i., p. 70, Pl. xi., fig. 85. Ralfs, in Pritch., p. 786, who describes the form as marine. Rab. Fl. Eur., sect. 1, p. 132, where the form is stated to be submarine, in which the author coincides with Smith.—Synedra fasciculata, Kütz. —Synedra saxonica, Kütz, according to Grunow, Verhand. der K. K. Zool. Bot. Gesel., Band xii., p. 391. Cleve regards this species as incidental to brackish water, and with Grunow considers it identical with Synedra fasciculata, Kütz, Om Svenska och Norska Diat., p. 220.

Stream, Port-na-Crush, Co. Donegal. Carnlough, Co. Antrim.

Breaches, near Newcastle. On moist rock, Black Castle, Co. Wicklow. Tacumshane, Co. Wexford.

Var. acicularis, (Wm. Sm.) Fresh water.
Resembling Synedra pulchella, only longer and narrower. (Pl. 28, fig. 19.)
Wm. Sm., B. D., Vol. i., p. 70, Pl. xi., fig. 86, who regards it as a brackish water form.—Synedra lævis, Kütz. Bac., p. 65, T. xv., fig. 8. 2. 3. 4. Were this the case, the variety should be attributed to Kützing, and be called var. lævis; but Kützing's figure is not sufficiently distinct to enable me to identify the variety with it, and therefore I deem it better to retain the name given by Smith, who figures it with accuracy.—Synedra Smithii, Ralfs, in Pritch., p. 786. Grunow, Verhand. der Zool. Bot. Gesel., Band xii., 1862, p. 392, who remarks, "that it is probably only a very long variety of (what he calls) Synedra fasciculata, mixed up with which he found it upon Cladophora flavida, Kütz., on the Peene at Woolgart, and in such manner that no clear distinction existed between the two." Rab. Fl. Eur., sect. 1, p. 131.

River Slaney, Killurin, Co. Wexford. Lough Gill, Co. Kerry. Carrickhugh, Co. Derry. Kilcool, moist rock, Black Castle, Co. Wicklow. In the last named locality, in which this form was found abundantly, marine influence was scarcely possible.

Var. lanceolata, (Wm. Sm.) Fresh water.
Resembling the typical form, but shorter and broader in proportion. (Pl. 28, fig. 20.)
Synedra minutissima, Wm. Sm., B. D., Vol. i., p. 70, Pl. xi., fig. 87, who ascribes the species to Kützing, but the form so called by the last named author, Bac., p. 63, T. iii., fig. 30, can scarcely be identical with it. More likely it is the same as that which Kützing describes as Synedra lanceolata: but whether or not this be the case, the designation is adopted because of its appropriateness, and the species attributed to Wm. Smith, whose figure admits of no mistake. Ralfs, in Pritch., p. 786. Heiberg, De Danske Diat., p. 65, who attributes the form to fresh or brackish water. Rab. Fl. Eur., sect. 1, p. 139.—Synedra vaucheriæ, Grunow, who adopts this view with doubtfulness, Verhand. der K. K. Zool. Bot. Gesel., Band xii., 1862, p. 393, T. v., fig. 9. This last named author regards Synedra vaucheriæ, Kütz., as distinct from the form so named by Wm. Sm., and the former identical with that figured as Synedra minutissima, by Wm. Smith.

River Slaney, Killurin, Co. Wexford. River at Port-na-Crush, and stream, Fintragh, Co. Donegal. Stream, Howth, Co. Dublin. Stream near Giants' Causeway, Co. Antrim. Kilcool, Black Castle, Co. Wicklow.

Var. linearis, (Wm. Sm.) Fresh water.
Smaller than the preceding var., and on side view somewhat linear. (Pl. 28, fig. 21.)
Synedra fasciculata, Wm. Sm., B. D., Vol. i., p. 73, Pl. xi., fig. 100, who has inaccurately confounded this fresh water species with Synedra fasciculata, Kütz. Bac., p. 68, T. xv., fig. 5, which is clearly a marine species.—Synedra parvula, Kütz., according to Grunow, Verhand. der Zool. Bot. Gesel., Band xii., 1862, p. 392, T. iv., fig. 17, where the form is accurately figured; but as it is impossible to identify it with Kützing's figure of the species so named, I consider it more conducive to accuracy to refer this species to Smith, who has so accurately described it; and as his specific name must be abandoned for the reason given, and that adopted by Grunow is not quite certain, I have given it a name characteristic of its general appearance. It is to be noted that Smith separates this form from those with which it stands related; but Grunow and Rabenhorst coincide with me as to its intimate relation to the group of which Synedra pulchella is the type.

Tacumshane, Co. Wexford. Tide pool, Malahide. In both which marine and fresh water forms were mixed up, but I found it likewise mixed with the preceding variety on the surface of wet rocks at Black Castle, Co. Wicklow.

(d.) *Striæ interrupted by a narrow longitudinal sulcus; valves linear.*

Synedra capitata, (Ehr.) Fresh water.
Frustule on front view linear, expanded slightly at the ends; on side view linear, with expanded triangular head. (Pl. 28, fig. 22.)
Ehr. Infus. T. xxi., fig. 29. Kütz. Bac., p. 67, T. xiv., fig. 19. Wm. Sm., B. D., Vol. i., p. 72, Pl. xii., fig. 94. Rab. Süssw. Diat., p. 55, T. iv., fig. 6. Ralfs, in Pritch., p. 788, Pl. iv., fig. 29, and x., fig. 185. Grunow, Verhand. der K. K. Zool. Bot. Gesel., Band xii., 1862, p. 394. Heiberg, De Danske Diat. p. 65. Cleve, Om Svenska och Norska Diat., p. 220.
In Smith's figure there appears a short median line terminating towards the centre in small pear-shaped nodules, and also a central free space; the same features appear in the figure of Ralfs, in Pritchard, but these peculiarities do not occur in the numerous specimens which have come under my observation.

Tacumshane, Co. Wexford. Ditch at railway station, Dundalk, Co. Louth. Stream, Crossdoney, Co. Cavan. Lucan. Dundrum. Boat harbour, Dolphin's barn, Co. Dublin. Royal Canal, Enfield, Co. Meath. Royal Canal, Kilcock, Co. Kildare. Kilcool, Co. Wicklow. The Callows, Ballinasloe, Co. Galway. Limestone quarry, Mullingar, Co. Westmeath. Lough Mourne deposit.

Var. longiceps, (Ehr.) Fresh water.

Like the preceding, but longer, more slender, the ends not so large; not triangular, but rounded off. (Pl. 28, fig. 23.)

Synedra longiceps, Rab. Süssw. Diat., p. 55. Ralfs, in Pritch., p. 788. Grunow, Verhand. der K. K. Zool. Bot. Gesel. Band xii., 1862, p. 386.—Synedra notarisii, Castracane, Dialogo di Diat. raccolte nell Val. Intrasca, p. 9.

Twyford Lough, near Athlone, Co. Westmeath, unmixed with the former, and mixed with it in ditch near railway station, Dundalk, Co. Louth.

Synedra ulna, (Ehr.) Fresh water.

Frustules on front view linear; on side view linear, suddenly contracted at the ends, which are slightly constricted and rounded; striæ interrupted in the centre by a quadrangular vacant space. (Pl. 28, fig. 24.)

It is not easy to comprehend how Smith could have regarded as one species the two forms described by him under this name, B. D., Vol. i., p. 71, Pl. xi., figs. 90 and 90 *B*, than which no two forms of the genus seem to be more distinct. The result is, that great confusion has been introduced, which may be dispelled by a careful comparison of Kützing's description and figure of the species with the actual forms. It is questionable whether the form figured by Smith, as above, fig. 90 *B*, really belongs to Synedra ulna; but, unqestionably, that of fig. 90 must be excluded from its limits.

Kütz. Bac., p, 66, T. xxx., fig. 28. Rab. Süssw. Diat., p. 54, T. iv., fig. 4. Ralfs, in Pritch., p. 788, Pl. x., fig. 184, in which only the front view is given, and the mode of growth is on a short stipes, and scattered. Grunow, Verhand. der K. K. Zool. Bot., Gesel. Band xii., 1862, p. 397, where he identifies this species with Smith's fig. 90*B*, as above cited, and makes fig. 90 a variety marked by the name of lanceolata. Heiberg refers to the species as identical with that of Smith's fig. 90; De Danske Diat., p. 64. Rabenhorst Fl. Eur., sect. 1, p. 133, does not refer to Smith's figures, and follows Grunow, only that he includes Synedra salina, a very distinct species, as a variety of Synedra ulna. Castracane identifies the form so named with that of Rabenhorst Süssw. Diat., T. iv., fig. 4, as well as with that of Smith, fig. 90. Catalogo di Diat. raccolte nell Vall. Intrasca, p. 10.

Tacumshane, Co. Wexford. Caum Lough, near Tralee, Glencar, Co. Kerry. River Dodder, Co. Dublin. Ditch near Wicklow. Feighcullen, Maynooth, Co. Kildare. River Moy, Foxford, Co. Mayo. Well, Farraghy, Co. Cork.

Var. oxyrhynchus, (Kütz.) Fresh water.

Much longer than the typical species, and ends on side view sharper. (Pl. 28, fig. 25.)

Kütz. Bac., p. 66, T. xiv., fig. 11. Ralfs, in Pritch., p. 788.

Grunow makes Synedra oxyrhynchus a distinct species, which he identifies with Synedra oxyrhynchus, Wm. Sm., B. D., Vol. i., p. 71, Pl. xi., fig. 91, and figures a variety distinguished as amphicephala, which appears identical with Synedra ulna, Wm. Sm., B. D., Vol. i., p. 71, Pl. xi., fig. 90 B. The form under consideration seems different from both. Rab. Fl. Eur., sect. 1, p. 135, who follows Grunow.

River Dodder, near Dublin. River Moy, Foxford, Co. Mayo.

Var. amphirhynchus. Ehr. Fresh water.

Like the typical species, from which it differs chiefly by the absence of the quadrangular unstriate space in the centre of the valve, on side view. (Pl. 28, fig. 26.)

Kütz. Bac., p. 66, T. xiv., fig. 15. Rab. Süssw. Diat., p. 55, T. iv., fig. 7. Ralfs, in Pritch., p. 788. Grunow, Verhand. der K. K. Zool. Bot., Gesel., Band xii., 1862, p. 397.

River Moy, Foxford, Co. Mayo. Bohernabreena, River Dodder, pond, Botanic Gardens of Trinity College, Co. Dublin. Greenane, Kilcool, Powerscourt, Co. Wicklow. Feighcullen, Co. Kildare. Killeshin, Queen's County. Well, Farraghy, Co. Cork. Stream near Giants' Causeway, Co. Antrim.

Mr. Kitton of Norwich, and Rev. George Davidson, have supplied me with specimens which would appear to belong to this variety, but growing in short filaments, after the manner characteristic of Fragilaria. I find no description of the stipes in any of the authors who have referred to this form, nor have I ever seen it myself *in situ;* but not unfrequently have I noticed it aggregated in tablets, but not parallel at the ends, as if the aggregation were accidental.

Synedra longissima, (Wm. Sm.) Fresh water.
Frustules very long on front view, quadrangular; on side view linear, till near the ends, towards which it is almost imperceptibly attenuated; ends constricted and then dilated, without any central free space; valves sometimes slightly arcuate. (Pl. 28, fig. 27.)

Smith's description of this species is tolerably accurate; but the figure, B. D., Vol. i., Pl. xii., fig. 95, is calculated to mislead. The form possesses no median line, nor is there a central free space, such as this figure represents.

Wm. Sm., B. D., Vol. i., p. 72. Ralfs, in Pritch., p. 786, who asks "is this distinct from Synedra biceps?" to which I reply, certainly it is. The forms differ greatly in their general appearance, and may be discriminated by the fact that the striæ in Synedra biceps are pervious—in Synedra longissima they are separated by a median sulcus. Cleve, Om Svenska och Norska Diat., 220. Rab. Fl. Eur., sect 1, p. 130, who remarks that "it appears to him an elongated, gently-undulate form of Synedra biceps," and strangely adds, that "he considers Grunow has rightly regarded it as a variety of Synedra splendens."—Synedra splendens, var. longissima, Grunow, Verhand. der. K. K. Zool. Bot. Gesel., Band xii., 1862, p. 397. Grunow considers this form identical with Synedra biceps, Kütz. Bac., p. 66, T. xiv., figs. 18 and 21, and Rab. Süssw. Diat., p. 55, T. v., fig. 9. But however this may be, Synedra longissima and Synedra biceps are in reality distinct species.

Pond in Botanic Gardens, Belfast. Malahide. St Fenton's Well, Sutton. Streamlet, Newcastle Lyons, Co. Dublin. Twyford Lake, near Athlone, Lake Belvidere, Co. Westmeath. Ditch near railway station, Dundalk, Co. Louth. Ditch near Wicklow.

Synedra obtusa, (Wm. Sm.) Fresh water.
Similar to the preceding species, but much shorter; not so much constricted or expanded at the rounded ends. (Pl. 28, fig. 28.)
Wm. Sm., B. D., Vol. i., p. 71, Pl. xi., fig. 92, who regards it as = Synedra ulna, Ehr. Inf., T. xvii., fig. 1; but of this he is doubtful; and Synedra æqualis, Kütz. Sp. Alg., p. 45, ad speciem quæ dedit amico De Brébisson. If Synedra æqualis, Kütz., just referred to, be the same as that described by the same author, Bac., p. 66, T. xiv., fig. 14, it is scarcely identical with the present species.—Synedra splendens, var. obtusa, Grunow, Verhand. der K. K. Zool. Bot. Gesel., Band xii., 1862, p. 397.—Synedra splendens, var. æqualis, Rab. Fl. Eur., sect. 1, p. 134. The linear form of the side view appears to me to distinguish this from the form named Synedra splendens by both the authors last referred to, which Grunow describes as generally, small lanceolate, and less frequently linear, and Rabenhorst as linear, lanceolate. If this form can be regarded as a variety of any other, I think it should be of Synedra longissima, which it very closely resembles.

Tacumshane, Co. Wexford ; Ditch near railway station, Londonderry. Limestone quarry, Mullingar. Twyford Lake, near Athlone. Lake Belvidere, Co. Westmeath.

(c). *Striæ interrupted by a narrow, longitudinal sulcus; valves, narrow elliptical.*

Synedra splendens, (Kütz.) Fresh water.
Frustules long: on front view usually wider at the ends than in the middle ; on side view, narrow elliptical, gradually attenuated to the slightly capitate ends. (Pl. 28, fig. 29).
I have found it impossible to discriminate between this species and Synedra ulna, as described by Wm. Sm., B. D., Vol. i., p. 71, Pl. xi., fig. 90. The latter species, as described by Kützing Bac., p. 66, T. xxxx., fig. 28., is on side view perfectly linear; and although I have occasionally seen specimens which exhibit a ten-

dency towards the elliptical outline, I am disposed to regard these as abnormal, the normal character being linear. Smith indeed distinguishes the two forms by the fact that, in the latter, the frustules are loose and scattered, whereas in the former they are arranged radiately; and, although such a feature of growth is not to be wholly overlooked, it is scarcely sufficient to distinguish the species, especially in the earlier stages of growth, where the frustules are few in number. I am inclined to think the form which Smith describes as Synedra ulna is really Synedra splendens. It seems strange that this form should have been attributed to Wm. Smith, although he regards what he calls Synedra radians as equivalent to Synedra splendens, Kütz.

Kütz., Bac., p. 66, T. xiv., fig. 16; Rab. Sussw. Diat., p. 54, T. iv., fig. 4? Ralfs, in Pritch., p. 788. Grunow, Verhand. der K. K. Zool. Bot. Gesel., Band xii., p. 394.—Synedra radians, Wm. Sm., B.D., Vol. i., p. 71, Pl. xi., fig. 89. Heiberg, De Danske Diat., p. 64. Castracane, Catalogo di Diat. raccolte nell Val Intrasca, p. 10. Cleve, Om Svenska och Norska Diat., p. 220.

Stream, Crossdoncy. Derrylane Lough, Co. Cavan. Lucan. Friarstown, Bohernabreena, Malahide, Co. Dublin. Tacumshane, Co. Wexford. Killeshin, Queen's Co. Royal Canal, Enfield, Co. Meath. Glencar. Pedlar's Lough, near Dingle, Co. Kerry. Ditch near railway station, Dundalk, Co. Louth. River Suck, Ballinasloe, Co. Galway.

Var. radians, (Kütz.) Fresh water.
Like the typical species, but smaller, and the ends more acute on side view. (Pl. 28, fig. 30.)
Kütz. Bac., p. 64, T. xiv., fig. 7. Ralfs, in Pritch., p. 787.—Synedra radians, Wm. Sm., B. D., Vol. i., p. 71, Pl. xii., fig. 89 B, and 89 y.

Friarstown, Co. Dublin. Derrylane Lough, Co. Cavan. Pedlar's Lough, near Dingle, Co. Kerry. Ditch near Dundalk, Co. Louth. Ditches in the Callows, Ballinasloe, Co. Galway.

Var. danica, (Kütz.) Fresh water.
Frustules longer and narrower than the typical species, the striation finer, and the valves on front view more gradually attenuated towards the ends, which are broadly rounded off, and not capitate. (Pl. 28, fig. 31.)
Kütz. Bac., p. 66, T. xiv., fig. 13.—Ralfs, in Pritch., p. 788; Synedra radians var. debilis, Rab. Fl. Eur., sect. 1, p. 134? Grunow considers this var. = Synedra radians, Wm. Sm., B. D., Vol. i., p. 71, Pl. xii., figs. 89 B, and 89 y; Verhand. der K. K. Zool. Bot., Gesel., Band xii., p. 396; but Synedra danica is much longer than that variety, less lanceolate, and with broader rounded apices.

River Moy, near Foxford, C. Mayo. Bantry Well, Farraghy, Co. Cork. Donoughmore, Co. Tyrone. Coolnamuck, parish of Dysert, Co. Waterford.

Synedra salina, (Wm. Sm.) Marine.
Valve lanceolate, gradually attenuated towards the ends, which are rounded off, and broader than in Synedra splendens. (Pl. 28, fig. 32.) Wm. Sm., B. D., Vol. i., p. 71, Pl. xi., fig. 88. Ralfs, in Pritch., p. 787. Grunow, Verhand. der K. K. Zool. Bot. Gesel. Band xii. p. 398.—Synedra ulna, var. marina Rab. Fl. Eur., sect. 1, p. 134.

Tacumshane, Co. Wexford. Malahide, Clontarf, Co. Dublin. Rostrevor, Co. Down. Stomachs of Ascidians, Roundstone Bay, Co. Galway.

Synedra gallionii, (Ehr.) Marine.
Frustules on front view slightly attenuated at the ends, on side view shorter, broader, and more obtuse at ends than in case of Synedra salina. (Pl. 28, fig. 33.)
Kütz. Bac., p. 68, T. xxx., fig. 42. Wm. Sm., B. D., Vol. i., p. 74. Supp. Pl. xxx., fig. 265, who describes a shorter and stouter var. *ib.*, Supp. Pl. xxx., fig. 265 B. Ralfs, in Pritch, p. 788, Pl. xii., figs. 34–36. Grunow, Verhand der K. K., Zool. Bot. Gesel., Band xii., 1862, p. 401. Rab. Fl. Eur., sect. 1, p. 137, who attributes the species to Bory.

On seaweeds, Bannow, and Tacumshane, Co. Wexford. On seaweeds, Malahide, Co. Dublin. Seaweeds, Larne, Co. Antrim. Seaweeds, Dundrum Bay, Co. Down. Arran Islands, Co. Galway, and from seaweeds at different parts of the coast in the Co. Clare.

The smaller variety has been found at Malahide, Howth, Co. Dublin. On seaweeds, Larne, Co. Antrim, and in the other localities where the larger species has occurred.

Synedra spathulata, N. S. Fresh water.
Frustules very large; length, ·0130; on front view wider at ends than middle; greatest breadth, ·0012; ends straight; on side view wider in the middle, and gradually attenuated towards the ends, at some distance from which ·0028, bending inwards and then outwards, then suddenly constricted towards the broadly capitate rounded extremities. Striæ course, costate. (Pl. 28, fig. 34.)

Ditch at bank of Royal Canal, near Kilcock, Co. Kildare. An undulate variety of the species occurs in a well, Newcastle, Lyons, Co. Dublin.

Synedra barbatula, (Kütz.) Marine.
Frustules short, on front view quadrangular; on side view broadly elliptical; striæ fine, but distinct. (Pl. 28, fig. 35.)
Kütz. Bac., p. 68, T. xv., fig. 104. Ralfs, in Pritch., p. 789.— Synedra gracilis, var. barbatula, Grunow, Verhand. der K.K. Zool. Bot., Gesel., Band xii., p. 402.

Salthill, Co. Dublin. Stomachs of Ascidians, Roundstone Bay, Co. Galway. Seaweeds, Tramore, Co. Waterford.

(f.) *Striæ marginal.*

Synedra tabulata, (Agardh.) Marine.
Frustules large, adhering in tablets on a short stipes; on front view wider at middle than at the ends; on side view nearly linear, very slightly attenuated towards the constricted and rounded ends; striæ broader than in the succeeding species. (Pl. 28, fig. 36.)
Kütz. Bac., p. 68, T. xv., figs. 101-3, where the form is described more in accordance with my specimens than that of Wm. Sm., B. D., Vol. i., p. 72, Pl. xii., fig. 96. Ralfs, in Pritch., p. 788; Grunow, Verhand. der K. K. Zool. Bot. Gesel., Band xii., 1862, p. 403. Rab. Fl. Eur. Alg., sect. 1, p. 137. Cleve, Om Svenska och Norska Diat., 220. According to Kützing = Diatoma tabulatum, Agardh, on which authority I attribute the species to Agardh, as do also Ralfs and Rabenhorst, while Smith, Cleve, and Grunow, the latter doubtfully, refer it to Kützing.

On seaweeds, Bannow, Co. Wexford, as well as on seaweeds near the town of Wexford. Seaweeds, Rostrevor, Co. Down. Seaweeds, Malahide, Co. Dublin. Laytown, Co. Meath. Breaches near Newcastle, Co. Dublin. Seaweeds, Larne, Co. Antrim.

Synedra arcus, (Kütz.) Marine.
Frustules much smaller than those of the preceding species, and not dissimilar in their mode of growth; on front view slightly arcuate; on side view slightly sigmoid; striæ short. (Pl. 28, fig. 37.)
Kütz. Bac., p. 68, T. xxx., fig. 50. Wm. Sm., B. D., Vol. i., p. 70, Pl. xi., fig. 98, Pl. xii., fig. 98, in which latter the front view and manner of growth are accurately depicted. Ralfs, in Pritch., p. 789, Pl. iv., fig. 27, where the front view is represented as straight and perfectly quadrangular, and the side view as arcuate, and with a median line, the striæ reaching the latter; in all these particulars the figure is not correct. Grunow, Verhand. der K. K. Zool. Bot. Gesel., Band xii., p. 405. Heiberg, De Danske Diat., p. 65. Rab. Fl. Eur., sect. 1, p. 138.

On seaweeds, Malahide, Monkstown, Bray, Co. Dublin.

Synedra affinis, (Kütz.) Marine.
Frustules in mode of growth similar to the preceding; on front view attenuated at ends; on side view lanceolate; striæ short. (Pl. 28, fig. 38.)
Kütz. Bac., p. 68, T. xv., fig. 6. Wm. Sm., B. D., Vol. i., p. 73, Pl. xii., fig. 97. Ralfs, in Pritch., p. 788. Grunow, Verhand. der K. K. Zool. Bot. Gesel., Band xii., 1862, p. 403. Rab. Fl. Eur., sect. 1, p. 138.

Tide-pool, Wexford. Tacumshane, Co. Wexford. On sea-weeds, Malahide and Clontarf, Co. Dublin. Camlough Bay, Co. Antrim.

Rostrevor and Dundrum Bay, Co. Down. Breaches near Newcastle, Co. Wicklow. Mouth of the Nannywater, Laytown, Co. Meath.

Synedra nitzschioides, (Grun.) Marine.

Frustules on front view slightly attenuated towards the ends; on side view narrow, linear lanceolate. (Pl. 28, fig. 39.)

Grunow does not describe the mode of growth, nor can I say anything on this subject, as the form has been observed by me only after treatment with acid. This species may be distinguished from the last by the linear and slightly apiculate form of the side view.

Grunow, Verhand. der K. K. Zool. Bot. Gesel., Band xii., p. 403, T. v., fig. 18. This species was found by Grunow only in the Pacific Ocean.

From stomachs of Ascidians, Roundstone Bay, Co. Galway. From seaweeds, Rush, Co. Dublin, where it occurs in tolerable abundance.

Synedra frauenfeldii, (Grun.) Marine.

Frustules much larger than the three preceding species on front view, but very slightly attenuated at the ends; on front view narrow, lanceolate, much attenuated from the middle towards the ends, which are slightly dilated; striæ fine, marginal in the middle, but as the valves become narrow towards the ends, they seem to meet. (Pl. 28, fig. 40.)

Grunow, Verhand. der K. K. Zool. Bot. Gesel., Band xii., 1862, p. 406, T. iv., fig. 26. The only habitat given by Grunow is the Red Sea.

Seaweeds, Dundalk, Co. Louth. The form is more slender than that figured by Grunow as above, the apex less dilated, and the striæ shorter; but in the main features the forms are so like as to leave but little doubt of their identity.

Synedra putealis, N. S. Fresh water.

Frustules in length ·0045, very narrow; on front view slightly attenuated towards the ends; on side view narrow, lanceolate, gradually tapering towards the rostrate ends; striæ short; stipes short; on which the frustules are crowded in small tablets containing about ten in each. (Pl. 28, fig. 41.)

This form possibly may be identical with that described as Synedra tenuis, by Kützing, Bac., p. 65, T. xiv., fig. 10, but in some respects it is so different as to warrant the conclusion that it is specifically distinct. Kützing does not describe the mode of growth nor the character of the striæ, and moreover alleges that in the species referred to, the frustules are exactly linear on front view, whereas in the present case they are obviously attenuated.

St. Fenton's Well, Sutton, Co. Dublin. Well near the Roman Catholic Chapel, Ballinasloe, in both which localities it occurs in great abundance, mixed with other forms.

Synedra Smithii, N. S. Fresh water.
Frustules small; on front view quadrangular; on side view narrow, linear; accuminate at the ends; striæ short. (Pl. 28, fig. 42.)

Synedra vaucheriæ, Wm. Sm., B. D., Vol. i., p. 73, Pl. xi., fig. 99, who identifies the species with that so named by Kützing, Bac., p. 65, T. iv., fig. 4, 1, 2a, 3; and so far as the description of it is concerned, not without warrant: but although in some respects the figures cited seem to agree with the form under notice, in other respects there is such a difference as to cast a doubt on the correctness of the identification. Kützing represents the striation in his form as pervious, whereas in that figured and described by Smith the striæ are marginal and very short. Rabenhorst describes and figures a form under the name of S. vaucheriæ; but although from the description it might fairly be supposed to be the same as the present form, the figure renders the identity more than doubtful; Süssw. Diat., p. 55, T. iv., fig. 15. Again, Grunow describes a form as identical with Kützing's Synedra vaucheriæ; Verhand. der K. K. Zool. Bot. Gesel., Band xii., 1862, p. 393, T. v., fig. 9, which seems to differ widely from Kützing's figure, as well from that so named by Wm. Smith. He remarks:—
"The species here referred to, which exhibits a decided relationship to Synedra pulchella, I regarded for a long time as the identical Synedra vaucheriæ of Kützing and recently had my impression on the subject confirmed through means of some specimens of De Brébisson's, kindly sent to me by Professor A. Braun. I find Smith's figure widely different from Synedra vaucheriæ, Kütz., which might much rather be regarded as a form of Synedra affinis, although Synedra vaucheriæ also possesses a tolerably broad unstriate space between the striæ, but in the description I find no allusion to the unstriate very fine ring-formed-pseudo-nodule." These remarks make it obvious that it is impossible to identify Smith's form with Synedra vaucheriæ, Kütz., from which it differs considerably. I have therefore adopted a new specific name, that of Synedra Smithii.

Tacumshane, Co. Wexford. River at Port-na-Crush, Co. Donegal. Malahide, Portmarnock, St. Fenton's Well, Sutton, Co. Dublin.

(g.) *Striæ obsolete.*

Synedra debilis, (Kütz.) Fresh water.
Frustules very minute; on front view regularly quadrangular; on side view elliptical-lanceolate. (Plate 28, fig. 43.)
Kütz. Bac., p. 65, T. iii., fig. 45. Ralfs, in Pritch., p. 787.—Synedra radians, var. debilis, Rab. Fl. Eur., sect. 1, p. 136.

Twyford Lake, near Athlone, Co. Westmeath. River Dour, Co. Cork.

FAMILY VI. STRIATELLEÆ, Kütz.

Frustules precisely as in the immediately preceding family, and distinguished by the possession of internal diaphragms, which, springing from the connecting membrane, are interposed between the two opposite valves.

This family, since it was constituted by Kützing, has been adopted by successive authors, but with some divergence respecting the species comprehended within its limits. As here defined, it embraces not only the genera included in Kützing's family Striatelleæ, but also those of the family Tabellarieæ, which, though generically distinct, come properly within the same limits. The Genera Gephyria and Eupluria, which were included by Ralfs, are here excluded from the family; because in whatever other respects they may agree, they stand remote in consequence of the unsymmetrical structure of the opposite valves. And for a similar reason I exclude Podosphenia, which Heiberg placed in the family, the frustules being unsymmetrical both on front and side view.

Thus defined, the family is precisely equivalent to Grunow's subgroup of Diatomeæ, and stands out distinguished by two very decided features, namely, the perfect symmetry of the valves, and the interposition between them of diaphragms more or less numerous.

The diaphragms constitute so important a feature in the family, that some observations are needed to explain their nature and mode of growth. As far as I know, Ralfs was the first who described these organs with any tolerable approach to accuracy. He says:—"The appearance of longitudinal striæ is in fact produced by silicious plates, arising internally from the margins of the filament, and extending towards, but not reaching, the centre. The interior is thus divided into chambers opening into a central space. When viewed laterally, this central space resembles a canal, especially as the inner edge of each plate has a concave outline." Ralfs, in Pritch., p. 803. If there be anything vague in this description, it is greatly elucidated by the observations of Wm. Smith, as well as by the figures of these diaphragms in the case of Rhabdonema, Tetracyclus, and Tabellaria, B. D., Vol. ii., pp. 32-34, Pl. xxxviii., fig. 306 h and 305†, Pl. xxxix., fig. 308 h and h', Pl. xliii., fig. 316† and 317†.

In these cases, the diaphragms may be regarded as compressed rings corresponding externally with the outline of the valves; but Heiberg has called attention to the fact that, in the case of Striatella, the diaphragms are somewhat differently constructed. "Smith's representation of the structure of this species is in the main correct, but he has misapprehended the form of the diaphragms, considering them to be closed rings (as his figure 307 h, as well as the descriptive term, "Annuli" indicate), whereas in reality they are open at one end. The form of them would naturally be best seen by preparing them out separately. One can, however, satisfy himself that the diaphragms are open at one end, by observing a perfect frustule in transverse view, when one diaphragm is seen from the open, and the other from the closed, side."—De Danske Diat., p. 72. In the case of the diaphragms of Striatella, it may be noticed that the silicious plate is thicker at one end, and becomes gradually thinner as it recedes from it. This fact may serve to illustrate the mode of growth in the diaphragms in other species, as well as in Striatella. Springing from opposite ends, the two contiguous diaphragms in some cases appear much thicker at the starting point, and as they proceed parallel to each other become thinner and thinner as they approach the opposite end of the frustule. The strong lines which appear as costæ on the front view may seem to mark the extreme length to which the diaphragms project into the cell; but the compressed rings are, except in the case of Striatella, complete, and can by proper focusing be traced through their entire course.

Genus I. GRAMMATOPHORA, (Ehr.)

Frustules attached, united in zig-zag filaments; diaphragms two in number; open in the centre, and equally developed at both sides of the same. Valves narrow, elliptical; sometimes slightly expanded in the middle; striæ obvious, and appearing on front view as a narrow striate border.

Although the species of this genus are by the experienced eye easily discriminated, it is not easy to describe their characteristics in words so as satisfactorily to obviate confusion with other forms belonging to the same family, especially with Tabellaria, which they resemble, not only in the mode of growth in zig-zag filaments, but also in the general formation of the diaphragms, which are equally developed on both sides of the central portion. Whether we view the frustules on the front or side views, they may be distinguished by the following characters:—In Grammatophora the valves are sometimes slightly expanded in the middle, but in no case so much so as in Tabellaria; the striæ, too, are ever noticeable, which is not the case with the last-named genus. And on the front view the narrow margin of striæ noticeable in the species of Grammatophora are never to be seen in those of Tabellaria.

Grammatophora marina, (Lyngb.) Marine.
Frustules on front view regularly quadrangular; on side view narrow, elliptical; striæ obvious; diaphragms curved near the ends, and thence running in a straight line towards the middle. (Pl. 29, fig. 1.)
Kütz. Bac., p. 128, T. xvii., fig. 24, who regards the species as identical with Diatoma marina, Lyngb. Wm. Sm., B. D., Vol. ii.,

p. 42, Pl. xlii., fig. 314. Ralfs, in Pritch., p. 808, Pl. iv., fig. 47, Pl. xi., fig. 52 and 53. Grunow, Verhand. der K. K. Zool. Bot. Gesel., Band. xii., 1862, p. 415. Heiberg, De Danske Diat., p. 71. Rab. Fl. Eur., s. 1, p. 303. Cleve, Om Svenska och Norska Diat., p. 222.

Sea-weeds, Malahide. Sea-weeds, Portmarnock, Co. Dublin. Sea-weeds, Portrush; and same, Co. Antrim. Arran Islands, Co. Galway. Tacumshane, Co. Wexford.

Grammatophora macilenta, (Wm. Sm.) Marine.

Frustules on front view quadrangular, but sometimes slightly arcuate; generally much longer than the preceding species; on side view nearly linear; diaphragms similar to the last, except that the foramen is more elliptical, and the striæ finer.

Wm. Sm., B. D., Vol. ii., p. 43. Supp. Pl. lxi., fig. 382. Ralfs, in Pritch., p. 808. Rab. El, Eur., sect. 1, p. 304. Cleve, Om Svenska och Norska Diat., p. 222.—Grammatophora oceanica, var. macilenta, Grunow, Verhand. der K. K. Zool. Bot. Gesel., Band xii., 1862, p. 417.

Salt ditch, near Wexford. Tacumshane, Co. Wexford. Carnlough Bay, Portrush. Waterfoot, Co. Antrim. Dundrum Bay, Co. Down. Arran Islands, Co. Galway.

Grammatophora serpentina, (Ralfs.) Marine.

Frustules on front view regularly quadrangular; on side view linear elliptic; striæ obvious; diaphragms undulate, and seen on front view spiral. (Pl. 29, fig. 2.)

Kütz. Bac., p. 129, T. xxix., fig. 82. Wm. Sm., B. D., Vol. ii., p. 43, Pl. xlii., fig. 315. Ralfs, in Pritch., p. 808, Pl. iv., fig. 48. Grunow, Verhand. der K. K. Zool. Bot. Gesel., Band xii., 1862, p. 420. Rab. Fl. Eur., sect. 1, p. 304. Cleve, Om Svenska och Norska Diat., p. 222.—Striatella serpentina, Ralfs. An. Nat. Hist., Vol. ii., Pl. ix., fig. 5.

Malahide, Co. Dublin. Sea-weeds near town of Wicklow. Tacumshane, Co. Wexford. Portrush, Co. Antrim. Arran Islands, Co. Galway.

Grammatophora balfouriana, (Wm. Sm.) Fresh water.

Frustules small; on front view quadrangular; on side view linear, elliptical; diaphragms direct, without curvature; striæ fine.

Ralfs, following Greville, establishes a new genus Diatomella to receive this single form, and is followed in this view by Grunow and Rabenhorst; but, as it appears to me, the characters are not such as to distinguish the new genus from Grammatophora.

Wm. Sm., B. D., Vol. ii., p. 43, Supp. Pl. lxi., fig. 383. Ralfs, in

Pritch., p. 810, Pl. iv., fig. 51, 52. Grunow, Verhand. der K. K. Zool. Bot. Gesel., Band xii., 1862, p. 319. Rab. Fl. Eur., sect. 1, p. 300.

Lough Derg, Co. Galway. Ulster Canal, near Newry, Co. Armagh. Only a few forms were found in these localities, the species being one of the rarest in Ireland.

Genus II. TABELLARIA, Ehr.

Frustules attached in zig-zag filaments; valves expanded at the middle and ends; striæ faint.

Tabellaria flocculosa, (Roth.) Fresh water.
Diaphragms numerous, thickened ends alternately placed, and varying in length. (Pl. 29, fig. 3.)
Kütz. Bac., p. 127, T. xvii., fig. 21. Rab. Süssw. Diat., p. 63, T. x., fig. 2. Wm. Sm. B. D., Vol. ii., p. 45, Pl. xliii., fig. 316. Ralfs, in Pritch., p. 807, Pl. xiii., fig. 29. Grunow, Verhand. der K. K. Zool. Bot. Gesel., Band xii., 1862, p. 410. Heiberg, De Danske Diat., p. 70. Castracane, Catalogo di Diat. raccolte nell Val Intrasca, p. 15. Cleve, Om Svenska och Norska Diat., p. 221.—Tabellaria ventricosa, Kütz. Bac., p. 127, T. xxx., fig. 74, does not differ from the present species.

Frequent, especially in sub-Alpine and boggy pools. Kützing regards this species as identical with Conferva flocculosa, Roth., on which authority the species is attributed to Roth.

Tabellaria fenestrata, (Lyngb.) Fresh water.
Diaphragms few, and of equal thickness on both sides of the central expansion; frustules much longer than in the preceding species.
Kütz. Bac., p. 127, T. xvii., fig. 22, T. xviii., fig. 2, and T. xxx., fig. 73, who regards the species as identical with Diatoma fenestratum Lyngbye. Rab. Süssw. Diat., p. 63, T. x., fig. 1. Wm. Sm., B. D., Vol. ii., p. 46, Pl. xlviii., fig. 317. Ralfs, in Pritch, p. 807. Grunow, Verhand. der K.K. Zool. Bot. Gesel., Band xii., 1862, p. 410. Heiberg, De Danske Diat., p. 71. Castracane Catalogo di Diat. raccolte nell Val Intrasca, p. 16. Cleve, Om Svenska och Norska Diat., p. 321.

Common in the same localities as the preceding, with which it is usually mixed.

Genus III. TETRACYCLUS, Ralfs.

Frustules united in parallel filaments; filaments free; thickened ends of the diaphragms alternate; valves much expanded in middle; strongly costate; costæ pervious.

Tetracyclus lacustris, (Ralfs.) Fresh water.
Middle expansion of the valve rounded. (Plate 29, fig. 4.)
Ralfs, Ann. Nat. Hist., Vol. xii., 1843, Pl. ii., fig. 2. Kütz. Bac., p. 127, T. xxix., fig. 70. Rab. Süssw. Diat., p. 68, T. ix., fig. 1. Wm. Sm., B. D., Vol. ii., p. 38, Pl. xxxix., fig. 308. Ralfs, in Pritch, p. 806, Pl. viii., fig. 10, and Pl. xi., fig. 24, 25. Grunow, Verhand der K. K. Zool. Bot. Gesel., Band xii., 1862, p. 412. Cleve, Om Svenska och Norska Diat., p. 222.

River Erne, Crossdoney, Co. Cavan. Lake near Castlewellan, Co. Down. River Bann, Verner's Bridge, Co. Armagh. Tonabrick Mountain, Co. Cork; Wm. Smith.

Tetracyclus emarginatus, (Ehr.) Fresh water.
"Valves constricted towards the extremities, which are rounded and sub-apiculate; inflections deeply notched or emarginate; otherwise like the last species."—Wm. Smith.
Wm. Sm. B. D., Vol. ii., p. 38. Ralfs, in Pritch., p. 806. Grunow, Verhand. der K. K. Zool. Bot. Gesel., Band xii., 1862, p. 412. Rab. Fl. Eur., sect. 1, p. 302. Cleve, Om Svenska och Norska Diat., p. 222. Smith supposes this species identical with Biblarium emarginatum, Ehr. Mic. T. xxxiii. 2, fig. 6. On his authority I attribute the species to Ehrenberg.

Gap of Dunloe, Killarney. Wm. Smith. This species is extremely rare, not a single specimen having ever come under my notice from any locality in Ireland.

Genus IV. RHABDONEMA, Kütz.

Stipes short; diaphragms numerous, on the external margin strongly costate, broad; extremity of the valves unstriate.

Smith alleges that in this genus the valves have a median line, a statement which does not appear to be sustained by the facts of the case.

Rhabdonema arcuatum, (Lyngb.) Marine.
Frustules short; on side view broadly elliptical; costate, with moniliform striæ interposed between the costæ; striæ pervious; diaphragms numerous, parallel, with a single foramen. (Pl. 29, fig. 5.)
Kütz. Bac., p. 126, T. xviii., fig. 6, who states that the species is

identical with Diatoma arcuatum, Lyngbye. Wm. Sm. B. D., Vol. ii., p. 34, Pl. xxxviii., fig. 305. Ralfs, in Pritch., p. 804. Grunow, Verhand. der K. K. Zool. Bot. Gesel., Band xii., p. 423. Heiberg, De Danske Diat., p. 70. Rab. Fl. Eur., sect. 1, p. 306. Cleve, Om Svenska och Norska Diat., p. 221.

Salt ditch, near Wexford. Tacumshane, Co. Wexford. Malahide, Ballybrack, Co. Dublin. Carnlough Bay. Sea-weeds, Portrush, Co. Antrim. Sea-weeds, Dundalk, Co. Louth. Sea-weeds near Galway town. Arran Islands, Co. Galway.

Rhabdonema minutum, (Kütz.) Marine.
Valves small; expanded in the middle; attenuated towards the rounded ends; striæ moniliform, pervious; diaphragms few; apparently alternate, with a single foramen.
Kutz. Bac., p. 126, T. xxi., fig. 2, 4. Wm. Sm., B. D., Vol. ii., p. 35, Pl. xxxviii., fig. 306. Ralfs, in Pritch., p. 804, Pl. iv., fig. 41. Grunow, Verhand. der K. K. Zool. Bot. Gesel., Band xii., 1862, p. 423. Heiberg, De Danske Diat., p. 70. Rab. Fl. Eur., sect. 1, p. 306. Cleve, Om Svenska och Norska Diat., p. 221.

Sea-weeds, Malahide; on piles of wooden bridge, Dollymount Strand, Ballybrack, Salt Hill, Co. Dublin. Sea-weeds, Portrush. Larne, Co. Antrim. Tacumshane, Co. Wexford. Dundalk, Co. Louth.

Rhabdonema adriaticum, (Kütz.) Marine.
Frustules very large; valves narrow, linear elliptical; striæ moniliform; diaphragms numerous, not so wide on margins nor so strongly costate as on R. arcuatum, with two or more foramina.
Kütz. Bac., p. 126, T. xviii., fig. 7. Wm. Sm., B. D., Vol. ii., p. 35, Pl. xxxviii., fig. 305 a, b. Ralfs, in Pritch., p. 805, Pl. xiii., fig. 27. Grunow, Verhand. der K. K. Zool. Bot. Gesel., Band xii., 1862, p. 424. Rab. Fl. Eur., sect. 1, p. 306. Cleve, Om Svenska och Norska Diat., p. 221.

Malahide, Co. Dublin. " Cork Harbour. Belfast Bay, near Carrickfergus." Wm. Smith.

Genus V. STRIATELLA, Agardh.

Frustules stipitate; stipes long; valves elliptical, lanceolate, with a median line, without central or terminal nodule; striæ obsolete; diaphragms numerous, on front view linear, unstriate, strongly marked at one end, and gradually attenuated towards the other; not reaching the entire breadth of the valves; arranged alternately; on side view not reaching the full length of valve; open the greater part of the length.

Striatella unipunctata, (Lyng.) Marine.
Diagnosis same as that of the genus. (Pl. 29, fig. 6.)
Kütz. Bac., p. 125, T. xviii., fig. 5, who considers the form identical with Fragilaria unipunctata, Lyngbye. Wm. Sm., B. D., Vol. ii., p. 36, Pl. xxxix., fig. 307. Ralfs, in Pritch., p. 803, Pl. iv., fig. 40. Grunow, Verhand. der K.K. Zool. Bot. Gesel., Band xii., 1862, p. 427. Heiberg, De Danske Diat., p. 72. Rab. Fl. Eur., sect. 1, p. 307. Cleve, Om Svenska och Norska Diat., p. 222.

Sea-weeds, Bray, Howth, Salt Hill, Co. Dublin. Stomachs of Ascidians, Co. Clare. Sea-weeds, Co. Galway. "Larne and Belfast Bays, Cork Harbour," Wm. Smith.

Genus VI. TESSELLA, Ehr.

Frustules stipitate, stipes short; not filamentous; diaphragms apparently reaching not further than the middle of the valve, alternate, arched, and in opposite directions on the opposite sides of the frustule; external edges of the diaphragms slightly striate.

Tessella interrupta, (Ehr.) Marine.
Diagnosis of the species same as that of the genus. Of the side view of this species, I have never been able to obtain a satisfactory observation. (Pl. 29, fig. 7.)
Kütz. Bac., p. 125, T. xviii., figs. 41, 2. This author states with hesitation that there is no stipes in this species, as also does Ralfs, in Pritch., p. 804, Pl. vii., fig. 5.—Striatella interrupta, Grunow, Verhand. der K. K. Zool. Bot. Gesel., Band xii., 1862, p. 427. It is to be noticed that this species cannot be confounded with Striatella interrupta, as described and figured by Heiberg, De Danske Diat., p. 75, T. v., fig. 15, and Rab. Fl. Eur., sect. 1, p. 307.

Sea-weeds, Co. Galway. Sea-weeds, Co. Clare; in both which localities it occurs in company with Striatella unipunctata.

FAMILY VII. AMPHIPLEUREÆ, Kütz.

Frustules free; lanceolate on side view, with median line and long narrow end nodules, but without central nodule, and exhibiting a sub-marginal keel at each side.

Genus I. AMPHIPLEURA, Kütz.

The characters of this genus may be regarded as those of the family. It will be found that the structure of the frustules in this genus has not hitherto been described with sufficient accuracy for their satisfactory diagnosis, and consequently its relations with other genera have been very variously represented. Kützing includes it among the Naviculeæ; Smith places it between Amphiprora and Navicula, while Ralfs, Grunow, and Heiberg, agree in assigning to it a position of near relationship to the Nitzschieæ. The remarks of the last named author are noteworthy:—" Amphipleura is a genus which stands in need of a more precise revision. Grunow, in his first treatise, placed the genus in the group Surirelleæ, with which it has no very close relationship; but subsequently this author established the genus as the type of a special group, Amphipleureæ, and at the same time gave a valuable contribution towards a more precise limitation of the genus: but notwithstanding, much remains still to be done. I have placed the genus with the Nitzschieæ, because Amphipleura sigmoidea, the only species thoroughly examined by me, seems to agree essentially with Nitzschia, and in fact to possess the same unsymmetrical relation of the connecting membrane with the front view. As to the other of the undernamed species (Amphipleura pellucida), I have not as yet had sufficient material to institute a more exact examination, and have been able only to satisfy myself as to its identity with the species of the author named."—De Danske Diat., p. 116. The above remarks indicate the source of the confusion which exists, namely, the supposition that the form described as Amphipleura sigmoidea belongs to the genus Amphipleura; I regard it as not at all distinguishable from Nitzschia sigma. Assigning this latter form to its proper place, we have a distinct and satisfactory diagnosis of the genus Amphipleura, founded on the presence of the median line without a central nodule, and the elongated character of the end nodules, as well as the presence of the submarginal lines. Referring to the last named peculiarity of structure, Smith notices Ehrenberg's ideal transverse section of the frustule, "which represents the ridges as springing from the surface of a convex valve, having between them a depression which corresponds with the ordinary median line of the Naviculæ," and adds, "I am unable to confirm this description."—B. D., Vol. i., p. 45. Grunow, however, asserts that "each valve has three keels; the two submarginal ones springing out so far in one aspect as to stand on the valves at right angles with the margin. In the aspect of the entire frustule as seen from the side, the submarginal keels appear, and the median line forms the contour of the valves."—Verhand. der K. K. Zool. Bot. Gesel. Band xii., 1862, p. 467.

Amphipleura pellucida, (Kütz.) Fresh water.
Valves narrow, lanceolate; striæ obscure. (Pl. 29, fig. 8.)
Kütz. Bac., p. 103, T. iii., fig. 52, T. xxx., fig. 84. In neither of these figures is the peculiar form of the end nodules noticed. Wm. Sm., B. D., Vol. i., p. 45, Pl. xv., fig. 127. Here the valve is repre-

sented without the median line, and having a longitudinal row of moniliform puncta interposed between the margin and the submarginal keels: the latter I have never been able to detect. Ralfs, in Pritch., p. 783, Pl. iv., fig. 30, Pl. ix., fig. 140, and Pl. xiii., fig. 1. Grunow, Verhand. der K. K. Zool. Bot. Gesel., Band xii., 1862, p. 468. Heiberg, De Danske Diat., p. 117. Rab. Fl. Eur., sect. 1, p. 143.

Limestone quarry near Mullingar, Co. Westmeath. Marl-pit, Inch, near Gorey, Co. Wexford. Feighcullen, Co. Kildare.

Amphipleura danica, (Kütz.) Marine.
Similar to the preceding in all respects, save that it is shorter and relatively broader.
Kütz. Bac., p. 103, T. xxx., fig. 38. Ralfs, in Pritch., p. 783. Grunow, Verhand. der K. K. Zool. Bot. Gesel., Band xii., 1862, pp. 468 and 470. Grunow is uncertain as to whether the median line has the elongated end nodules; but of this there is no doubt, my specimens invariably exhibiting the same: and he seems to regard the species as identical with Amphipleura rigida, Kütz, this latter being in fact the same as Amphipleura sigmoidea, Wm. Sm., and belonging not to the genus Amphipleura, but to Nitzschia.

Stomachs of Ascidians, Co. Clare.

FAMILY VIII. NAVICULEÆ, Kütz.

Frustules oblong, having both valves furnished with a median line, central, and two terminal nodules.

In this group I include all those forms with symmetrical frustules, more or less oblong elliptical in their outline, and having both valves furnished with a median line, also with a central and two end nodules; quite irrespective of their mode of growth, in tubes, stipitate, or free, filamentous or simple. So limited, Gomphonema, and Cocconeis, included by Heiberg as Naviculeæ cuneatæ, are necessarily excluded on account of the unsymmetrical structure of their valves; while the species which normally occur, surrounded by a more or less amorphous mass of gelatinous investment, as Dickiea and Mastogloia, as well as those which grow in tubes more or less composite, as Berkleya, Colletonema, Schizonema; Doryphora, which is stipitate, Diadesmis, which is filamentous, as well as the genera which grow free, and without any investment, are included, because their frustules, however varying in minor details, ever exhibit the same general features. If Kützing, Smith and others, assigning too much value to the secondary modes of growth, have widely separated genera which are intimately related by a common structure, Heiberg on the other hand regards as of little or no significance these peculiarities of growth, which, although subordinate to the general structure of the frustules, should not be overlooked. These differences, as they occur normally, are doubtless assignable to some peculiarity in the structure of the plants which regularly develop them. They therefore demand the careful attention of the students of nature, and, as I think, ought to be marked by a special designation.

(a). *Chlamydiæ—Frustules enveloped in a more or less definite frond.*

Genus I. MASTOGLOIA, Wm. Smith and Thwaites.

Mucous frond in such species, as have been observed *in situ*, papillate, the frustules imbedded in the top of the papillæ; frustules furnished with narrow-marginal silicious plates interposed between the valve and the connecting band.

Kützing, (Bac. p. 92, T. xxx., fig. 37,) describes a form under the name of Navicula meleagris, which evidently belongs to this genus. Thwaites, Ann. Nat. Hist., March, 1848, gives a description of another form belonging to this genus, under the name of Dickiea danseii, but when the characteristic difference in the form of the mucous investment was pointed out by Smith, (B. D., vol. ii., p. 64), he established the genus Mastogloia to receive a new form discovered by himself, as well as some others that had meanwhile been brought under his notice. The genus therefore may in some measure be attributed to Smith; the more so because he first seems to have noticed and described one of the most important features in the structure of the frustule. He says, "The frustules of Mastogloia are notably distinct from those of any other genera of the tribe having the annulate structure, described under the genus Rhabdonema with the conspicuous canaliculi of a Surirella. In the present case, the canaliculi which take the form of loculi are, however, formed differently from those of Surirella, not being connected with the valve, but with the annulus, which projects as a septum into the body of the frustule." And again, "Normally the annular septum extends only partially across the interior of the frustule, but occasionally the loculi are seen to reach nearly as far as the median line of the valve." —B. D., Vol. ii., p. 63. In reference to this description, Grunow remarks, "I have been unable to convince myself of the correctness of Smith's supposition, that the costæ which according to him form diaphragms are attached to the connecting membrane. After numerous observations, I find they are quite analogous to the costæ of other Diatoms, and are an inner layer of the silicious plate which in this instance separates itself from the outer layer more easily than in other Diatoms."—Verhand. der K. K. Zool. Bot. Gesel., Band x., 1860, p. 574. Heiberg's views on the subject of dispute are thus expressed: "Smith on the contrary took an erroneous view of the genus as such, inasmuch as he regarded the inner layer of the valves on which the characteristic costæ are situated as an annulus or diaphragm of the same structure as that which we find in the Striatelleæ : also he considered the costæ to be canaliculi, which does not correspond with the actual facts of the case. Grunow has the merit of having been the first to point out the error of the opinion of Smith above referred to."—De Danske Diat., p. 92. Whether the plate bearing the loculi is more intimately associated with the connecting membrane, as Smith thought, or with the valve itself, as Grunow and Heiberg are of opinion it is, this is certain, so far as my observation extends, that, as Grunow remarks, the plate seems to attach itself more frequently to the valve than to the connecting membrane; but as the valves frequently occur without the plate, and the plate is often found detached, I am disposed to consider it not so much an inner layer of the silicious epiderm as a separate formation, and much more intimately related to the diaphragms of the Striatelleæ than to the inner layer which bears the costæ in the Epithemiæ. Smith describes the loculi as opening by foramina along the line of suture, a statement which Ralfs repeats. I have however failed to notice any such openings, the plate having ever appeared to be perfectly solid. Inasmuch as Thwaites considered the occurrence of the frustules in gelatinous cushions the distinctive character of the genus Mastogloia, and other distinguished writers have entertained the same opinion, Grunow's remark on the subject is deserving of attention : " Whether the species of the genus Mastogloia occur invariably in a gelatinous investment, is a matter concerning which I am very doubtful, as in a fresh collection I observed Mastogloia Smithii free, while I found no specimens in a gelatinous cushion"—Verhand. der K. K. Zool. Bot. Gesel., Band x., 1860, p. 575. However this may be, the occurrence of the plate with loculi in the perfect frustule is a mark of distinction which identifies the genus. Further, it was considered by Grunow, that the occurrence of the inner layer with its costate striation, so different from the sculpture of the valve, constitutes a strong bond of affinity between Mastogloia and Cocconeis. If, however, the opinion I have expressed as to the distinctness of the plate from the valve be correct, this resemblance fails, and in the general details of structure the two genera are widely distinct. The process of reproduction in this genus has been observed by Lüders : according to his observations, two mother cells produce two auxospores. Pfitzer, Untersuchungen über Bau und Entwicklung der Bacillariaceen, p. 74, remarks, "that in this feature the genus corresponds with the Naviculeæ, and not with the Cocconcideæ in which Grunow placed it; for the latter, out of two mother cells, develop but a single auxospore."

Mastogloia lanceolata, (Thwaites.) Marine or brackish water.
Valves lanceolate ; marginal plate wide at middle, and gradually tapering to the ends; loculi narrow, and numerous; median line slightly undulate ; strongly marked at the central nodule, and greatly

attenuated towards the ends; striæ linear, fine; slightly radiate; not quite reaching the median line, but terminated by two strongly developed sulci, which bend in slightly towards the central nodule at either end, leaving a narrow lanceolate space about the median line free from striæ.

Smith and Grunow, the former doubtfully, regard this form as identical with Navicula meleagris, Kütz. Bac., p. 92, T. xxx., fig. 37. Rabenhorst, however, regards Kützing's form as distinct from the present; and in this I am disposed to agree with him, as I have seen specimens exactly corresponding with that of Kützing, and as I think quite distinct from Mastogloia lanceolata.

Wm. Sm., B. D., Vol. ii., p. 64, Pl. liv., fig. 340. The figure and description are correct, as far as they go, but neither the longitudinal sulci about the median line, nor the striæ are described. Ralfs, in Pritch., p. 924. Grunow, Verhand. der Zool. Bot. Gesel., Band x. 1860, p. 576. Heiberg, De Danske Diat., p. 94. Rab. Fl. Eur., sect. 1, p. 261. Cleve, Om Svenska och Norska Diat., p. 230.

Tacumshane, Co. Wexford. Lough Gill, Co. Kerry. Salt marsh, Kilcool, Co. Wicklow. Salt marsh near the town of Galway. Dollymount Strand, Co. Dublin.

Mastogloia convergens, N. S. Marine or brackish water.

Valve broadly elliptical; length ·0018; breadth ·0008; rounded at ends; median line straight, strongly marked, and of equal breadth throughout; central nodule small and round: marginal plates broad in the middle, gradually attenuated towards the ends, at some distance from which they bend outwards; the space between the plates is broadly lanceolate at either end, and narrower in the middle, where the boundary line curves very gently towards the margin; loculi broader than in the last; striæ fine, linear, convergent in the middle of the valve, where they are stronger and farther apart, and for the remainder gently radiate. (Pl. 29, fig. 9.)

On first view, this form might readily be confounded with the preceding; but the more carefully it is examined, the more apparent are its distinctive characteristics. In its outline, it is broader for the length than Mastogloia lanceolata; its ends are broader, and more round. In the latter, the loculi are more numerous, shorter in the middle, and gradually diminishing towards the ends; in the present case, the loculi are wider in the middle, and suddenly become attenuated towards the ends. The longitudinal sulci near the median line, so marked a feature of M. lanceolata, are wanting in this. In M. lanceolata, the striæ are uniformly radiate; in M. convergens, they are convergent in the middle, and for the rest more decidedly radiate than in the other.

Salt marsh near the town of Galway. Lough Gill, Co. Kerry, accessible to the tide.

Mastogloia closeii, N. S. Marine or brackish water.

Valve somewhat rhomboid; length ·0018; breadth ·0008; ends narrow, lanceolate; median line straight; central nodule very small; marginal plates wide in the middle for a short space, and rapidly attenuated long before reaching the ends; loculi generally four in number, two large in the middle, and one at either side narrow, attenuated; space between the inner margin of plates wide, shaped somewhat like an hour-glass, with pointed ends; striæ fine, linear, radiate, reaching the median line. (Pl. 29, fig. 10.)

Found first in a gathering by Rev. Maxwell H. Close, from rock pools in the bay called Lough Kay, between Cahirciveen and Doulus Head, Co. Kerry. Lough Gill, Co. Kerry. Sea-weeds, Giants' Causeway, Co. Antrim.

Mastogloia portierana, (Grunow.) Marine.

Valves narrow, lanceolate; slightly produced at the apex; marginal plates narrow; gradually attenuated towards the ends; loculi numerous; striæ very obscure. (Pl. 29, fig. 11.)

This form is very similar in some respects to large specimens of Mastogloia lanceolata, but differs in many details; it is longer, and proportionately narrower; the sulci at either side of median line in the case of M. lanceolata are absent in this; the apices, too, are slightly produced, and the striæ much finer than in that species. Grunow states that, with an amplifying power of 400 times, the striæ are scarcely noticeable; but in the several specimens examined by me with a one-eighth objective and deep eye-piece, the striæ could not be discovered. Grunow, Verhand. der K. K. Zool. Bot. Gesel., Band xii.; 1863, p. 157, T. iv., fig. 13. Rab. Fl. Eur., sect. 1, p. 236.

From stomachs of Ascidians, Roundstone Bay, Co. Galway.

Mastogloia danseii, (Thwaites.) Marine or brackish water.

Valve linear, elliptical; broadly rounded at ends; striæ reaching the median line, but slightly shortened around the central nodule; radiate, formed of close puncta; marginal plates on inner margin straight till near the ends, where they are suddenly attenuated; loculi numerous, parallel; space between the plates narrow, and slightly expanded at the ends.

Wm. Sm., B. D., Vol. ii., p. 64, Supp. Pl. lxii., fig. 388. Ralfs, in Pritch., p. 924, Pl. xv., fig. 30. Grunow, Verhand. der K. K. Zool. Bot. Gesel., Band x., 1860, p. 576. Rab. Fl. Eur., sect. 1, p. 261.—Dickieadanseii, Thwaites, Ann. Nat. Hist., March, 1848, p. 171. Smith seems to think that this species hardly differs from Mastogloia lanceolata, but a careful consideration of the two forms will, I think, prove that in all the details they are essentially different.

Tacumshane, Co. Wexford. Lough Foyle, Co. Londonderry. Larne, Co. Antrim. Salt marsh, Kilcool, Co. Wicklow.

Mastogloia apiculata, (Wm. Sm.) Marine.

Valves broadly elliptical; slightly produced at the ends; median line fine, with two sulci, one at either side, and very close to it; parallel for greater part of length, and converging towards the ends; central nodule small; marginal plates narrow, gradually attenuated towards the ends, where they suddenly decrease in breadth; loculi numerous; space between the inner margins broadly elliptical, and slightly expanded at the ends; striæ fine, closely punctate, slightly radiate.

Wm. Sm., B. D. Vol. ii., p. 65. Supp. Pl. lxii., fig. 387. Ralfs, in Pritch., p. 925. Grunow, Verhand. der K. K. Zool. Bot. Gesel., Band x., 1860, p. 577, T. vii., fig. 9. Rab. Fl. Eur., sect. 1, p. 262.

Dollymount Strand, Co. Dublin. Stomachs of Ascidians, Roundstone Bay, Co. Galway.

Mastogloia smithii, (Thwaites.) Fresh or brackish water.

Valves elliptical; frequently produced at the ends; marginal plates relatively broad; attenuated at the ends; space included between the inner margins narrow; slightly expanded at the ends; striæ fine, linear; slightly radiate. (Pl. 29, fig. 12.)

This form varies greatly in size and shape, as well as in the habitat. It seems essentially a fresh water form, for I have found it frequently in localities far remote from marine influences; and also in places where, so far as I could judge, there was no likelihood of mixture of fresh water with the salt. Under the circumstances, I was anxious to submit the forms to the most rigid examination, but could detect no specific difference between them. Grunow observes that, in the specimen that came under his notice, there was even a tolerably wide transversely expanded central nodule, which he considers should be established as the characteristic distinction between this species and Mastogloia lanceolata. I may mention that this feature, though frequently noticeable, is not of universal occurrence.

Wm. Sm., B. D., Vol. ii., p. 65, Pl. liv., fig. 341. Ralfs, in Pritch., p. 925. Grunow, Verhand. der K. K. Zool. Bot. Gesel., Band x., 1860, p. 575, T. vii., fig. 11. Rab. Fl. Eur., sect. 1, p. 261. Cleve, Om Svenska och Norska Diat., p. 230.

Tacumshane, Co. Wexford. Lough Gill, Co. Kerry. Kilcool, Co. Wicklow. Newtownlimavady, Co. Derry. In all which gatherings there was a mixture of fresh and brackish forms. Tide pool, Greystones, Co. Wicklow, where the forms were mostly marine. Lough Corrib, Co. Galway, wholly free from marine influence.

Var. *capitata*, (Wm. Sm.) Fresh water.

Agreeing with the typical form, only that the produced ends are capitate; the striæ, also, which are similarly arranged, may easily be resolved into minute dots.

Wm. Sm., B. D., Vol. ii., p. 65, Pl. liv., fig. 341 B. In all probability, this is identical with the form described by Greville, Q. J. M. S., October, 1862, p. 235, Pl. x., fig. 11; although that author remarks that in his form the striæ were much more obscure than in the form figured by Smith as above.

Lough Corrib, Co. Galway, mixed with the typical form.

Mastogloia grevillii, (Wm. Sm.) Fresh water.

Valve linear; cuneate at the obtuse extremities; marginal plate nearly linear on the inner margin, suddenly attenuated towards the ends; loculi numerous; striæ fine, linear, radiate, shortened at the central nodule, so as to give a stauro-form appearance to the valve.

Wm. Sm. B. D. Vol. ii., p. 64, Supp. Pl. lxii, fig. 389. Ralfs, in Pritch., p. 925. Grunow, Verhand. der K. K. Zool. Bot. Gesel., Band x., 1860, p. 575. Heiberg, De Danske Diat., p. 94. Rab. Fl. Eur., sect. 1, p. 260.

Kilcool, Co. Wicklow. Lough Neagh, Co. Antrim. Ballyshannon, Co. Donegal. Carrickhugh, Co. Derry.

Mastogloia costata, N. S. Fresh water.

Valve linear; cuneate at ends; length ·0013, breadth ·0005; marginal plates broad, on inner margin perfectly linear till near the ends, where they very slightly expand, in shape of a spear head; loculi numerous; striæ strongly costate, converging in the middle, and for the rest radiate; shortened at the central nodule. (Pl. 29, fig. 13.)

In shape and size, this form is so like Mastogloia grevillii that it might easily be confounded with it; but, however, on closer investigation it will appear quite distinct. In M. grevillii, the fine linear striæ can by proper focusing be easily seen along with the loculi of the marginal plate. In the present species, either from the convexity of the valve, or the coarseness and closeness of the costate striæ, or perhaps owing to both these circumstances, the plates are not easily detected, except at the inner margin, where their boundary may be detected by the clear intervening space into which the ends of the strong costæ are seen to project.

On a moist rock, Ballyshannon, Co. Donegal.

Genus II. DICKIEIA, Berkeley.

Frond flat, leaf-like; unbranched; frustules scattered without regular arrangement.

Smith attributes this genus to Ralfs; but Ralfs himself ascribes it to Berkeley. It is adopted by Kützing, Smith, Grunow, and Rabenhorst, but Heiberg rejects it as being unnecessary, the forms being, as he thinks, ranged properly with the Naviculæ.

Dickieia ulvoides, (Berk.), Marine.
Gelatinous frond, more or less perfectly ovate; entire, and having a distinct pedicel; valves linear, elliptical; central nodule transversely dilated; striæ fine, parallel. (Pl. 29, fig. 14.)
Berkeley and Ralfs, Ann. Nat. Hist., Series 1., Vol. xiv., Pl. ix., Kütz. Bac., p. 119. Wm. Sm., B. D., Vol. ii., p. 66, Pl. liv., fig. 342. Ralfs, in Pritch., p. 925, Pl. xv., fig. 31. Rab. Fl. Eur., sect. 1, p. 264.

Greystones, Co. Wicklow.

Dickieia pinnata, (Ralfs), Marine.
Frond lasciniated; valves narrow, elliptical; striæ fine, parallel; nodule small, round.
Ralfs. Ann. Nat. Hist., 2nd Series, Vol. viii., Pl. v., fig. 6. Ralfs, in Pritch., p. 925. Wm. Sm., B. D. Vol. ii., p. 66, Pl. liv., fig. 343. Rab. Fl. Eur., sect. 1, p. 264.

On piles of the wooden bridge, Dollymount strand; Wooden piles on strand, Clontarf; Sea-weeds, Malahide; Ireland's eye; Rock-pools, Ballybrack, Co. Dublin: in the last named locality it occurs in greatest abundance. Larne, Co. Antrim.

Genus III. COLLETONEMA, De Bréb.

Gelatinous frond filiform, simple or sparingly divided at the ends.

The first known forms of this genus were discovered by Thwaites, and published by him in Ann. Hist., March, 1848, under the generic name of Schizonema. De Brébisson subsequently separated these forms from Schizonema, and instituted the present genus for their reception; the distinguishing characters being their fresh water habitat, and the simple tubular frond. Whatever value may attach to the latter peculiarity, the former is utterly untenable as a generic distinction. Smith alleges that in this genus the frustules are more firmly silicious than in Schizonema, a statement I cannot corroborate; but even though it admitted of no doubt, this fact could scarcely be regarded as a sufficient generic distinction. Rabenhorst, Süssw. Diat., p. 51, who himself observed none of the species, adopts the genus, characterising it by the fact of the frustules occurring in rows within a structureless gelatinous investment. Ralfs adopts Smith's definition, but doubts "if any of the above characters sufficiently distinguish Colletonema from the allied genera," in Pritch., p. 926. Grunow's observations on the genus are noteworthy; he says: "The genus

Colletonema is in a twofold aspect uncertainly founded. On the one hand, it can scarcely be rightly separated from Schizonema, in which small forms occur in simple sheaths, and on the other hand its separation from Navicula is very uncertain. It appears to me that many species of Naviculæ may, under certain conditions, occur, as well in gelatinous masses as inclosed in gelatinous tubes, and two of the forms which I have with some hesitation placed in this genus appear to me to confirm this impression." Farther on, in his observations on Colletonema neglectum, he remarks : " I once observed this species in an unused mill-stream in which Navicula gracilis occurred in uncommon abundance, and for the most part certainly in a free state; very frequently also were found gelatinous tubes filled with perfect frustules of Navicula gracilis, just as Smith has described it, and also very unfrequently bands consisting of double rows of the same Navicula without any sheaths; nor could I by the most careful examination discriminate between these forms and those of Navicula gracilis from other localities, where no gelatinous tubes were discovered."—Verhand. der K. K. Zool. Bot. Gesel., Band x., 1860, pp. 570, 571. These observations coincide with the supposition of Wm. Smith, that " Pinnularia radiosa may be merely a free state of Colletonema neglectum and Navicula crassinervia, the same condition of Colletonema vulgare." B. D., Vol. ii., p. 69. I take the opportunity of remarking that, in a gathering made by me from Lough Aron, on the summit of the Slieveanieran mountain, Co. Antrim, in the summer of 1872, Navicula rhomboides occurred in great abundance ; some of the forms were free and active, others were inclosed in gelatinous tubes, invariably arranged in single files, and by no means uncommonly the frustules were seen in long files, attached apparently one to another by the ends, without the slightest appearance of tubes, just as in Grunow's case of Navicula gracilis. Rabenhorst restores the species of this genus to Schizonema ; and Heiberg, rejecting the generic distinction founded on the gelatinous tubes in which the frustules are invested, unites them with Navicula.

Reproduction has been observed by Thwaites in the case of Colletonema subcoherens; he says: "The Sporangia of this species are produced by the conjugation of a pair of frustules outside the filaments ; but sporangial frustules are frequently found in a filament intermixed with ordinary frustules, from which they differ only in size."—Ann. Nat. Hist., March, 1848. Pfitzer superadds, that "two cells produce two auxospores."—Untersuchungen, p. 73.

Colletonema eximium, (Thwaites), Fresh water.
Frond filiform, frustules arranged in one or more rows; valve sigmoid, striæ fine, parallel.
Rab. Süssw. Diat., p. 51. Wm. Sm., B. D., Vol. ii., p. 69, Pl. lvi., fig. 350. Ralfs, in Pritch., p. 926, Pl. viii., fig. 43. Grunow, Verhand. der K. K. Zool. Bot. Gesel., Band x., 1860, p. 573, who remarks, regarding this species: "it must either be transferred to Pleurosigma,

or a new genus established to receive it."—Schizonema eximium, Thwaites, Ann. Nat. Hist., March, 1848. Rab. Fl. Eur., sect. 1, p. 266.—Gloionema sigmoides, Ehr. Abh., 1845, p. 78.—Encyonema sigmoides, Kütz. Alg., p. 62.—Endosigma eximium, De Bréb.

Tacumshane, Co. Wexford. Near Railway station, Newtownlimavady, Co. Derry.

Colletonema vulgare, (Thwaites). Fresh water.
Frond occasionally divided; frustules elliptical, lanceolate, striæ very fine.
In Smith's figure the striæ are described as radiate, but I have never been able to resolve them.
Wm. Sm., B. D., Vol. ii., p. 70, Pl. lvi., fig. 351. Grunow, Verhand. der K. K. Zool. Bot. Gesel., Band x., 1860, p. 572. Ralfs, in Pritch., p. 926.—Schizonema vulgare, Thwaites, Ann. Nat., Hist., 2nd Series, Vol. i., p. 10, Pl. xii., fig. H. Rab. Fl. Eur., sect. 1, p. 265.—Navicula vulgaris, Heiberg, De Danske Diat., p. 83.

Carrickmacreilly Mountain near Glanealy, Wicklow: the species is very uncommon.

Colletonema neglectum, (Thwaites.) Fresh water.
Frond slightly divided; frustules closely packed; elliptical, lanceolate; extremities obtuse; striæ finely costate, radiate. (Pl. 29, fig. 15.)
Wm. Sm., B. D., Vol. ii., p. 70, Pl. lvi., fig. 352. Ralfs, in Pritch., p. 926. Grunow, Verhand. der K. K. Zool. Bot. Gesel., Band x., p. 571.—Schizonema neglectum, Thwaites, Ann. Nat. Hist., 2nd Series, Vol. i. p. 11, Pl. xii., J. Rab. Fl. Eur., sect. 1, p. 265.

Genus IV. BERKELEYA, Greville.

Frond branched, the branches springing from a basal tubercle.

Most authors adopt this genus, but Heiberg rejects it as unnecessary, and includes the species under Navicula.

Berkeleya fragilis, (Greville.) Marine.
Frustules closely packed in the tubes. Valves elliptical, lanceolate, broadly rounded at the ends. Striæ obscure. (Pl. 29, fig. 16.)
Grev. Scot. Crypt. Flora. tab. 294. Do. Brit. Flora. p. 416. Ralfs, Ann. Nat. Hist., 1st Series, Vol. xvi., Pl. iii., fig. 2. Do., in Pritch., p. 926. Kütz. Bac., p. 109. Wm. Sm., B.D., Vol. ii., p. 67, Pl. liv., fig. 344. Grunow, Verhand. der K. K. Zool. Bot. Gesel., Band x., 1860, p. 512. Rab. Fl. Eur., sect. 1, p. 264.—Navicula fragilis, Heiberg, De Danske Diat., p. 84. Bangia micans, Lyngbye, Tent. Hydro-

phyt., p. 84. This last synonym is given on the authority of Heiberg, who had the opportunity of inspecting authentic specimens.

Cork Harbour, Wm. Smith. Rock-pool, Salt Hill, Co. Dublin. Coast of Galway, from collections by M'Calla, in the Herbarium, Trinity College, Dublin.

Genus V. Schizonema, Agardh.

Frond usually much divided. Frustules arranged in one or more files within the gelatinous tubes which constitute the frond.

Smith remarks justly that "the fronds in this extensive genus were amongst the earliest Diatomaceous organisms recognised by naturalists, and have been the perplexity of all subsequent observers." Nor is this to be wondered at, when the difficulties attendant on their examination are taken into consideration. The frustules enveloped in the fronds are generally minute, so that even though they were free it would be no easy matter to examine them satisfactorily, and the difficulty is much enhanced by the intervention of the fronds as well as by the manner in which the frustules are packed within them. Kützing attempted to arrange the species on the basis of the characters of the fronds, but with how little success the student will be convinced who endeavours to make himself master of the subject by the aid of his minute descriptions, and of his very indefinite figures. Heiberg falls into a mistake the very opposite to that of Kützing— discarding from consideration not only the characters of the fronds in the various species, but regarding the fact of the frustules being normally incased within fronds as an unreliable generic distinction, and so he ranks the species under the genus Navicula. De Brébisson had observed that "the greater part of the species needed reconsideration, and to be studied with regard to the character of the frustules." and Smith, with his characteristic sagacity, taking this hint, at the same time not overlooking any reliable character exhibited by the fronds, dispelled the confusion which had hitherto existed, and reduced the species into an order, which seems, all the circumstances considered, to admit of little improvement.

As to the mode of reproducing the sporangia in the genus, opinions differ, as the following extract from Pfitzer will sufficiently show:— "In Schizonema Grevillii, according to Smith, a single mother-cell produces a single auxospore, while according to Lüders this occurs but seldom, namely, when one auxospore becomes defunct; usually, on the contrary, two cells co-operate, and form two auxospores. The development of the latter occurs outside the tubes in a large and fine mucous investment. The mode of proceeding, according to Lüders, is that each mother-cell divides itself, and the halves unite in pairs. However, in other forms in which, according to Lüders, a similar state of things occurs, I have not found this view confirmed. So that probably Schizonema does not differ in this respect from the rest of the Naviculæ."—Untersuchungen über Bau und Entwicklung der Bacillariaceen, p. 73.

(†) *Frustules with parallel striæ.*

Schizonema crucigerum, (Wm. Sm.) Marine.
"Frond filiform; filaments implicate below, free above, much divided. Frustules crowded. Valves with a distinct stauros, lanceolate, acute" (Wm. Smith) on side view; on front view wider in the middle than at ends. Striæ distinct, close, linear. (Pl. 29, fig. 17.)
In Smith's figure, the striæ are described as slightly radiate, but in my specimens, I find them parallel.
Wm. Sm., B. D., Vol. ii., p. 74., Pl. lvi., fig. 354, and Pl. lvii., fig. 356. Ralfs, in Pritch., p. 928. Rab. Fl. Eur. sect. 1, p. 266. —Stauroneis crucigera, Heiberg, De Danske Diat., p. 88.

Tacumshane, Co. Wexford. Malahide, Portmarnock, Salt-hill, Co. Dublin. Rostrevor, Co. Down. Lough Gill, Co. Kerry.

Schizonema smithii, (Agardh.) Marine.
"Frond, filiform, robust, simple below, much divided, fasciculated and fastigiate above. Frustules in numerous closely set files. Valves elliptico-lanceolate, acute."—Wm. Smith. To which I would add, striæ, obvious, extending to median line. Front view of frustule regularly quadrangular. (Pl. 29, fig. 18.)
Agardh. Conspectus, p. 18. Kütz. Bac., p. 114, T. xxvii., fig. 5. Wm. Sm., B. D., Vol. ii., p. 75, Pl. lvii., fig. 362. Rab. Fl. Eur., sect. 1, p. 269.—Micromega Smithii, Ralfs, in Pritch., p. 930.

Howth, Salt Hill, Malahide, Co. Dublin. Sea coast, Co. Antrim.

Schizonema divergens, (Wm. Sm.) Marine.
"Frond, simple below, sparingly divided, or by cohesion irregularly submembranous above; ultimate ramuli short, obtuse."—Wm. Smith. Valve, shorter and wider than the last, and more rounded at the ends. Striæ fine, linear, reaching the median line.
Wm. Sm., B. D., Vol. ii., p. 76, Pl. lvii., fig. 363. Rab. Fl. Eur. sect. 1, p. 269.—Micromega divergens, Ralfs, in Pritch., p. 931.

Besides the locality named by Wm. Smith, Larne Lough, where it was collected by Dr. Dickie, this species has been gathered by myself at Malahide and Salt-hill, Co. Dublin; and by Dr. David Moore, at Carrickfergus and Carnlough Bay, Co. Antrim.

Schizonema mucosum, (Kütz.) Marine.
"Frond filiform, gelatinous, simple below, by cohesion sub-mem-

branous above. Margin irregularly ramulous. Frustules in files, few, sub-distant. Valve elliptical, delicately striate." Wm. Smith. Not unlike the last, except that it is more delicately striate, shorter, broader, and more rounded at ends.

Kütz. Bac., p. 115, T. xxvi., fig. 9. Wm. Sm., B. D., Vol. ii., p. 75, Pl. lvii., fig. 360. Rab. Fl. Eur., sect. 1, p. 268.—Micromega mucosum, Ralfs, in Pritch., p. 933.

With seaweeds, Galway, Dr. David Moore. Malahide, Howth, Co. Dublin.

Schizonema ramosissimum, (Agardh.) Marine.
" Frond filiform, much divided from the base, and irregularly sub-membranous by cohesion above. Ramuli short, obtuse. Frustules numerous, in closely packed files. Valves elliptico-lanceolate, acute."—Wm. Smith. Striæ fine, linear.

Agardh. Syst., p. 11. Harvey's Manual, p. 210, who, according to Smith, had the opportunity of inspecting authentic specimens. Wm. Sm., B. D., Vol. ii., p. 78, Pl. lix., fig. 369. Rab. Fl. Eur. p. 272.—Micromega ramosissimum, Agardh. Consp., p. 22. Ralfs, in Pritch., p. 934.

Near Larne, Carnlough, Co. Antrim, collected by Dr. David Moore.

(††). *Frustules having radiate striæ.*

Schizonema grevillii, (Agardh.) Marine.
" Frond filiform, much divided from the base, Ultimate ramuli acute, larger divisions with several files; ultimate ramuli with a single file of frustules. Valve lanceolate."—Wm. Smith. Striæ fine, gently radiate. On the front view, frustules are very wide, quadrangular. The side view appears nearly as far as the median line. The central nodule thus seen is depressed. The connecting band exhibits longitudinal lines. (Pl. 29, fig. 19.)

Agardh. Conspect., p. 19. Kütz. Bac., p. 114, T. xxvi., fig. 4., T. v., fig. 1. Wm. Sm., B. D., Vol. ii., p. 77, Pl. lviii., fig. 364. Ralfs, in Pritch., p. 928. Rab. Fl. Eur., sect. 1, p. 267.—Schizonema quadripunctatum, Harvey's Manual, p. 214.

Larne, Carrickfergus, Co. Antrim, collected by Dr. David Moore. Malahide, Merrion, Co. Dublin. River Nannywater, near Laytown, Co. Meath.

Schizonema helmintosum, (Chauvin.) Marine.
" Frond filiform, or by cohesion irregularly sub-membranous; much and irregularly divided; ultimate divisions short, abrupt."—Wm. Smith. Frustules linear, elliptical, sometimes sharp, sometimes more rounded

at the ends. Striæ fine, obscurely punctate, convergent about the central nodule, and for a considerable distance from it, towards the ends straight and radiate.

Agardh. Conspect., p. 20. Grev. Brit. Flora, p. 412. Harvey's Manual, p. 210. Kütz. Bac., p. 114, T. xxvii., fig. 6. Wm. Sm., B. D., Vol. ii., p. 74, Pl. lvi., fig. 355. Rab. Fl. Eur., sect. 1, p. 268.—Micromega helmintosum, Ralfs, in Pritch., p. 830.

Howth, Malahide, Co. Dublin. Carnlough Bay, collected by Dr. David Moore.

Schizonema comoides, (Agardh.) Marine.
"Frond filiform, simple below, much divided and fasciculated above. Frustules crowded."—Wm. Smith. Frustules small, length about ·0010, somewhat rhombic on front view, rounded slightly at the ends. Striæ strong and distant at centre, finer and closer towards the end; on front view linear, in outline rounded at ends.

Agardh. Conspect., p. 19. Harvey's Manual, p. 213. Wm. Sm., B. D., Vol. ii., p. 75, Pl. lvii., fig. 358. Rab. Fl. Eur., sect. i., p. 268.—Schizonema aruncosum, Kütz. Bac., p. 113, T. xxiv., fig. 2, T. xxv., fig. ix.—Micromega comoides, Ralfs, in Pritch., p. 934.

Carnlough Bay, Co. Antrim, collected by Dr. David Moore. Howth, Malahide, Co. Dublin.

Schizonema parasiticum, (Harvey.) Marine.
"Frond capillary, branched, filaments slightly cohering above. Ramuli short, patent. Mucus often rugose. Frustules crowded in files, more or less distant. Valves elliptico-lanceolate, acute. Length of frond 5"; length of frustule ·0011; breadth of valve ·0002."—Wm. Smith. Striæ extremely fine. Frustule on front view subquadrangular.

Harvey's Manual, p. 213. Wm. Sm. B. D., Vol. ii., p. 79, Pl. lix., fig. 37. Rab. Fl. Eur., p. 273.—Micromega parasiticum, Kütz. Bac., p. 116, T. xxvii., fig. 2. Ralfs, in Pritch., p. 932.

Malahide, Salt Hill, Co. Dublin.

Schizonema laciniatum, (Harvey.) Marine.
"Frond filiform, much branched, filaments often adhering into rope-like tufts. Ramuli very long. Frustules numerous, crowded in irregular files. Valves elliptical, somewhat acute. Length of frustule ·0018; breadth of valve ·00035."—Wm. Smith. Valves striate; striæ punctate, gently radiate. On front view frustules broader at middle than at ends, ends rounded off; side view coming largely into sight when observed in front, the inner margins nearly meeting the connecting membrane, and at the ends receding therefrom.

On careful inspection of authentic specimens of Schizonema implicatum (Harvey), I find the frustules on side and front view so like one another in all respects that, judging from the frustules alone, I am disposed to consider that it is not distinct from the present; nor does the general appearance of the fronds differ so much as to be irreconcilable with this impression.

Harvey's Manual, p. 210. Wm. Sm., B. D., Vol ii., p. 79, Pl. lix., fig. 370. Rab. Fl. Eur., sect. i., p. 273.—Schizonema scoparium, Kütz. Bac., p. 114, T. xxvii., fig. 1.—Micromega laciniatum, Ralfs, in Pritch., p. 932.

Carrickfergus to Antrim, collected by Dr. David Moore. Galway, collected by M'Calla.

Schizonema gracillimum, (Wm. Sm.) Marine.

"Frond capillary, simple below; sparingly branched and sub-membranous towards the apices. Frustules crowded in irregular files. Valves elliptico-lanceolate. Length of frustule .0009, breadth of valve ·00015."—Wm. Smith. Striæ linear, very slightly radiate. Frustule on front view narrow, quadrangular. So far as the frustules are concerned, in outline and general appearance the species differs little from Schizonema parasiticum. The striæ may be a little coarser and the valve somewhat narrower.

Wm. Smith, B. D., Vol. ii., p. 79, Pl. lix., fig. 372.—Micromega gracillimum, Ralfs, in Pritch., p. 934.

Nannywater, Laytown, Co. Meath.

(†††). *Frustules without striæ.*

Schizonema obtusum, (Grev.) Marine.

"Frond filiform, sparingly branched, apices abrupt. Frustules exceedingly numerous, in irregular files; valves elliptical. Length of frond 1"; length of frustule ·0011; breadth of valve ·00025." Wm. Smith. To which should be added that the valves are rounded at the ends. (Pl. 29, fig. 20.)

Greville, Brit. Fl., p. 413. Harvey's Manual, p. 209. Rab. Fl. Eur., sect. 1, p. 272.—Micromega obtusum, Ralfs, in Pritch., p. 931.

Near Dunluce Castle, Portballintrae, Co. Antrim, collected by Dr. David Moore. Merrion, Malahide, Co. Dublin. Galway.

Schizonema dilwynii, (Agardh.) Marine.

"Frond capillary throughout, sparingly branched, tenacious; apices acute. Frustules exceedingly crowded towards the apices, scattered and remote in the older portions. Valves lanceolate, acute. Length of frond 2" to 5", or upwards; length of frustule ·0008; breadth of valve ·0002." Wm. Smith. So far as the frustules are concerned there is but little difference between this and the preceding species; the only difference being that while in the former case the valve is rounded at the ends, in the present case they are acute. I have sometimes found both species in the one gathering.

Agardh. Syst., p. 10. Id. Consp., p. 20. Grev. Brit. Fl., p. 412. Harvey's Manual, p. 212. Kütz., Bac., p. 118, T. xxvi., fig. 3. Wm. Sm., B. D., Vol. ii., p. 77, Pl. lviii., fig. 366. Ralfs, in Pritch., p. 928. Rab., Fl. Eur., sect. 1, p. 272.

Rathlin Island, Carrickfergus, Carnlough Bay, Co. Antrim—all collected by Dr. David Moore. River Nannywater, Laytown, Co. Meath. Merrion, Co. Dublin.

(b). *Achlamydiæ. Frustules without a gelatinous investment.*

Genus VI. DIADESMIS, Kütz.

Frustules united in a filament.

Diadesmis williamsonii, (Wm. Sm.) Marine.

On front view margins of frustules undulate, and exhibiting the striation of the valve; on side view, valve linear, acuminate at the ends. Striæ moniliform. (Pl. 29, fig. 21.)

This form was first partially described by Wm. Smith, B. D., Vol. ii., p. 14, Pl. xxxiii., fig. 287, who, having seen only the front view so accurately figured by him, doubtfully referred it to the genus Himantidium. Subsequently Gregory, who had opportunity of more thoroughly investigating it, transferred it to the genus Diadesmis, to which it properly belongs. Grunow refers this species to the genus Dimeregramma, and makes the following observations:—" Of the Eunotia-like structure of the same there is no question; the margins of the front view are never so distinctly triundulate as in Smith's description; for the most part the middlemost elevation is found much stronger than the other two, in consequence of which it approaches Dimeregramma minor."—Verhand. der K. K., Zool. Bot. Gesel., Band xii., 1862, p. 377.

Gregory, Diat. of Clyde, p. 25, Pl. x., fig. 40, in which both side and front views are accurately delineated. Ralfs, in Pritch, p. 923. Rab. Fl. Eur., sect. 1, p. 260.

From stomachs of Ascidians, Roundstone Bay, Co. Galway.

Genus VII. BREBISSONIA, Grunow.

Frustules simple, stipitate.

The only species of this genus was by Smith described and figured under the name of Doryphora Boeckii. The genus Doryphora had been adopted by Kützing for the reception of a single species which was named by him Doryphora amphiceros. His definition of the genus was, "frustules simple, depressed on the secondary side, punctate, elliptico-lanceolate, stipitate." Bac. p. 74. Influenced, no doubt, by the consideration of the last named characteristic, Wm. Smith adopted the genus as the proper place for another form named by him Doryphora Boeckii, and to some extent amended the definition : "Frustules stipitate, lanceolate, or elliptical; valve with a median line; nodules obsolete."—B. D., Vol. i., p. 77. This definition is not quite correct as respects either of the species included under this generic designation, for Doryphora amphiceros has no median line, properly so called; and the nodules, though small, are not obsolete in the case of Doryphora Boeckii. The latter species, Ralfs, as Ehrenberg had done before, refers to the genus Cocconema, but properly remarks, "This species is, no doubt, wrongly referred to Cocconema, since both margins of the lateral valves are symmetrical. We regard it as a stalked Navicula; and find a central, though inconspicuous nodule, a fact which forbids it being placed in Doryphora, as Professor Smith proposed."—In Pritch., p. 878. Grunow transfers Doryphora amphiceros to his new genus Rhaphoneis, and recognising the intimate relationship of Doryphora Boeckii to Navicula, suggested the adoption of a new generic designation, Brebissonia. defining it simply as a stipitate Navicula.

Heiberg recognises the proper relationship of the species, as Ralfs and Grunow had done, but rejecting the stipitate character as of no consequence, described the form as Navicula Boeckii.—De Danske Diat., p. 85. At all events, it is better to drop the genus Doryphora, which has been so ill defined, lest confusion should arise from maintaining it, even though with a more precise definition; and, as I think that the stipitate mode of growth should not be regarded as of no importance, I adopt the suggestion of Grunow above referred to.

Brebissonia boeckii, Ehr. Marine.

Valve on side view lanceolate. Striæ costate, close, radiate, median line obvious, with large end nodules, and ending towards the central nodule, in pin-head-like expansions; central nodule long and narrow, with a narrow free space at each side of the median line. (Pl. 29, fig. 22.)

Grunow, Verhand. der K. K., Zool. Bot. Gesel., Band x., 1860, p. 512.—Cocconema boeckii, Ehr. Infus., T. xix., fig. 5. Kütz. Bac., p. 81, T. vi., fig. 5. Ralfs, in Pritch., p. 878, Pl. vii., fig. 48. Rab. Fl. Eur., sect. i., p. 83.—Doryphora boeckii, Wm. Sm., B. D., Vol. i., p. 77, Pl. xxiv., fig. 223.—Navicula boeckii, Heiberg, De Danske Diat., p. 85.

Stomachs of Ascidians, Roundstone Bay, Co. Galway. Salt ditch on banks of Slaney, near Wexford. River Slaney, Killurin, Co. Wexford.

Genus VIII. NAVICULA, Bory.

Frustules simple, free.

Ehrenberg separated the forms included in this genus into two distinct genera, Navicula and Pinnularia, founded on the fact that in the former the striæ are moniliform, in the latter costate. Considerable difference of opinion has existed as to whether or not this distinction is tenable. Kützing rejected it, while Wm. Smith and Rabenhorst maintained its validity. Ralfs, in Pritch., p. 892, included the species of Pinnularia under the genus Navicula for the following reasons:— " Were the costæ always plainly developed, as in Pinnularia nobilis and its allies, no difficulty could occur in determining the genera; but in many of the more minute species it is often very difficult to distinguish between striæ and costæ. We have not admitted Pinnularia here, partly for the reason just given, but principally because we cannot decide to which genus a large number of Ehrenberg's species should be referred." The existence of the distinctive characteristic is here admitted, but the genus founded upon it is discarded on account of the difficulty of applying it in many cases. Grunow regards the distinction between costate and moniliform striæ, in this case, as founded on insufficient observation. He says, "The so-called costæ in the Pinnulariæ are quite distinct from the ribs of other genera of Diatomaceæ, and consist of a union of more or less confluent puncta, which cannot, indeed, be clearly discriminated, except by the help of good amplification and well-managed illumination."—Ueber neue oder ungenügend gekannte Algen, Verhand der K. K. Zool. Bot. Gesel., Band x., 1860, p. 513. This eminent author thus discards the distinction between Navicula and Pinnularia, and is followed by Heiberg, Cleve, and others. Schumann, who adopts the same view, indicates a peculiarity in some of the larger forms of Pinnularia, (P. nobilis and P. major, for example,) which is worthy of special notice here, namely, the interposition of very fine striæ between the costæ, which he says are indistinct in P. nobilis, but quite distinct in P. major; these interstitial markings I have never been able to discover, and Pfitzer makes the same remark concerning them. The last-named author, in his treatise " Untersuchungen ueber Bau und Entwicklung der Bacillariaceen" maintains the distinctiveness of the genus Pinnularia, not on the ground of the different character of the striation, but on the following peculiarities:—1st. The so-called costæ are depressions on the surface of the valve. 2nd. The valves themselves are unsymmetrical. 3rd. The arrangement of the cell-contents exhibits a marked difference from those of Navicula, as well in the normal condition as also in the process of self-division.—Regarding the characteristics just named, some remarks are here required. As to the first, supposing it to be true, there is great difficulty in applying it in the more minute forms.

As to the second, Pfitzer is at variance with most other authors who have regarded the forms included under the genus Pinnularia as perfectly symmetrical, and to me they have ever appeared just as symmetrical as those of Navicula. The third characteristic is that which is most worthy of notice, but the forms in which the peculiarity has been observed are comparatively few. So that we are not as yet in a position to regard it as satisfactorily established. For myself I have long since regarded the distinction between Navicula and Pinnularia as unsatisfactory, and have felt obliged to abandon it in consequence of having observed forms in which the costate character of the Pinnulariæ is combined with the moniliform striæ of the Naviculæ. In consequence of this there is no alternative but the abandonment of the genus Pinnularia, or the adoption of a new genus to receive these forms in which the characteristics of Navicula and Pinnularia are combined. The former appears the more satisfactory course, which I have accordingly pursued. The forms belonging to this genus are now so very numerous some more satisfactory grouping of them than that of Smith and Ralfs, founded on the outline of the valves, is necessary. Grunow has done much towards supplying this desideratum, and, if I have succeeded in effecting an improved arrangement, I am indebted to the hints supplied by that distinguished naturalist.

Conjugation has been observed in some species of Navicula. Two mother cells produce two sporangial cells or auxospores, as Pfitzer designates them, which latter are found to lie in a position parallel to that of the former.

(a.) *Nobiles.*

Striæ strongly costate, not extending to the median line, but leaving a broad, smooth, longitudinal middle space, which is expanded around the central nodule, and occasionally extending to the margin.

Navicula nobilis, (Ehr.) Fresh water.

Valve large, varying in length from ·012 to ·015; oblong, inflated both at the middle and ends; costæ broad, converging in the middle, and slightly radiate towards the ends; longitudinal free median space expanded greatly at the centre and ends. (Plate 30, fig. 1.)

Kütz. Bac., p. 98, T. iv., fig. 24. Ralfs, in Pritch., p. 895. Grunow, Verhand. der K. K. Zool. Bot. Gesel., Band x., 1860, p. 515. Cleve, Om Svenska och Norska Diat., p. 223.—Pinnularia nobilis, Ehr. Proc. Berl. Acad., 1840. Wm. Sm., B.D., Vol. i., p. 54, Pl. xvii., fig. 161. Rab. Süssw. Diat., p. 44, T. vi., fig, 2; Rab. Fl. Eur., Alg., sect. 1, p. 209.

Bantry, Co. Cork. Featherbed Mountain, Co. Dublin. Lugnaquilla, Co. Wicklow. Lough Mourne deposit, Co. Antrim. Dromore sub-peat deposit, Co. Down. River Bann, at Coleraine, Co. Derry. Drumoughty Lough, near Kenmare, Co. Kerry.

Navicula major, (Kütz.) Fresh water.
Valve about the same length as that of N. nobilis; oblong, but very slightly expanded in the middle, and at the rounded, somewhat conical, ends; longitudinal free space narrower than that of N. nobilis; costæ broad, converging in the middle, and nearly parallel for the remainder. On front view frustule linear with rounded angles.

Kütz. Bac., p. 97, T. iv., fig. 19. Ralfs, in Pritch., p. 896. Grunow, Verhand. der K. K. Zool. Bot. Gesel., Band x., 1860, p. 515. Heiberg, De Danske Diat., p. 80. Cleve, Om Svenska och Norska Diat., p. 223.—Pinnularia major, W. Sm., B. D., Vol. i., p. 54, Pl. xviii., fig. 161. Rab. Süssw. Diat., p. 42, T. vi., fig. 5. Do. Fl. Eur. Alg., sect. 1, p. 210.

Lower Lake, Killarney, River near Glencar, Co. Kerry. River Bann, near Coleraine, Co. Derry. Marl pit, near Arklow, Streamlets on Carrickmacreilly Hill, Greenane, Co. Wicklow. Derrylane Lough, Co. Cavan. Killakee, Featherbed Mountain, Co. Dublin. Slieve Donard, Co. Down. Lough Mourne deposit. Dromore Sub-peat deposit. Lough Islandreavy deposit. Pond near Camolin, Co. Wexford.

Navicula cardinalis, (Ehr.) Fresh water.
Valve oblong-linear, length about ·0125; breadth about ·0022, rounded at the ends; median line undulate; end nodules large; free intermediate space wide, reaching the margin in the middle, forming a broad stauroform space; costæ broad, converging in the middle, nearly parallel for the remainder. (Pl. 30, fig. 2.)

Ralfs, in Pritch., p. 806, Pl. xii., fig. 72. Grunow, Verhand. der K. K. Zool. Bot. Gesel., Band x., 1860, p. 515.—Pinnularia cardinalis, Ehr. Wm. Sm., B.D., Vol. i., p. 55, Pl. xix., fig. 166. Rab. Fl. Eur. Alg., sect 1, p. 220.—Stauroneis cardinalis, Kütz. Bac., p. 106, T. xxix., fig. 10.

Lough Mourne deposit; found also living in a pond near the city of Armagh.

Navicula viridis, (Nitzsch.) Fresh water.
Valve varying much in size; linear elliptical, with rounded ends; intermediate free space narrower than in the three preceding species, and not so much expanded in the middle; costæ broad, but not so much so as in the preceding. (Pl. 30, fig. 3.)

This species has been attributed to various authors, but if Kützing be right in supposing it to be = Bacillaria viridis, Nitzsch, 1817, it should be attributed to the last named author, as Heiberg has done. Smith assigns the species to himself, although regarding it as = Navicula viridis, Ehr. Rabenhorst attributes it to himself, while Grunow attributes it to Kützing. Grunow makes this form the type of the group Virides, but seems to regard Navicula major, which he includes among the Nobiles, to be only a variety of Navicula viridis. Speaking of this former, he says, "it appears to me to be only a variety of Nav. viridis, tolerably numerous figures (especially from specimens out of the Kieselguss of Franzensbad), which lie before me, present such manifold transitions, as well in respect to the appearance of the striation as to the outline of the form, that in most cases it is difficult to decide whether the specimen should be referred to one or the other." Verhand. der K. K. Zool. Bot. Gesel., Band x., 1860, p. 515.

The correctness of this remark is obvious to all careful observers, but still the species seem to be distinct. The following characters seem to distinguish Navicula viridis from N. major; the costæ are finer and less radiate; the median free space is narrower and less expanded around the central nodule, and the normal outline is linear elliptical.

Kütz. Bac., p. 97, T. iv., fig. 18. Ralfs, in Pritch., p. 907, Pl. ix., figs. 135, 136. Grunow, Verhand. der K. K. Zool. Bot. Gesel., Band x., 1860, p. 518. Heiberg, De Danske Diat., p. 80. Cleve, Om Svenska och Norska Diat., p. 223.—Pinnularia viridis, Wm. Sm., B. D., Vol. i., p. 54, Pl. xviii., fig. 163. Rab. Süssw. Diat., p. 42, T. vi., fig. 4.

Featherbed Mountain, Friarstown, Co. Dublin. River Erne, near Crossdoney, Derrylane Lough, Co. Cavan. Ditch near Cushendun, Co. Antrim, Drumoughty Lough, near Kenmare, Lower Lake, Killarney. River near Glencar, Co. Kerry. Greenane Carrickmacreilly Hill, Lugnaquilla, Co. Wicklow. Lough Corrib, Co. Galway. Lough Mourne deposit, Sub-peat deposit, Dromore, Co. Down.

Navicula alpina, (Wm. Sm.) Fresh water.

Length of valves about ·0060, breadth about ·0018; broadly elliptical, with rounded ends; intermediate free space wide, but slightly expanded around the central nodule; costæ broad, convergent in the middle, and radiate towards the ends. (Pl. 30, fig. 4.)

Grunow, Verhand. der K. K. Zool. Bot. Gesel., Band x., 1860, p. 522.—Pinnularia alpina, Wm. Sm., B. D., Vol. i., p. 55, Pl. xviii., fig. 168. Rab. Fl. Eur. Alg., sect. 1, p. 213.

On the slopes of Slieve Donard, Co. Down. Killakee, Featherbed Mountain, Co. Dublin.

Navicula pachyptera, (Ehr.) Fresh water.

Frustules regularly quadrangular on front view; length of valve about ·0034, breadth about ·0013; slightly inflated in the middle, rounded at the ends; intermediate free space but slightly expanded in the middle; costæ broad, slightly converging in the middle, and nearly parallel for the remainder. (Plate 30, fig. 5.)

Kütz. Bac., p. 98, T. xxviii., fig. 58. Ralfs, in Pritch., p. 896, who considers the species distinct from Pinnularia lata, Wm. Smith, which latter he refers to as Navicula lata, p. 908. Grunow, Verhand. der K. K. Zool. Bot. Gesel., Band x., 1860, p. 515.—Pinnularia pachyptera, Rab. Süssw. Diat., p. 44, T. vi., fig. 11.—Pinnularia lata, Wm. Sm., B. D., Vol. i., p. 55, Pl. xviii., fig. 167. Kützing describes a form as Navicula lata, Bac., p. 92, T. iii., fig. 51, which is obviously different from the present.

Pool, Glencree, Co. Wicklow. River Dodder, Featherbed Mountain, Co. Dublin. River Bann, near Hilltown, Co. Down.

Navicula distans, (Wm. Sm.) Marine.
Frustule on front view slightly constricted in the middle, and gently attenuated at the ends; valve lanceolate, length about ·0045, breadth about ·0010; costæ not so robust as in the preceding; convergent; intermediate free space lanceolate, much expanded in the middle and narrow towards the ends. (Plate 30, fig. 6.)
Grunow, Verhand. der K. K. Zool. Bot. Gesel., Band x., 1860, p. 523. Ralfs, in Pritch., p. 907. Cleve, Om Svenska och Norska Diåt., p. 224. —Pinnularia distans, Wm. Sm., B. D., Vol. i. p. 56, Pl. xviii., fig. 169. Rab. Fl. Eur. Alg., sect. 1, p. 214.

Sea-weeds, Bannow, Co. Wexford. Sea-weeds, Malahide, Stomachs of Pectens, Dalkey, Piles of wooden bridge, Dollymount Strand, Sea-weeds, Howth, Co. Dublin. Stomachs of Ascidians, Belfast Lough, Co. Antrim. Stomachs of Ascidians, Co. Clare. Seaweeds, Kilkee, Co. Clare.

Navicula undulata, N. S. Marine.
Length of valve ·0060, breadth, ·0015; lanceolate with rounded ends; median line undulate, intermediate free space lanceolate, greatly expanded in the middle; costæ strong, convergent. (Pl. 30, fig. 7.)

Sea-weeds, Giants' Causway, Co. Antrim.

Navicula rectangulata, (Gregory.) Marine.
Valve linear; length about ·0040, breadth about ·0010; slightly expanded at the middle and ends, which latter are rounded; intermediate free space narrow at ends, but roundly expanded in the middle; costæ strong, converging in the middle, and radiate towards the ends; frustule on front view constricted in the middle. (Plate 30, fig. 8.)
Gregory, Diat. of Clyde, p. 479, Pl. ix., fig. 7. Donkin, N. H. Brit. Diat., p. 66, Pl. x., fig. 5.—Pinnularia rectangulata, Rab. Fl. Eur. Alg., sect. 1, p. 215.

Stomachs of Ascidians, Broadhaven, Co. Galway.

Navicula trevelyana, (Donkin.) Marine.

Frustule on front view deeply constricted, with truncate extremities; middle and end nodules apparent, with a narrow slightly lunate unstriate band at either side of the central nodule; valve linear, rounded at ends; length about ·0048, breadth about ·0008; median line somewhat undulate; intermediate free space narrow, except around the median nodule, where it is much and roundly expanded; costæ strong, converging in the middle, and radiate towards the ends. (Plate 30, fig. 9.)

Donkin, Q. J. M. S., 1861, p. viii., Pl. 1, fig. 2. Do. N. H. Brit. Diat., p. 66, Pl. 10, fig. 6.—Pinnularia trevelyana, Rab. Fl. Eur. Alg. sect. i., p. 210.

Bannow, Co. Wexford. Malahide, Co. Dublin.

Navicula oblonga, (Kütz.) Fresh water.

Frustules on front view quadrangular, narrow; valve narrow, elliptical; length about ·0058, breadth about ·0007; apices broad, rounded; costæ strong, convergent; intermediate free space narrow, except in middle, where it is roundly expanded. (Pl. 30, fig. 10.)

Kütz. Bac., p. 97, T. iv., fig. 21. Ralfs, in Pritch., p. 907. Grunow, Verhand. der K. K., Zool. Bot. Gesel, Band x., 1860, p. 523. Cleve, Om Svenska och Norska Diat., p. 225.—Pinnularia oblonga, Wm. Sm. B. D., Vol. i., p. 54, Pl. xviii., fig. 165. The form described by Rabenhorst, Süssw. Diat., p. 45, T. vi., fig. 6, as Pinnularia oblonga, is obviously different from the present species.

Castlebridge, Co. Wexford. River near Glencar, Co. Kerry. Pond, Newcastle-Lyons, Co. Dublin. Powerscourt Demesne, Kilcool, Co. Wicklow.

Navicula oblonga, var. *lanceolata*, (Grunow.) Fresh water.

Valve shorter and broader than in the typical form, lanceolate, with rounded ends; intermediate free space narrow.

Grunow remarks that this variety "stands near to Pinnularia peregrina, as described by Wm. Smith," but it is certainly distinct, being found in localities beyond the reach of marine influence. It may be distinguished from Navicula peregrina by the intermediate free space, expanded in the middle, which that form does not exhibit.

Grunow, Verhand. der K. K. Zool. Bot. Gesel., Band x., 1866, p. 523, T. iv., fig. 25.

Lough Mourne deposit, Co. Antrim.

Navicula longa, (Gregory.) Marine.

Valves lanceolate; length about ·0060; breadth about ·0010; costæ strong, distant, slightly radiate in the middle, more radiate

towards the ends; intermediate free space narrow, except in the centre, where it is somewhat rhombically expanded. (Pl. 30, fig. 11.)
Ralfs, in Pritch., p. 906. Donkin, N. H. Brit. Diat., p. 55, Pl. viii., fig. 3.—Pinnularia longa, Gregory, Q. J. M. S., Vol. iv., 1856, p. 47, Pl. 5, fig. 18. Rab. Fl. Eur. Alg., sect. i., p. 218.

Arran Islands; Stomachs of Ascidians, Roundstone Bay, Co. Galway.

Navicula divergens, (Wm. Sm.) Fresh water.
Valve oblong; length from about ·0035 to ·0055, breadth, from about ·0007 to ·0012. Gibbous in the middle, attenuated towards the slightly constricted and rounded extremities. Costæ strong, convergent in the middle, and radiate towards the ends. Intermediate free space narrowed towards the ends, where there is a slight expansion; greatly expanded in the middle, reaching the margin in a tolerably broad stauroform band.
Ralfs, in Pritch., p. 896. Grunow, Verhand. der K. K. Zool. Bot. Gesel., Band x., 1860, p. 523. Cleve, Om Svenska och Norska Diat., p. 225.—Pinnularia divergens, Wm. Sm., B. D., Vol. i., p. 57; Pl. xviii., fig. 177. Rab. Fl. Eur. Alg. sect. i., p. 221.

Drumoughty Lough, near Kenmare, County Kerry. Featherbed Mountain, Killakee, County Dublin. Bantry, County Cork. Lake near Castlewellan, County Down. Lough Mourne deposit, County Antrim.

Navicula divergens, var. *longa*, (O'Meara.) Fresh water.
Valve oblong, linear. Length about ·0059; breadth about ·0008; very slightly expanded in the middle and at the rounded ends. Costæ as in the typical form; intermediate free space as in typical form, but scarcely reaching the margin, compared with which it is relatively narrower in middle, and broader at the ends. (Pl. 30, fig. 13.)

Pond near the City of Armagh.

Navicula divergens, var. *elliptica*, (O'Meara.) Fresh water.
Like the typical species but broadly elliptical.

Lough Mourne deposit, Co. Antrim.

Navicula borealis, (Ehr.) Fresh water.
Valve narrow, elliptical, with rounded ends. Length about ·0015; breadth about ·0004. Costæ short, parallel; intermediate free space relatively wide, elliptical. (Pl. 30, fig. 14.)
Kütz. Bac. p. 96. T. xxviii., figs. 68 72, (where it is identified with Pinnularia borealis, Ehr.) Grunow, Verhand. der K. K. Zool. Bot. Gesel., Band x., 1860, p. 518.—Pinnularia borealis, Rab. Süssw.

Diat., p. 42, T. vi., fig. 19. Do. Fl. Eur. Alg., sect. 1, p.216 (where it is identified with Pinnularia latestriata.) Gregory Q. J. M. S., Vol. ii., 1854, Pl. iv., fig. 13. Wm. Sm., B. D., Vol. ii., p. 94.

Drumoughty Lough, near Kenmare, Co. Kerry. Pond near Glenchree, Co. Wicklow. Ulster Canal, near Poyntzpass, Co. Armagh. Loughbrickland, Co. Down. Cushendon, Lough Neagh, Co. Antrim, Featherbed Mountain, Co. Dublin.

Navicula menapiensis, N. S. Marine.
Valve small; length ·0016; breadth ·0005; linear, ends rounded and slightly conical. Costæ marginal, distant; intermediate free space tolerably wide, linear elliptical. (Pl. 30, fig. 15.)
This form is, in some respects, similar to the last, but striæ are longer; otherwise distinguished by its marine habitat.

Sea-weeds, Bannow, Co. Wexford. Stomachs of Ascidians, Broadhaven Bay, Co. Galway.

Navicula tabellaria, (Ehr.) Fresh water.
Valve oblong, slightly expanded at the middle and ends. Length about ·0050; breadth about ·0007. Costæ strong, convergent in the middle, then parallel and radiate towards the ends; intermediate free space wide, roundly expanded in the middle. (Plate 30, fig. 12.)
Kütz. Bac., p. 98, T. xxviii., figs. 79, 80, where the costæ are described incorrectly as reaching the median line; also T. xxx., fig. 20, where the costæ are represented as marginal, whereas they extend much further towards the median line. Grunow, Verhand. der K. K. Zool. Bot. Gesel., Band x., 1860, p. 516. Ralfs, in Pritch., p. 896, Pl. xii., fig. 21. Cleve, Om Svenska och Norska Diat., p. 224. Donkin., N. H. Brit. Diat., p. 70, Pl. xii., fig. 4.—Pinnularia tabellaria, Ehr. Wm. Sm., B. D., Vol. i., p. 58, Pl. xix., fig. 181. Rab. Süssw. Diat., p. 44, T. vi., fig. 24. Do. Fl. Eur. Alg., sect. i., p. 211.

Friarstown, Piperstown, Featherbed Mountain, Killakee, Co. Dublin. Glenchree, Lugnaquilla Mountain. Co. Wicklow. Glencar, Co. Kerry. Lough Corrib, Co. Galway. Lough Mourne deposit, Co. Antrim.

Navicula tabellaria, var. *acrosphæria*, (De Brèb.) Fresh water.
Like the typical form. The costæ, however, are marginal.
Navicula acrosphæria, Kütz. Bac., p. 97, T. v., fig. 11, where it is alleged that the form is identical with Frustulia acrosphæria, De Brèbisson, to whom, on this account, I attribute the species. Ralfs, in Pritch., p. 896.—Navicula tabellaria, Grunow, who observes, that "Wm. Smith's figures and descriptions of Navicula acrosphæria and N. tabellaria differ only in the different size and the somewhat

thicker striation of the former species." Verhand. der K. K. Zool. Bot. Gesell., Band x., 1860, p. 516.—Navicula acrosphæria. De Brébisson, Consid. sur les Diat., 1838, p. 19. Donkin, N. H. Brit. Diat., p. 72, Pl. xii., fig. 2.—Pinnularia acrosphæria, Wm. Sm., B. D., Vol. i., p. 58, Pl. xix., fig. 183.—Pinnularia tabellaria, var. acrosphæria, Rab. Fl. Eur. Alg., sect. i., p. 211.

Carnew, Greenane, Co. Wicklow. Lake near Castlewellan, Co. Down. Camolin, Co. Wexford.

(b.) *Gibbosæ*.

Similar to the *Nobiles*; the *striæ* finer; the intermediate free space narrower, expanding around the central nodule, and sometimes extending to the margin in a stauriform band.

Navicula clepsydra, (Donkin). Marine.
Frustules on front view constricted in the middle; ends angular; side view largely apparent. Valves narrow, elliptical; ends rounded. Length about ·0040; breadth about ·0009. Striæ punctate, converging in the middle; slightly radiate towards the ends; intermediate free space linear, narrow, except in the centre, where it is roundly expanded. (Plate 30, fig. 16.)
Donkin, Q. J. M. S., 1857, p. 8, Pl. i., fig. 3. Do., N. H. Brit. Diat., p. 63, Pl. x., fig. ii. Rab. Fl. Eur. Alg., sect. i., p. 181.

Ireland's Eye, Co. Dublin.

Navicula rupestris, N. S. Fresh water.
Valve in length ·0025; breadth ·0008; linear, elliptical, very gently attenuated towards the rounded ends. Striæ costate, fine, waved, converging in the middle, radiate towards the ends; intermediate free space narrow, except in the middle, where it is expanded in a rhomboid form. (Pl. 30, fig. 17.)

Found on moist rock, Portrush, Co. Antrim.

Navicula ceres, (Schumann). Marine.
Valve linear, elliptical; gently attenuated towards the rounded ends. Length ·0022; breadth ·0007. Striæ costate, in some lights appearing as if closely moniliform; convergent in the middle; slightly radiate towards the ends; intermediate free space narrow, except in the middle, where it is greatly expanded. (Pl. 30, fig. 18.)
Schumann, Preussische Diatomeen; Zweite Nachtrag, p. 56, T. ii., fig. 38.
Stomachs of Ascidians, Broadhaven Bay, Co. Galway.

Navicula gibba, (Ehr.) Fresh water.

Valve nearly linear; very slightly constricted towards the ends, and very gently expanded in the middle. Length about ·0044; breadth about ·0008. Striæ finely costate; convergent in the middle, and radiate towards the ends. Intermediate free space narrow, except in the middle, where it is roundly expanded. (Pl. 30, fig. 19.)

Kützing, (Bac., p. 98, T. xxviii. fig. 70), has described a form under this name, which he regards as Pinnularia gibba, Ehr. With this the form so named by Rabenhorst (Süssw. Diat., p. 45, T. vi., fig. 27), agrees. Ralfs' description seems tolerably well to correspond, "lanceolate, with dilated capitate ends." In the above cases the figures represent the form more gibbous in the middle than the present species, and with capitate ends; the striæ also are parallel, while in the present form they are convergent in the middle, and radiate at the ends, just as Wm. Smith has figured Pinnularia gibba, B. D. Vol. i., p. 58, Pl. xix., fig. 180. The present form is less capitate at the ends, and the intermediate free space more roundly expanded in the middle than in Smith's figure. Grunow, comparing the species he has named Navicula gibba with Navicula tabellaria, says it stands distinct from it "by the narrower expansion of the ends, and the more gradual tapering in the middle." Verhand. der K. K. Zool. Bot. Gesell., Band x., 1860, p. 517. This description corresponds exactly with the present form.

Lough Corrib, Co. Galway. Drumoughty Lough, near Kenmare, Co. Cork. Carn Lough, near Tralee, Co. Kerry. Derrylane Lough, Co. Cavan. Carrickmacreely Hill, Lugnaquilla Mountain, Rathdrum, Co. Wicklow. Featherbed Mountain, Co. Dublin. Lough Mourne deposit, Co. Antrim.

Navicula gibba, var. boeckii, (Rab.) Fresh water.

Valve smaller than the typical species; length ·0032, breadth ·0007; margin very slightly gibbous; ends somewhat capitate; striæ finely costate; intermediate free space narrow, except at the middle, where it expands considerably, sometimes reaching the margin at one side, but not at the other. (Plate 30, fig. 20.)

Grunow, Verhand. der K. K. Zool. Bot. Gesell., Band x., 1860, p. 517, T. iv., fig. 17. This author regards the form as identical with Staurophora peckii, Rab. Bacil. Sachs.

Lough Corrib, Co. Galway. Pond near the city of Armagh.

Navicula gibba, var. parva, (O'Meara). Fresh water.

Valve small; length ·0015, breadth ·0003; slightly gibbous at the margins; much attenuated towards the somewhat-capitate ends; striæ costate, fine, convergent in the middle, and slightly radiate towards the ends; intermediate free space relatively broad, expanding at the middle, and sometimes reaching to the margin. (Plate 30, fig. 21.)

There is a form somewhat similar to this described by Grunow under the name of Navicula stauroptera, var. parva, Verhand. der K. K. Zool. Bot. Gesell., Band x., 1860, p. 517, T. iv., fig. 19. The striation in the present form is, however, coarser than in Grunow's figure, the latter also being more robust, for which reasons I hesitate to identify the present form with that of Grunow.

Lough Neagh, near Lurgan, Co. Armagh. Camolin, Co. Wexford.

Navicula hemiptera, (Kütz). Fresh water.
Valve linear, elliptical, with rounded ends; length ·0025, breadth ·0005; striæ costate linear, convergent at the middle, and radiate towards the ends; intermediate free space narrow, somewhat expanded in the middle. (Plate 30, fig. 22.)
Kütz. Bac., p. 97, T. xxx., fig. 11. Ralfs, in Pritch., p. 908; Grunow, Verhand. der K. K. Zool. Bot. Gesell., Band x., 1860, p. 519. This author considers the form may be only a variety of Navicula viridis, which it greatly resembles, except that it is smaller, and the striation very much finer. Cleve, Om Svenska och Norska Diat., p. 223.—Pinnularia hemiptera, Wm.'Sm., B.D., Vol. ii., p. 95. Rab. Süssw. Diat., p. 42, T. vi., fig. 17. Do. Fl. Eur. Alg., sect. i. p. 212.

Lucan, Featherbed Mountain, Friarstown, Co. Dublin. River Erne, near Crossdoney, Derrylane Lough, Co. Cavan. Lough Erne, Co. Fermanagh. Lough Neagh, near Lurgan. Ulster Canal, near Poyntzpass, Co. Armagh. Pool near Glengarriff, Co. Cork. Streamlet, Cushendun, Co. Antrim. River Bann, near Coleraine, Co. Derry. Sub-peat deposit, Dromore, Co. Down.

Navicula apiculata, (De Bréb.) Marine.
Valve linear in the middle, gradually tapering towards the ends, which run out into acute short beaks; length ·0026, breadth ·0008; costæ fine, converging in the middle, radiate towards the ends; intermediate free space narrower towards the ends, expanded in the middle. (Pl. 30, fig. 23.)
Pinnularia rostellata, Gregory, Diat. of Clyde, p. 488, Pl. ix., fig. 20, 1857.—Navicula apiculata, De Brébisson Diat. du Littoral de Cherbourg, p. 16, Pl. i., fig. 5, 1867. Ralfs, in Pritch., p. 903. Donkin N. H. Brit. Diat., p. 56, Pl. viii., fig. 6. Kützing has described a form as Navicula rostellata, which is quite distinct from the present; it is therefore necessary to drop the specific name adopted by Gregory, and substitute for it De Brébisson's name, Navicula apiculata.
Gregory and De Brébisson describe the striæ as reaching the median line; Donkin more correctly represents them as falling short of it, but does not describe the central expansion of the free intermediate space.

Navicula brébissonii, (Kütz). Fresh water.

Valve linear, elliptical; ends somewhat rounded; length ·0016, breadth ·0005; costæ fine, radiate; intermediate free space narrow, except in the middle, where it expands, reaching the margin in a stauroform band widening towards the margin. (Plate 30, fig. 24.)
Kütz. Bac., p. 93, T. iii., fig. 49. Ralfs, in Pritch., p. 897. Grunow, Verhand. der K. K. Zool. Bot. Gesell., Band x., 1860, p. 519.
—Pinnularia stauroneiformis, Wm. Sm., B.D., Vol. i., p. 57, Pl. xix., fig. 178. Rab. Fl. Eur. Alg., sect. i., p. 222.

Drumoughty Lough, near Kenmare, Bantry, Co. Cork. Derrylane Lough, Co. Cavan. Rathdrum, Featherbed Mountain, Co. Wicklow. Killakee, Co. Dublin. Lough Gill, Co. Kerry.

Navicula brébissonii, var. angusta, (Grun.) Fresh water.

Valve narrow, elliptical; ends attenuated, and slightly rounded; length ·0016, breadth ·00025; costæ fine, radiate; intermediate free space narrow, except in the middle, where it expands, reaching the margin in a stauroform band narrower than in the typical species. (Plate 30, fig. 25.)
Grunow, Verhand. der K. K. Zool. Bot. Gesell., Band x., 1860, p. 519, T. v., fig. 18.

Derrylane Lough, Co. Cavan. Camolin, Co. Wexford.

Navicula icostauron, (Ehr.) Fresh water.

Valve linear, elliptical; length ·0028, breadth ·0006; costæ fine, radiate; intermediate free space narrow, except in the middle, where it expands into a narrow stauroform parallel band reaching the margin. (Plate 30, fig. 27.)
Stauroptera icostauron, Ehr., as Grunow suggests, Verhand. der K. K. Zool. Bot. Gesell., Band x., 1860, p. 519.—Stauroneis icostauron, Kütz. Bac., p. 106, T. xxix., fig. 10.—Pinnularia viridis, var. B., Wm. Sm., B.D., Vol. i., p. 54, Pl. xviii., fig. 163 B.

Derrylane Lough, Co. Cavan. Adrigoole, Co. Kerry. Featherbed Mountain, Co. Dublin. Lake near Castlewellan, Co. Down.

Navicula stauroptera, (Grunow). Fresh water.

Valve linear, elliptical, with rounded ends; length ·0025, breadth ·0007; costæ coarse, convergent in the middle, radiate towards the ends; intermediate free space narrow, except in the middle, where it is much expanded, appearing sometimes to reach the margin, but really not so. (Plate 30, fig. 28.)
Grunow, Verhand. der K. K. Zool. Bot. Gesell., Band x., 1860, p. 516. Stauroptera parva, Ehr., according to Kützing.—Stauroneis parva, Kütz. Bac., p. 106, T. xxix., fig. 23. Gregory has described a form as Pinnularia parva, Q. J. M. S., 1854, p. 98, Pl. iv., fig. 11. To

avoid confusion, the specific name adopted by Ehrenberg and Kützing for this species had best be abandoned, and the designation proposed by Grunow as above substituted for it.

Raphoe, Co. Donegal. Lough Neagh, near Lurgan, Co. Armagh. Sub-peat deposit, Dromore, Co. Down.

Navicula bacillum, (Ehr.) Fresh water.
Valves linear; ends rounded; costæ fine, strongly marked in the middle, radiate; intermediate free space narrow, slightly expanded in the middle; length about ·0018, breadth about ·0005. (Plate 30, fig. 29.)

Ehrenberg has given many figures of a species so named, some of which are utterly undistinguishable; one from a marine habitat indicated cannot be the same. Two, however, of his figures are plain enough for satisfactory identification.

Ehr. Mic. T. xv., A. fig. 38; T. ii., 2. fig. 14. Kütz. Bac., p. 96, T. xxviii., fig. 69. Wm. Sm., B.D., Vol. ii., p. 91. Ralfs, in Pritch., p. 907. Grunow, Verhand. der K. K. Zool. Bot. Gesell., Band x., 1860, p. 551, T. iv., fig. 1. Rab. Süssw. Diat., p. 39, T. vi., fig. 76. Heiberg, De Danske Diat., p. 85.

Ditch near town of Wexford. Lower Lake, Killarney, Co. Kerry. Lough Neagh, near Lurgan, Co. Armagh. Cushendun, Co. Antrim. Derrylane Lough, Co. Cavan. Sub-peat deposit, Dromore, Co. Down. Lough Mourne deposit.

Navicula americana, (Ehr.) Fresh water.
Valve linear, oblong, with rounded ends; length ·0035, breadth ·0010; slightly constricted; costæ fine, convergent in the middle, and nearly parallel towards the ends; intermediate free space wide, greatly expanded in the middle; central nodule large, median line very strongly marked. (Plate 30, fig. 30.)

Ehr. Mic. T. II., II., fig. 16. Kitton, Science Gossip, June, 1868, p. 131.

This species in a fossil state is widely dispersed; besides the locality indicated by Ehrenberg, it has been found by Mr. Kitton of Norwich, in Perley's Meadow deposit, Sth. Bridgton, Maine, U. S. A. I found it in great abundance in a fresh water deposit discovered by Dr. Moss, R. N., in Vancouver's Island, as also in a sub-peat deposit from Dromore, Co. Down. Rev. George Davidson has furnished me with specimens found in a fossil state in Lough Canmore, near Aberdeen. I have found it in tolerable abundance in a living state in Lough Neagh, near Lurgan, Co. Armagh.

Navicula isocephala, (Ehr.) Fresh water.
Valve long, narrow; length ·0055, breadth ·0007; undulate on the margin, with three nearly equal and slight inflations; ends constricted

and capitate; costæ strong, convergent in the middle, and radiate towards the ends; intermediate free space narrow, except in the middle, where it is much expanded, reaching to the margin. (Plate 30, fig. 31.)

Kütz. Bac., p. 101, without a figure. This author identifies the species with Pinnularia isocephala, Ehr. Kitton, Science Gossip, June, 1868, p. 132.—Pinnularia monile, Rab. Fl. Eur. Alg., sect. i., p. 220.

Pond near the city of Armagh. Friarstown, Co. Dublin.

Navicula nodosa, (Ehr.) Fresh water.

Valve long and narrow; length ·0024, breadth ·0005; margin undulate, with three nearly equal inflations; costæ short, not very close, convergent in the middle, radiate towards the ends; intermediate free space wide, expanded in the middle. (Plate 30, fig. 26.)

Kütz. Bac., p. 101. T. xxviii., fig. 82. This author regards the form as identical with Navicula nodosa, Ehr. Infus., 1838, p. 179, T. xiii., fig. 9. Rab. Süssw. Diat., p. 41, T. vi., fig. 86. Gregory, Q. J. M. S., Vol. iv., 1856, p. 3, Pl. i., fig. 5. Pinnularia nodosa, Wm. Sm., B.D., Vol. ii., p. 96.

Friarstown, Featherbed Mountain, Co. Dublin. River Slaney, near Killurin. Camolin, Co. Wexford. Lake near Castlewellan, Co. Down. Kilcool, Lugnaquilla Mountain, Co. Wicklow.

Navicula nodosa, var. staurophora, (Grunow). Fresh water.

Valve smaller than in the typical species; length ·0016, breadth ·00025; inflations not so distinct; intermediate free space expanding in the middle into a distinct stauroform band reaching the margin. (Plate 30, fig. 26 a.)

Navicula nodosa, Grunow, Verhand. der K. K. Zool. Bot. Gesell., Band x., 1860, p. 521, T. ii., fig. 21.

Navicula bicapitata, (O'Meara). Fresh water.

Valves small; length ·0020, breadth ·0006; linear, attenuated towards the capitate ends; costæ fine, convergent at the centre, radiate towards the ends; intermediate free space narrow, except at the middle, where it is roundly expanded, not reaching the margin. (Plate 30, fig. 32.)

Pinnularia biceps, Gregory, Q. J. M. S., 1856, p. 8, Pl. i., fig. 28. Kützing has described a form under the name of Navicula biceps, Bac., p. 96, T. xxviii., fig. 51, which is widely different from the present. Gregory's specific name must therefore be dropped.

Drumoughty Lough, near Kenmare, Co. Cork. Cawn Lough, near Tralee, Co. Kerry. River Bannow, near Clonegal, Co. Carlow. Kilcool, Co. Wicklow. Camolin, Co. Wexford.

Navicula bicapitata, var. *crucifera*. Fresh water.
Valve linear in the middle, attenuated towards the capitate ends. Length ·0024; breadth ·0006. Costæ fine, radiate; intermediate free space narrow, except in the middle, where it expands into a narrow stauroform band, reaching to the margin, and wider there than at the centre. (Pl. 30, fig. 33.)

Pinnularia interrupta, Wm. Sm., B. D., Vol. i., p. 59, Pl. xix., fig. 184. Were it not for the figure of Smith, just referred to, it would be difficult to identify this form. Smith alleges that it is identical with Stauroneis parva, Kütz. Bac., p. 106, T. xxix., fig. 23; but that form, as described by Kützing, is elliptical, and has not capitate ends, in consequence of which I consider the species quite distinct. The specific name adopted by Smith was previously appropriated by Kützing for a form belonging to the genus Navicula, which that form still retains; for which reason I have changed the specific designation.—Navicula parva, Ralfs, in Pritch., p. 897. This description is given obviously on the supposition that Pinnularia interrupta, (Wm. Sm.,) was identical with Stauroneis parva, Kütz. But a comparison of the figures renders the accuracy of this supposition more than doubtful.

Pool near Glengarriff, Co. Cork. Lough Gill, Co. Kerry. River at Port-na-Crush, Co. Donegal. Ditch, Cushendun, Co. Antrim. Gavagh, Co. Derry. Pool near Glenchree, Co. Wicklow.

Navicula bicapitata, var. *constricta*, (Grunow). Fresh water.
Valves slightly incurved in the middle; ends much produced, narrowed, and but slightly capitate. Length ·0025, breadth in middle ·0006. Costæ fine, radiate. Intermediate free space narrow, except in the middle, where it expands to the margin in a narrow stauroform band, widening at margin. (Pl. 30, fig. 34.)

Navicula mesolepta, var. constricta, Grunow, Verhand. der K. K. Zool. Bot. Gesell., Band x., 1860, p. 521, T. iv., fig. 22, C. Inasmuch as the typical form of Navicula mesolepta has persistent costæ, whereas in the present case the costæ are obviously interrupted in the middle, I prefer to regard this form as a variety of Navicula bicapitata.

Featherbed Bog, Co. Dublin. Camolin, Co. Wexford.

Navicula termes, (Ehr.) Fresh water.
Valve narrow, oblong. Length ·0035, breadth ·0006; slightly incurved in the middle; ends much produced, slightly constricted. Costæ short, slightly radiate; intermediate free space wide, sometimes reaching the margin in a stauroform band. (Pl. 30, fig. 35.)

Navicula termes, var. nodulosa, Kütz. Bac., p. 101, T. xxviii., fig. 71, in which the costæ are represented as reaching the median line, whereas in the present form they are marginal. Kützing regards the species as Pinnularia termes, Ehr.—Navicula mesolepta, var. nodulosa, Grunow, Verhand. der K. K. Zool. Bot. Gesell., Band x., 1860, p. 320.

Featherbed Bog, Co. Dublin. Camolin, Co. Wexford.

Navicula microstauron, (Ehr.) Fresh water.
Valve linear, oblong, attenuated towards the broadly rounded ends, which are slightly, if at all, capitate. Length ·0026; breadth ·0006; costæ convergent in the middle, radiate towards ends; intermediate free space narrow, except in the middle, where it expands into a narrow stauroform band, slightly wider at the margin than towards the central nodule. (Pl. 30, fig. 36.)
Stauroneis microstauron, Kütz. Bac., p. 106, T. xxix., fig. 13. —Stauroptera microstauron, Rab. Süssw. Diat., p. 49, T. ix., fig. 7.

Featherbed Bog, Co. Dublin. Lough Gill, Co. Kerry.

Navicula crucifera, N. S. Fresh water.
Valve linear, oblong, narrow. Length ·0026, breadth ·0003. Slightly attenuated towards the scarcely capitate ends. Costæ convergent in the middle, slightly radiate towards the ends; intermediate free space relatively wide, expanding in the middle into a narrow stauroform band. (Pl. 30, fig. 37.)
This form strongly resembles one described by Schumann as Navicula nodulosa, β, Die Diat. der Hohen Tatra, p. 77, T. iv., fig. 53. It is, however, longer and narrower, the costæ shorter, and the stauroform band not so wide.

Featherbed Bog, Co. Dublin. Lough Mourne deposit, Co. Antrim.

Navicula pinnularia, (Cleve). Marine.
Valve linear, elliptical, ends rounded. Costæ strong, nearly parallel. Length from ·0020 to ·00034, breadth from ·0006 to ·0008. Intermediate free space very narrow, except in the middle, where it expands in a broad strauriform band. (Pl. 30, fig. 38.)
Cleve, Om Svenska och Norska Diat., p. 224, T. iv., fig. 1.

Arran Islands, Stomachs of Ascidians, Roundstone Bay, Stomachs of Ascidians, Broadhaven Bay, Co. Galway. Portmarnock, Co. Dublin.

Navicula scalaris, (Ehr.) Fresh water.
Valve linear, elliptical, ends rounded. Length ·0014, breadth ·0003. Striæ nearly parallel; intermediate free space very narrow, except in the middle, where it expands into a broad stauroform band, reaching the margin. (Pl. 30, fig. 39.)
Navicula borealis, var. scalaris, Grunow, Verhand. der K. K. Zool.

Bot. Gesell., Band. x., 1860, p. 518, T. iv., fig. 15, which represents the costæ as stronger and more distant than they are in my specimens. —Stauroneis scalaris, Kütz. Bac., p. 106, T. xxix., fig. 37. In this figure the form is wider than in my specimens, and the stauroform band is much narrower than in Grunow's figure, as well as in my specimens. —Stauroptera scalaris, Ehr., Rab. Süssw. Diat., p. 49, T. ix., fig. 8.

Camolin, Co. Wexford.

Navicula cuneata, N. S. Fresh water.
Valve linear, cuneate at the ends. Length .0025, breadth ·0006. Costæ strong, convergent in the middle, radiate towards the ends; intermediate free space broad, expanded in the middle. (Pl. 30, fig. 40.)
This form in outline much resembles Pinnularia acuminata, Wm. Sm., B. D., Vol. i., p. 55, Pl. xviii., fig. 164, but differs from it in the following details :—In the latter the striæ are coarser, shorter, and parallel, the intermediate free space is much wider than in this, and having no expansion such as is very obvious in the present form.

Featherbed Bog, Co. Dublin.

Navicula acuminata, (Wm. Sm.) Fresh water.
Valve linear, ends cuneate. Length ·0029, breadth ·0006. Costæ coarse, nearly parallel in the middle, and slightly radiate towards the ends; intermediate free space wide. (Pl. 30, fig. 41.)
Ralfs, in Pritch., p. 909.—Pinnularia acuminata, Wm. Sm., B. D., Vol. i., p. 55, Pl. xviii., fig. 164. Rab. Fl. Eur. Alg., sect. i., p. 216.

Featherbed Mountain, Killakee, Co. Dublin. Kilcool, Co. Wicklow. Rostrevor, Co. Down.

Navicula retusa, (De Brébisson). Marine.
Valve narrow, oblong, rounded at the ends; striæ course, distant, nearly parallel; intermediate free space relatively wide; length ·0026, breadth ·0004; frustule on front view constricted; angles much rounded. (Plate 30, fig. 42.)
De Bréb., Note sur Diat. de littoral de Cherbourg., p. 16, fig. 6. Ralfs, in Pritch., p. 908. Donkin, Q. J. M. S., 1857, p. 14, Pl. i., fig. 17. Do. N. H. Brit. Diat., p. 64, Pl. x., fig. 3. Rab. Fl. Eur. Alg., sect. i., p. 186. Donkin agrees with Walker Arnott in regarding this form as identical with Navicula pectinalis, Wm. Sm., B. D., Vol. ii., p. 91.

Malahide, Co. Dublin. Arran Islands, Stomachs of Ascidians, Roundstone Bay, Co. Galway.

Navicula integra, (Wm. Sm.) Fresh water.

Valve narrow, elliptic, incurved, then angularly expanded towards the ends which are narrow and papillate; striæ fine, radiate; intermediate free space narrow, except at the middle, where it is slightly expanded. (Plate 30, fig. 43.)

Ralfs, in Pritch., p. 895, who describes the striæ as reaching the median line. Donkin, N. H. Brit. Diat., p. 40, Pl. vi., fig. 8, where the character of the striæ is correctly delineated.—Pinnularia integra, Wm. Sm., B. D., Vol. ii., p. 96. Rab. Fl. Eur. Alg., sect. i, p. 220.

Powerscourt, Co. Wicklow.

Navicula pachycephala, (Rab.) Fresh water.

Valve elliptical, with capitate ends; length ·0022, breadth ·0006; costæ short, convergent; intermediate free space broad, reaching the margin in a narrow stauroform band. (Plate 30, fig. 44.)

Pinnularia pachycephala, Rab. Süssw. Diat., p. 43, T. vi., fig. 40.

Featherbed Mountain, Ballybrack, Co. Dublin.

Navicula subcapitata, (Gregory). Fresh water.

Valve narrow, linear, with subcapitate ends; costæ coarse and distant; intermediate free space relatively wide, linear; length ·0015, breadth ·0002. (Plate 30, fig. 45.)

Ralfs, in Pritch., p. 902.—Navicula gracillima, var. subcapitata, Rab. Fl. Eur. Alg., sect. i., p. 200.—Pinnularia subcapitata, Gregory, Q. J. M. S., 1856, p. 9, Pl. i., fig. 30.

Friarstown, Featherbed Mountain, Killakee, Co. Dublin. Glencar, Co. Kerry. Lake near Castlewellan, Co. Down.

Navicula gracillima, (Gregory). Fresh water.

Valve narrow, linear, with produced slightly capitate ends, length ·0018, breadth ·00025; costæ very fine, convergent in the middle, slightly radiate towards the ends; intermediate free space narrow, except in the middle, where it is roundly expanded. (Plate 30, fig. 46.)

Ralfs, in Pritch., p. 902. Rab. Fl. Eur. Alg., sect. i., p. 199. Schumann, Diat. der Hohen Tatra, p. 70, T. iv., fig. 49.—Pinnularia gracillima, Gregory, Q. J. M. S., 1856, p. 9, Pl. i., fig. 31. Wm. Sm., B. D., Vol. ii., p. 95.

Friarstown, Piperstown, Featherbed Mountain, Co. Dublin. Rathdrum, Lugnaquilla Mountain, Co. Wicklow. Drumoughty Lough, near Kenmare, Co. Cork. Glencar, Co. Kerry. Lake near Castlewellan, Co. Down.

Navicula macula, (Gregory). Marine.
Valve broadly elliptical, with narrowed truncate ends; length ·0014, breadth · 0008; costæ fine, parallel; intermediate free space narrow, except in the middle, where it expands greatly in quadrangular form. (Plate 30, fig. 47.)
Gregory, Q. J. M. S., 1856, p. 43, Pl. v., fig. 9. Ralfs, in Pritch., p. 896. Rab. Fl. Eur. Alg., sect. i., p. 189.

Lough Gill, Co. Kerry.

Navicula zellensis, (Grunow). Fresh water.
Valve narrow; length ·0016, breadth ·0003; ends produced; margin triundulate; striæ very fine; intermediate free space narrow, except at the middle, where it expands in a short narrow stauroform band. (Plate 30, fig. 48.)
Grunow, Verhand. der K. K. Zool. Bot. Gesell., Band x., 1860, p. 521, T. iii., fig. 34. Rab. Fl. Eur. Alg., sect. 1, p. 207.

Lough Derryvaragh, Co. Westmeath. Camolin, Co. Wexford.

(c.) *Cuspidatæ*.

Valves more or less distinctly lanceolate; ends sometimes produced; median line distinct; intermediate free space narrow, bounded by two well-defined longitudinal ridges, one on either side of the median line.

Navicula cuspidata, (Wm. Smith). Fresh water.
Valve large, lanceolate; ends cuspidate; length about ·0070, breadth ·0015; striæ close, fine, linear, parallel; median line with slightly elongated expansions near the central nodule. (Plate 31, fig. 1.)
Kütz. Bac., p. 94, T. iii., figs. 24 and 27. Wm. Sm. B. D., Vol. i., p. 47, Pl. xvi., fig. 131. Rab. Süssw. Diat., p. 37, T. vi., fig. 16. This latter author remarks, that this form is very like Navicula fulva, but never attains the same size. This observation is not borne out by the specimens I have had the opportunity of examining; Navicula cuspidata is usually the larger, sometimes very much so. Ralfs, in Pritch., p. 905, Pl. xii., fig. 5. Grunow, Verhand. der K. K. Zool. Bot. Gesell., Band x., 1860, p. 528. The form referred to by Grunow may possibly be different from the present, as he describes the striæ as somewhat radiate in the middle; the striæ in N. cuspidata being parallel all through. Heiberg, De Danske Diat., p. 82. Cleve, Om Svenska och Norska Diat., p. 228. Donkin, N. H., Brit. Diat., p. 39, Pl. vi., fig. 6.

Castlebridge, Tacumshane, Co. Wexford. Derrylane Lough, Stream, Crossdoney, Co. Cavan. Cushendun, Co. Antrim. Pond, Botanic Gardens, Belfast, Co. Down. Bellarena, Co. Derry. River

Dodder, Co. Dublin. Lough Gill, Co. Kerry. Powerscourt, Co. Wicklow. Lough Mourne deposit.

Navicula fulva. (Donkin). Fresh water.
Valve very much as the preceding, but smaller, and having the striæ somewhat radiate; length ·0032, breadth ·0007. (Pl. 31, fig. 2.)

There is great difficulty in identifying this form with that named Navicula fulva by Ehrenberg, which several authors identify with Navicula cuspidata.

This latter Smith has so accurately described, that there is no difficulty in identifying it, and therefore, under the circumstances, I attribute it to him. Donkin, too, has so figured Navicula fulva as to render it equally distinctive, and for this reason I assign the species to him.

Donkin, N. H., Brit. Diat,, p. 41, Pl. vi., fig. 9.

Lough Gill, Co. Kerry. Dysart, Co. Waterford.

Navicula cuspis, N. S. Marine.
Valves narrow, lanceolate; length about ·0044, breadth about ·0008; longitudinal sulci close to median line. Striæ linear, slightly radiate; ends cuspidate; dry valve a light straw colour. (Pl. 31, fig. 3.)

From stomachs of Ascidians, Co. Clare.

Navicula rhombica. (Gregory). Marine.
Frustules on front view subquadrate; slightly constricted angles, rounded. On side view, valve elliptical. Striæ fine, linear, converging in the middle, radiate; much finer and closer towards the ends; length ·0026, breadth ·0008. (Pl. 31, fig. 4.)

Gregory, Q. J. M. S., 1856, p. 38, Pl. v., fig. 1. Ralfs, in Pritch, p. 903. Rab. Fl. Eur. Alg., sect. i., p. 181.

Barrow, Co. Wexford. Malahide, Co. Dublin. Lough Gill, Co. Kerry. Seashore near town of Galway. Breaches, Co. Wicklow. Stomachs of Ascidians, Belfast Lough, Co. Antrim. Stomachs of Ascidians, Co. Clare.

Navicula cærulea, N. S. Fresh water.
Valve narrow, lanceolate: ends much produced. Length ·0022, breadth ·0005; longitudinal sulci close to median line. Striæ linear, convergent in middle, slightly radiate towards the ends; dry valve of a pale colour. (Pl. 31, fig. 5.)

Lough Mask, near Tourmakeady, Co. Mayo.

Navicula decipiens, N. S. Marine.
Valve narrow, elliptical, rounded at ends; length ·0030, breadth ·0008. Striæ fine, close, slightly radiate; in some lights apparently punctate; seemingly disappearing in the middle, and presenting the appearance of a narrow stauroform band, extending to the margins; this however is deceptive. (Pl. 31, fig. 6.)

Tide-pools, Galway Bay, near the town of Galway.

Navicula tumens. (Wm. Smith). Brackish or marine.
Valve elliptical; ends produced. Length from ·0024 to ·0040, breadth from ·0010 to ·0015. Striæ fine, punctate, slightly radiate; when not exactly in focus appearing to be moniliform. (Pl. 31, fig. 7.)

Smith has correctly described the character of the striæ in this species; but the figure represents the striæ as they appear when not in focus.

Donkin, N. H., Brit. Diat., p. 15, considers this form as identical with Navicula rostrata, Ehr., and Navicula sculpta, Ehr. These forms it appears were found by Donkin in the Bergmehl of Santa Fiore, and in the fossil deposit of Franzensbad, which I believe are both fresh water deposits, though that author assigns Navicula rostrata to brackish localities. The form under consideration has been found by Smith only in brackish water; and I have found it only in localities decidedly brackish or marine. However similar the forms may be, they seem to me perfectly distinct, and distinguishable by this feature, that in Navicula tumens the striæ run uninterruptedly from the margin to the longitudinal sulci, whereas in N. rostrata they are interrupted, and present an unstriate space between each sulcus and the ends of the striæ. Wm. Sm., B. D., Vol. i., p. 52, Pl. xvii., fig. 150. Ralfs, in Pritch., p. 900. Grunow, Verhand. der K. K. Zool. Bot. Gesell., Band x., 1860, p. 541. Rab. Fl. Eur. Alg., sect. i., p. 192.

Salt ditch, near Newtownlimavady Junction, Co. Londonderry. Salt ditch, near the town of Galway. Seaweeds, Salt Hill, Co. Dublin. Salt ditch, Breaches, Co. Wicklow. Lough Gill, Co. Kerry.

Navicula rostrata. (Ehr.) Fresh or brackish water.
Valves elliptical, produced into long rounded apices; length ·0046, breadth ·0015. Striæ punctate, slightly radiate, disappearing in the middle of the space between the margin and the longitudinal sulcus, and appearing again upon the edge of the sulcus. (Pl. 31, fig. 8.)

There is some doubt as to whether this species belongs to fresh or brackish water. The fact that Donkin identified the form, so well delineated by him, with specimens from the Santa Fiore deposit, as well as that of Franzensbad, would seem decisive as to its proper habitat being in fresh water. The localities, however, to which he has assigned the species found by him in a living state are brackish;

and the only three localities in which I have found it in Ireland, if not marine, are certainly brackish.

Kütz. Bac., p. 94, T. iii., fig. 55, who attributes the species to Ehrenberg. Ralfs, in Pritch., p. 901, who regards it as distinct from Navicula sculpta, Ehr. Grunow, Verhand. der K. K. Zool. Bot. Gesell., Band x., 1860, p. 540, who states that he did not find the form in the Santa Fiore Bergmehl. examined by him, but confirms Donkin's statement of having obtained it in the Franzensbad deposit. Donkin, N. H. Brit., Diat., p. 15, Pl. ii., fig. 9. Rab. Fl. Eur. Alg., sect. i., p. 197.

Seashore, Queenstown, Co. Cork. Breaches, Co. Wicklow. Salt Hill, Co. Dublin.

Navicula tenuirostris, N. S. Marine.

Valve elliptical, with long produced narrow apices; length ·0018, breadth ·0006; striæ fine, parallel in the middle, and slightly radiate towards the ends; less distinct midway between the margin and the longitudinal sulcus; intermediate free space narrow, apparently expanding in the middle in a short and very narrow stauroform band. (Plate 31, fig. 9.)

Stomachs of Ascidians, Broadhaven Bay, Co. Galway.

Navicula ambigua, (Ehr.) Fresh water.

Valves elliptical, ends produced and capitate; length ·0032, breadth ·0010; striæ fine, parallel. (Plate 31, fig. 10.)

Kütz. Bac., p. 95, T. xxviii., fig. 66, who attributes the species to Ehrenberg. Wm. Sm., B. D., Vol. i., p. 51, Pl. xvi., fig. 149. Rab. Süssw. Diat., p. 40, T. vi., fig. 59. Ralfs, in Pritch., p. 902. Grunow, Verhand. der K. K. Zool. Bot. Gesell., Band x., 1860, p. 529, T. iv., fig. 33. Cleve, Om Svenska och Norska Diat., p. 228. Donkin, N. H., Brit. Diat., p. 39, Pl. vi., fig. 5.

River Erne, near Crossdoney, Co. Cavan. Pool near Glencar, Co. Cork. River Bann, near Coleraine, Co. Londonderry.

Navicula sphærophora, (Kütz.) Fresh water.

Valve elliptical; ends considerably produced and capitate; striæ fine, punctate, slightly convergent; length ·0030, breadth ·0010. (Plate 31, fig. 11.)

Kütz. Bac., p. 95, T. iv., fig. 17. Wm. Sm., B. D., Vol. i., p. 52, Pl. xvii., fig. 148, who represents the striæ as moniliform, an appearance they present only when not in focus. Rab. Süssw. Diat., p. 40, T. vi., fig. 65a, 65b being, as it would appear, a very distinct form. Ralfs, in Pritch., p. 899. Grunow, Verhand. der K. K. Zool. Bot.

Gesell., Band x., 1860, p. 540, T. iv., fig. 34. Cleve, Om Svenska och Norska Diat., p. 227. Donkin, N. H. Brit. Diat., p. 34, Pl. v., fig. 10.

Tacumshane, Co. Wexford. Lough Gill, Co. Kerry. Moist rock, Portrush, Co. Antrim. River Bann, near Coleraine, Co. Londonderry.

Navicula quarnerensis, (Grunow). Marine.
Valve broadly elliptical, slightly produced towards the apiculate ends; striæ fine, obscurely punctate, radiate; length ·0028, breadth ·0012. (Plate 31, fig. 12.)
Grunow, Verhand. der K. K. Zool. Bot. Gesell., Band x., 1860, p. 530, T. iii., fig. 8, found in the Adriatic Sea, from two to four fathoms in depth.

Salt ditch, near Galway town. Stomachs of Ascidians, Roundstone Bay, Stomachs of Ascidians, Broadhaven Bay, Co. Galway.

Navicula Davidsoniana, N. S. Marine.
Valve broadly elliptical; ends slightly produced, apiculate; striæ fine, linear, parallel in the middle, and slightly radiate towards the ends; central nodule large, elongate, longitudinal; sulci very distinct, slightly expanded in the middle. (Plate 31, fig. 13.)
From stomachs of Ascidians, Co. Clare.

Navicula ovulum, (Grunow). Marine.
Valve broadly elliptical; striæ fine, linear, slightly radiate in the middle, and more so towards the ends; longitudinal sulci strongly marked, and quite parallel through their entire length; central nodule small; colour of dry frustule pale yellow; length ·0024, breadth ·0011. (Plate 31, fig. 14.)
Grunow, Verhand. der K. K. Zool. Bot. Gesell., Band x., 1860, p. 519, T. iii., fig. 19.—Navicula litoralis, Donkin; N. H. Brit. Diat., p. 5, Pl. i., fig. 2.
Malahide.

(d.) *Latiusculæ*.

Valves generally elliptical; ends sometimes produced; striæ fine; intermediate free space generally broad, and expanded in the middle; a submarginal longitudinal sulcus more or less distinctly developed.

Navicula latiuscula, (Kütz.) Fresh water.
Valve broadly elliptical; striæ delicate, parallel; length about ·0048, breadth ·0014; intermediate free space much expanded. (Plate 31, fig. 15.)
Kütz. Bac., p. 93, T. v., fig. 40. This form could scarcely have

been identified, were it not that authentic specimens were seen by Wm. Smith, who considers it identical with his Navicula patula, B. D., Vol. i., p. 49, Pl. xvi., fig. 139. Ralfs, in Pritch., p. 905. Rab. Süssw. Diat., p. 38, T. vi., fig. 61. If in this case the figure be correct, it can scarcely be identified with Navicula latiuscula, Kütz. Grunow, Verhand. der K. K. Zool. Bot. Gesell., Band x., 1860, p. 534, T. iv., fig. 38. Donkin, N. H., Brit. Diat., p. 27, Pl. iv., fig. 7. Rab. Fl. Eur. Alg., sect. i., p. 182.

Lough Corrib, Co. Galway. Killurin, Co. Wexford. Newtownlimavady, Co. Derry. Breaches, Newcastle, Co. Wicklow.

Navicula barkeriana, N. S. Marine.

Valve linear, elliptical, gradually attenuated towards the produced ends; striæ linear, fine, close, distinctly radiate; intermediate free space wide, greatly expanded in the middle; median terminating towards the central nodule in elongated expansions; length ·0052, breadth ·0014.

This form might be easily confounded with Navicula latiuscula, from which it differs in the following features: the intermediate free space is much wider, the ends are produced, and the striæ are radiate, and somewhat coarser. (Plate 31, fig. 16.)

On sea-weeds, Dalkey, Co. Dublin. Breaches near Newcastle, Co. Wicklow. In both these gatherings there was a considerable admixture of fresh water forms; the marine forms, however, greatly preponderated.

Navicula grunovii, (O'Meara). Fresh or brackish water.

Valve broadly elliptical, longitudinal, marginal sulci very distinct; intermediate free space wide, lanceolate, greatly expanded in the middle; median line slightly undulate; striæ fine, slightly radiate; length ·0040, breadth ·0016. (Plate 31, fig. 17.)

Navicula elegans, Grunow, Verhand. der K. K. Zool. Bot. Gesell., Band x., 1860, p. 534, T. iv., fig. 37. This author confounds this form with Navicula elegans, Wm. Sm., of which he states he had never seen a specimen; and suggests that in case it should prove to be different from the last-named species it should be designated Navicula lacustris. Cleve, in his Diatoms of the Arctic Sea, p. 17, perceiving that the form was obviously distinct from Navicula elegans, adopts Grunow's alternative designation, which, however, must be abandoned, as the name had been applied by Gregory to designate a very different form. Grunow found this species in fresh water as well as in slightly brackish water, so that there is a difficulty in ascertaining the habitat. I cannot clear up this difficulty, inasmuch as the only gathering in which the form occurred to me contained both marine and fresh water forms.

Bellarena, Co. Derry.

Navicula amphisbæna, (Bory). Fresh water.
Valve broadly elliptical, with produced capitate ends, longitudinal sulci close to the margin; intermediate free space lanceolate, broad in the middle. Striæ fine, linear, close, radiate; length ·0035, breadth ·2013. (Pl. 31, fig. 18.)
Kütz. Bac., p. 95, T. iii., figs. 41 and 42. This author regards the species as identical with Navicula amphisbæna, Bory, 1824, to whom, therefore, it should be attributed. Wm. Sm., B. D., Vol. i., p. 51, Pl. xvii., fig. 147. Ralfs, in Pritch., p. 899, Pl. vii., fig. 72. Rab. Süssw. Diat., p. 40, T. vi., fig. 66. Grunow, Verhand. der K. K. Zool. Bot. Gesell., Band x., 1860, p. 36. Heiberg, De Danske Diat., p. 82. Cleve, Om Svenska och Norska Diat., p. 227. Donkin, N. H. Brit. Diat., p. 36, Pl. v. fig. 13.

River Dodder, Dundrum, Blackrock, Malahide, Co. Dublin. River Bann, Coleraine, Bellarena, Co. Derry. Caumlough, near Tralee. Lough Gill, Co. Kerry. Breaches, near Newcastle, Co. Wicklow. Tacumshane, Co. Wexford.

Navicula subsalina, (Ehr.) Brackish water.
In all respects resembling Navicula amphisbæna, except that the ends are not capitate, nor so much produced.
Donkin, N. H. Brit. Diat., p. 24, Pl. iv., fig. 2.—Navicula amphisbæna, var. β. Wm. Sm., B. D., Vol. i., p. 51; Pl. xvii., fig. 147 β. The last-named author attributes the species to Ehrenberg. Cleve, Diatoms from Arctic Sea, p. 18. This form occurs frequently, mixed with Navicula amphisbæna, in places accessible to marine influences, but I have never found it in perfectly fresh water. So that, with Donkin, I am disposed to consider it may be a distinct species.

Tacumshane, Co. Wexford. Breaches, Co. Wicklow. Caumlough, near Tralee. Lough Gill, Co. Kerry. Malahide, Co. Dublin.

Navicula elegans, (Wm. Sm.) Marine or brackish water.
Valve elliptical, lanceolate; longitudinal sulci marginal. Striæ distinct, linear, convergent in the middle, afterwards radiate; intermediate free space narrow, except in the middle, where it expands considerably; length about ·0038, breadth about ·00065. (Pl. 31, fig. 19.)
Wm. Sm. B. D., Vol. i., p. 49. Pl. xvi. fig. 137. Ralfs, in Pritch., p. 907. Heiberg, De Danske Diat., p. 85. Rab. Fl. Eur. Alg., sect. i., p. 182. Donkin, N. H. Brit., Diat., p. 23, Pl. iv., fig. 1. This form is obviously distinct from that described under the name of Navicula elegans by Grunow, Verhand. der K. K. Zool. Bot. Gesell., Band x., 1860, T. iv., fig. 37.

Blackrock, Co. Dublin. Caumlough, near Tralee. Lough Gill, Co. Kerry. Galway Bay. Breaches, Kilcool, Co. Wicklow. Tacumshane, Co. Wexford.

Navicula palpebralis, (De Bréb.) Marine.

Valve broadly elliptical, lanceolate at the ends; striæ distinctly costate, linear, radiate, marginal; intermediate free space wide, elliptical-lanceolate; length ·0034, breadth ·0013. (Pl. 31, fig. 20.)

Wm. Sm., B. D., Vol. i., p. 50. Supp., Pl. xxxi., fig. 273. The figure represents the striæ as minutely punctate; in reality they are strongly costate. Ralfs, in Pritch., p. 905. Grunow, Verhand. der K. K. Zool. Bot. Gesell., Band x., 160, p. 536, T. iii., fig. 27. The form here described exactly resembles that of Smith, being very small, and with minutely punctate striæ. Donkin, N. H. Brit. Diat., p. 25, fig. 3. This author regards the species as identical with *Navicula barclayana*, Greg. Rab. Fl. Eur. Alg., sect. i., p. 182, who describes the striæ as distinctly granulate.

Stomachs of Ascidians, Broadhaven Bay, Arran Islands, Co. Galway.

Navicula angulosa, (Greg.) Marine.

Similar to the preceding, but striæ finer and closer, and longer, convergent in the middle, radiate towards the ends; intermediate free space, instead of being elliptical, is lanceolate; length ·0050, breadth ·0010.

Gregory, Q. J. M. S., 1856, p. 42, Pl. v., fig. 8. Ralfs, in Pritch., p. 905. Rab. Fl. Eur. Alg., sect. i., p. 176. Donkin, N. H. Brit. Diat., p. 26, Pl. iv., fig. 4.

River Slaney, Killurin, Tacumshane, Co. Wexford. Breaches, near Newcastle, Co. Wicklow. Malahide, Co. Dublin. Arran Islands, Co. Galway.

Navicula semiplena, (Gregory). Marine.

Valve as in the preceding form, but much narrower, and the intermediate free space not angular in the middle.

Donkin, N. H. Brit. Diat., p. 26, Pl. iv., fig. 5.—*Pinnularia angulosa*, var. β, Gregory, Q. J. M. S., 1856, p. 42, Pl. v., fig. 8*— *Pinnularia semiplena*, Greville, Q. J. M. S., 1859, p. 84, Pl. vi., fig. 12.

Malahide, Co. Dublin. Fintragh Bay, Co. Donegal. Rostrevor, Co. Down.

Navicula hebes, (Ralfs). Fresh water.

Valve gibbous in the middle, ends somewhat attenuated, but still broad, and rounded. Striæ fine, linear, nearly parallel; intermediate free space wide in middle, lanceolate towards the ends. (Pl. 31, fig. 21.)

Ralfs, in Pritch., p. 896, who regards the species as identical with *Navicula obtusa*, Wm. Sm., B. D., Vol. i., p. 50, Pl. xvi., fig. 140, with which I find it impossible to identify it. Donkin, N. H. Brit., Diat., p, 23, Pl. iii., fig. 12.

Marl, Co. Down. Lough Mourne deposit.

Navicula lineata, (Donkin). Marine.
Valve linear, elliptical, with cuneate ends; margin slightly curved. Striæ strong, convergent in the middle, and radiate towards the ends; longitudinal sulcus dividing the striæ into two nearly equal parts; intermediate free space broad, lanceolate towards either end, and expanded in the middle; length about ·0034, breadth about ·0010. (Pl. 31, fig. 22).
Donkin, Q. J. M. S., 1859, p. 32, Pl. iii., fig. 17. Also N. H., Brit. Diat., p. 8, Pl. i., fig. 8.

Seashore near the town of Galway.

Navicula liber, (Wm. Sm.) Marine.
Valve narrow elliptical, with rounded ends. Striæ fine, slightly radiate, divided into two nearly equal portions by the longitudinal sulcus; intermediate free space narrow towards the ends; slightly expanded in the middle; length from ·0030 to ·0045, breadth from ·0009 to 0012. (Pl. 31, fig. 23.)
Wm. Sm., B. D., Vol. i. p. 48, Pl. xvi., fig. 133. Ralfs, in Pritch., p. 907. Grunow, Verhand. der Zool. Bot. Gesell., Band x., 1860, p. 547. Cleve, Om Svenska och Norska Diat., p. 227. Rab. Fl. Eur. Alg., sect. i., p. 180. Donkin, N. H. Brit. Diat., p. 62, Pl. ix., fig. 5.

Salt ditch, near the town of Wexford. Lough Gill, Co. Kerry. Seaweeds, Kilkee, Co. Clare. Lough Foyle, near Newtownlimavady, Co. Derry. Breaches, near Newcastle, Co. Wicklow. Galway Bay.

Navicula bicuneata, (Grunow). Marine.
Valve deeply constricted in the middle, with long cuneate ends, somewhat rounded at the apex. Striæ linear, parallel; longitudinal sulcus nearer to the median line than to the margin; intermediate free space narrow, except in the middle, where it is slightly expanded; median line strongly developed; central nodule small, roundish; length ·0056, breadth at the shoulders ·0018, at the middle ·0015. (Pl. 31, fig. 24.)
Grunow, Verhand. der K. K. Zool. Bot. Gesell., Band x., 1860, p. 546, T. iii., fig. 4. This author considers the form may be only a variety of Navicula liber, from which, however, it differs both in form and structure. The striæ in this are parallel, in Navicula liber slightly radiate. My specimens are generally wider at the shoulders, and more constricted than Grunow's figure represents them. Cleve, Om Svenska och Norska Diat., p. 227, T. i., figs. 3 and 4. The form, as represented by this last-named author, is even less constricted than Grunow's figure represents it. Cleve remarks:—
"Grunow has not described the front view, which in the specimens examined by me were cuneate, as is the case in Gomphonema

or Novilla; for which reason this species ought to be transferred to a new genus, distinguished from Navicula by the cuneate front view. The side view was sufficiently conformable with Grunow's description." The cuneate appearance of the front view just referred to, I am inclined to think, was casual, arising from the separation of the valves at one end, while at the other end they retained their normal position. In the specimen I was able to observe on the front view, there was but a single valve, which did not exhibit any tendency to a cuneate outline.

Stomachs of Ascidians, Roundstone Bay, Arran Islands, Co. Galway. Bantry Bay, Co. Cork.

Navicula gründleriana, N. S. Marine.

Valve linear elliptical; somewhat cuneate at the ends; intermediate free space narrow, except in the middle, where it expands into a broad, subquadrangular area. Striæ linear, slightly radiate; longitudinal sulcus marginal. (Pl. 31, fig. 25.)

This form strongly resembles a Navicula figured by Schmidt, Atlas, T. vi., figs. 31 and 32; and by this author attributed to Gründler. It differs however, inasmuch as the striæ in the latter are described as punctate; in the present case they are linear. The free area around the central nodule in this form is much larger than in that figured by Schmidt. The strong similarity has suggested the specific name.

The present form upon first view might be easily confounded with Navicula macula, Greg., from which it may be discerned by the fact that the ends in the latter are contracted and rounded; in this they are cuneate. The striæ, too, in this are very much coarser and more distant than in Nav. macula.

Stomachs of Ascidians, Broadhaven Bay, Co. Galway.

(e) *Limosæ*.

Longitudinal sulci more numerous than in the last, and generally more highly developed; intermediate free space narrow.

Navicula iridis, (Ehr.) Fresh water.

Valve linear, elliptical, rounded off at the ends. Striæ fine, linear, parallel; intermediate free space narrow towards the ends, expanded in the middle; length from ·0046 to ·0072, breadth from ·0010 to ·0016. Longitudinal striæ distinct at the margin. (Pl. 31, fig. 26.)

Kütz. Bac., p. 92, T. xxviii., fig. 42. Ralfs, in Pritch., p. 907. Rab. Fl. Eur. Alg., sect. i., p. 171. Donkin, N. H. Brit. Diat., p. 30, Pl. v., fig. 6.—Navicula firma, Wm. Sm., B. D., Vol. i., p. 48,

Pl. xvi., fig. 138. Smith's figure does not represent the longitudinal striæ, which more particularly characterize this species. Kützing's figure, though representing this peculiarity, does not give to it its due prominence.

Drumoughty Lough, near Kenmare, Co. Cork. Marsh, Kilcool, Glenmalure, Co. Wicklow. Lower Lake, Killarney, Co. Kerry. Ditch, Cushendun, Co. Antrim. Pond in Botanic Gardens. Belfast. Lough Mourne deposit, Co. Down.

Var. amphigomphus, (Ehr.) Fresh water.
Like the typical form in its general characters, but linear in its outline and cuneate at the ends; length from ·0025 to ·0045, breadth from ·0010 to ·0016. (Plate 31, fig. 27.)
Kütz. Bac., p. 93, T. xxviii., fig. 40. Rab. Süssw. Diat., p. 38, T. vi., fig. 47.—Navicula firma, Ralfs, in Pritch., p. 909. Donkin, N. H. Brit. Diat., p. 31, Pl. v., fig. 7.—Navicula firma, var. cuneata, Lagerstedt, Sötv. Diat. från Spetsbergen och Beeren Eiland, p. 29.

Lower Lake, Killarney, Co. Kerry. Piperstown, Co. Dublin. River Erne, near Crossdoney, Co. Cavan. Kilcool, Co. Wicklow.

Var. affinis, (Ehr.) Fresh water.
Valve like the typical species, but narrow and linear in outline; ends produced, broad, rounded, and slightly constricted. (Plate 31, fig. 28.)
Navicula affinis, Kütz. Bac., p. 95, T. xxviii., fig. 65, who attributes the species to Ehrenberg. Wm. Sm., B. D., Vol. i., p. 50, Pl. xvi., fig. 143. Ralfs, in Pritch., p. 902, Pl. xii., fig. 32. Rab. Süssw. Diat., p. 40, T. vi., fig. 58. Cleve, Om Svenska och Norska Diat., p. 228. Donkin, N. H. Brit. Diat., p. 33, Pl. v., fig. 8. Lagerstedt, Sötv. Diat. från Spetsbergen och Beeren Eiland, p. 29.

River Erne, near Crossdoney, Co. Cavan. Drumoughty Lough, near Kenmare, Glengarriff, Co. Cork. Bellarena, Co. Derry. Pond, Botanic Gardens, Belfast, Co. Down. Near Newcastle, Kilcool, Lugnaquilla mountain, Co. Wicklow. Killakee, Co. Dublin.

Navicula dubia, (Ehr.) Fresh water.
Valve like that of Navicula iridis, var. amphigomphus, but much smaller and broader in proportion; the cuneate ends extended into short apices; striæ in many specimens seen very slightly radiate; length ·0018, breadth ·0008. (Plate 31, fig. 29.)
Navicula dubia, Kütz. Bac., p. 96, T. xxviii., fig. 61, who attributes the species to Ehrenberg. Rab. Süssw. Diat., p. 40, T. vi., fig. 60. This latter figure is quite unlike the present species. Ralfs, in Pritch., p. 902. Donkin, N. H. Brit. Diat., p. 30, Pl. v., fig. 5.—Navicula peisonis, Grunow, Verband. der K. K., Zool. Bot. Gesell.,

Band x., 1860, p. 544, T. iii., fig. 28 : and likely also identical with Navicula limosa, var. biauncata, Grunow, Verhand. der K. K. Zool. Bot. Gesell., Band x., 1860, p. 545, T. v., fig. 7.

Lough Mask, near Tourmakeady, Co. Mayo. Kilcool, Co. Wicklow. Lough Gill, Co. Kerry. Pond in Botanical Gardens of Trinity College, Dublin.

Navicula limosa, (Kütz.) Fresh water.

Valve triundulate on the margin, more expanded in the middle than at the ends; ends cuneate; striæ fine, parallel; longitudinal free space narrow, except in the middle, where it is slightly expanded; longitudinal striæ easily observed, with good illumination; length about ·0034, breadth in the middle ·0006. (Plate 31, fig. 30.)

Kütz. Bac., p. 101, T. iii., fig. 50. Rab. Süssw. Diat., p. 41, T. vi., fig. 31. Ralfs, in Pritch., p. 894, Grunow, Verhand. der K. K. Zool. Bot. Gesell., Band x., 1860, p. 544, T. v., fig. 86. Donkin, N. H. Brit. Diat., p. 73, Pl. xii., fig. 61. Cleve, Om Svenska och Norska Diat., p. 227. Lagerstedt, Sötv. Diat. från Spetsbergen och Beeren Eiland, p. 30, T. i., fig. 6.

Powerscourt, Co. Wicklow. Botanical Gardens of Trinity College, Dublin.

Var. gibberula, (Kütz.) Fresh water.

Like the typical species, differing only in this, that the ends instead of being cuneate are rounded.

Grunow, Verhand. der K. K. Zool. Bot. Gesell., Band x., 1860, p. 544, T. v., fig. 8a. Donkin, N. H. Brit. Diat., p. 73, Pl. xii., fig. 6a. —Navicula gibberula, Kütz. Bac., p. 101, T. iii., fig. 50. Wm. Sm., B. D., Vol. i., p. 51, Pl. xvii., fig. 160. Schumann, Diat. der Hohen Tatra, p. 76. Lagerstedt, Sötv. Diat. från Spetsbergen och Beeren Eiland, p. 38.

River Erne, Crossdoney. Derrylane Lough, Co. Cavan. Glengarriff, Co. Cork. Lough Neagh, near Lurgan, Co. Armagh. Streamlet in Powerscourt demesne, Co. Wicklow. Lough Mourne deposit.

Var. truncata, (Kütz.) Fresh water.

Valve nearly linear, with rounded ends; the longitudinal sulci waved; length ·0025, breadth ·00055. (Plate 31, fig. 31.)

Grunow, Verhand. der K. K. Zool. Bot. Gesell., Band x., 1860, p. 545, T. v., figs. 8c and 9.—Navicula truncata, Kütz. Bac., p. 96, T. iii., fig. 34, and T. v., fig. 4. Rab. Süssw. Diat., p. 39, T. vi., fig. 67.

Friarstown, River Dodder, Co. Dublin. Lough Neagh, near Lurgan, Co. Armagh. Lough Mask, near Tourmakeady, Co. Mayo. Dundalk, Co. Louth. Wet rock, Ballyshannon, Co. Donegal. Castlegregory, Co. Kerry.

Navicula undosa, (Ehr.) Fresh water.

Valve broadly elliptical, slightly triundulate; apices produced, very narrow, and slightly capitate; longitudinal striæ distinct; transverse striæ obscure; length ·0016, breadth ·0006. (Plate 31, fig. 32.) Kütz. Bac., p. 101, T. xxviii., fig. 83. Rab. Süssw. Diat., p. 41, T. vi., fig. 56.

River Erne, near Crossdoney, Co. Cavan.

Navicula esox, (Ehr.) Habit. doubtful.

Valve lanceolate, with an angular expansion in the middle; margin slightly triundulate; ends cuneate; striæ distinct, linear, punctate, nearly parallel in the middle, slightly radiate and closer towards the ends; median line strongly developed; terminal nodules at some distance from the ends; length ·0034, breadth ·0010. (Plate 31, fig. 33.)

Kütz. Bac., p. 94, T. xxviii., fig. 53, who regards the species as identical with Pinnularia esox, Ehr. Ralfs, in Pritch., p. 896, Pl. xii., fig. 43. The description in this case is tolerably accurate, but the figure is incorrect.—Pinnularia esox, Rab Süssw. Diat., p. 45, T. vi., fig. 7. This figure does not at all represent the peculiarities of the species.

It is doubtful whether this is a fresh-water or marine form. Rabenhorst includes it among the former; the only gathering in which I found it was marine, yet containing some fresh water forms.

Mud from salt water, coast of Clare, supplied by Doctor Sullivan, President Queen's College, Cork.

Navicula trochus, (Ehr.) Fresh water.

Valve inflated in the middle, greatly contracted towards the ends, which are slightly capitate; transverse striæ indistinct; longitudinal striæ distinct; intermediate free space narrow, except in the middle, where it is expanded. (Plate 31, fig. 34.)

Kütz. Bac., p. 99, T. iii., fig. 59. Ralfs, in Pritch., p. 899.— Navicula follis, Donkin, N. H. Brit. Diat., p. 44, Pl. vi., fig. 15. There is considerable difficulty as to the synonymy of this species. Donkin considers it identical with Navicula follis, Ehr., Navicula crux, Ehr., and Navicula inflata, Kütz. Supposing the figures of the last named as delineated by Kützing (Bac., T. iii., fig. 36), and by Rabenhorst (Süssw. Diat., p. 41, T. v., fig. 10), to be correct, and that the former author was correct in supposing Navicula inflata to be identical with Navicula follis, Ehr., I cannot think that the latter is likely to be identical with Navicula trochus. Kützing has figured Navicula trochus so accurately, that it is easily recognisable; it is identical with that under consideration, and also, as it appears to me, with that named Navicula follis, by Donkin.

Lough Mourne deposit.

Navicula producta, (Wm. Sm.) Fresh water.

Valve linear, elliptical; ends produced and slightly capitate; transverse striæ distinct; linear-punctate parallel; longitudinal striæ distinct; intermediate free space very narrow; length ·0040, breadth ·0010. (Plate 31, fig. 35.)

Wm. Sm., B. D., Vol. i., p. 51, Pl. xvii., fig. 144. Ralfs, in Pritch., p. 902, Pl. vii., fig. 62. Grunow, Verhand. der K. K. Zool. Bot. Gesell., Band x., 1860, p. 543.—Navicula affinis, var. producta, Rab. Fl. Eur. Alg., sect. i., p. 197.

Botanical Gardens of Trinity College, Dublin. Lower Lake, Killarney, Co. Kerry. Sub-peat Deposit, Dromore, Co. Down.

Navicula coccononeiformis, (Gregory). Fresh water.

Valve elliptical; transverse striæ very fine, linear slightly radiate; longitudinal striæ more obvious; intermediate free space narrow, lanceolate; length ·0016, breadth ·0008. (Plate 31, fig. 36.)

None of the authors I am acquainted with have alluded to the longitudinal striæ, which notwithstanding are very obvious when the valve is observed in a dry state. When mounted in balsam, they are quite undistinguishable, except with very high powers, and with good illumination.

Gregory, Q. J. M. S., 1856, p. 6, Pl. i., fig. 22. Wm. Sm., B. D., Vol. ii., p. 92. Ralfs, in Pritch., p. 896. Grunow, Verhand. der K. K. Zool. Bot. Gesell., Band x., 1860, p. 550, T. iv., fig. 9. Rab. Fl. Eur. Alg., sect. 1, fig. 186 and p. 189. Donkin, N. H. Brit. Diat., p. 22, Pl. iii., fig. 11. Lagerstedt, Sötv. Diat. från Spetsbergen och Beeren Eiland, p. 32, T. ii., fig. 8.

Lough Mask, near Toumakeady, Co. Mayo. Lough Mourne deposit.

Navicula Kotzchyi, (Grunow). Fresh water.

Valve small, elliptical, lanceolate; ends slightly produced, and occasionally slightly constricted; central nodule large and quadrangular; striæ fine, linear, in the middle more distinct than towards the ends, radiate; longitudinal striæ distinct; length ·0013, breadth ·0005.

Grunow, Verhand. der K. K. Zool. Bot. Gesell., Band x., 1860, p. 538, T. iv., fig. 12. This author represents the striæ as moniliform, but in the few forms that came under my notice I could not verify this representation. The longitudinal striæ are not noticed by Grunow, but with careful manipulation they were very apparent in my specimens. Grunow gives three figures of this species; of these the shortest and broadest, and that in which the striæ are not so distinct is the form with which my specimens are most in accordance.—Navicula Kotschyana, Rab. Fl. Eur. Alg., sect. i., p. 193.

Lough Mask, near Tourmakealy, Co. Mayo.

Navicula maxima, (Gregory). Marine.
Frustules on front view slighly constricted in the middle, rounded at the ends; valve linear, ends rounded; transverse striæ fine, linear, parallel; longitudinal striæ two or three; intermediate free space narrow, slightly expanded in the middle; length about ·0050, breadth about ·0011. (Pl. 31, fig. 38.)
Gregory, Q. J. M. S., 1855, p. 41, Pl. iv., fig. 10. Ralfs, in Pritch., p. 909, Pl. vii., fig. 75. Donkin, N. H. Brit. Diat.—The last named author regards this species as identical with Navicula bicuneata, Grunow. There is certainly a strong resemblance between the two forms in many particulars, but nevertheless they seem to me perfectly distinct. Navicula bicuneata is much broader, ever constricted, sometimes very much so, but one longitudinal sulcus is noticeable in it, whereas in Navicula maxima the longitudinal lines are more numerous, and not so distinctly marked. Rab. Fl. Eur. Alg., sect. i., p. 172.

Portmarnock, Ireland's Eye, Co. Dublin. Breaches near Newcastle, Co. Wicklow. Seaweeds, Kilkee. Stomachs of Ascidians, Co. Clare.

Var. linearis, (Grunow). Marine.
Valve much narrower and shorter than the typical form, transverse striæ finer; longitudinal striæ obvious; intermediate free space, narrow, not expanded in the middle; length ·0032; breadth ·0005. (Pl. 31, fig. 39.)
Navicula linearis, Grunow, Verhand. der K. K. Zool. Bot. Gesell., Band x., 1860, p. 546, T. iii., fig. 2. Rab. Fl. Eur. Alg., sect. i., p. 180.

Stomachs of Ascidians, Co. Clare. Stomachs of Ascidians, Roundstone Bay. Arran Islands, Co. Galway.

Var. lata, (O'Meara). Marine.
Valves as in the typical form, but relatively shorter and wider, the ends somewhat cuneate; length ·0030; breadth ·0010.

Stomachs of Ascidians, Co. Clare.

Navicula subula, (Kütz.) Marine.
Valve lanceolate, transverse striæ very obscure, longitudinal, obvious; the dry valve pale straw-colour; intermediate free space very narrow; length about ·0024; breadth about ·0004. (Pl. 31, fig. 40.)
Kütz. Bac., p. 91, T. xxx., fig. 19. Grunow, Verhand. der K. K. Zool. Bot. Gesell., Band x., 1860, p. 548, T. iii., fig. 24. Rab. Fl. Eur. Alg., sect. i., p. 175. The specimens I have met with are much shorter than that figured by Kützing, and agree with the figure of Grunow.

Stomachs of Ascidians, Co. Clare. Stomachs of Ascidians, Roundstone Bay, Co. Galway. Malahide, Co. Dublin.

Navicula translucida, N. S. Marine.
Valve lanceolate, transverse striæ obvious, costate, radiate; longitudinal striæ, two or three obvious; length, ·0020, breadth, ·0003. (Pl. 31, fig. 41.)

Stomachs of Ascidians, Co. Clare.

Navicula papillifera, N. S. Marine.
Valve elliptical-lanceolate, ends produced, papilliform; median line incurved and expanded towards the central nodule; intermediate free space narrow; transverse striæ obsolete, longitudinal striæ obvious, numerous; length ·0020, breadth ·0006. (Pl. 31, fig. 42.)

Stomachs of Ascidians, Roundstone Bay.

Navicula liburnica, (Grun.) Marine.
Valve elliptical, lanceolate, transverse striæ fine, linear, slightly radiate; longitudinal striæ indistinct, yet with good light noticeable; intermediate free space narrow, lanceolate. (Pl. 31, fig. 43.)
Grunow, Verhand. der K. K. Zool. Bot. Gesell., Band x., 1860, p. 547, T. iii., fig. 25. Rab. Fl. Eur. Alg., sect. i., p. 172.

Stomachs of Ascidians, Co. Clare. Stomachs of Ascidians, Roundstone Bay. Stomachs of Ascidians, Broadhaven Bay, Co. Galway.

Navicula plumbicolor, N. S. Marine.
Valve linear, with rounded ends; length, ·0018; breadth, ·0007; transverse striæ very obscure, punctate, radiate, longitudinal sulcus sub-marginal; longitudinal striæ more easily observed than the transverse; intermediate free space narrow, linear; dry valve of a leaden colour. (Pl. 31, fig. 44.)

Stomachs of Ascidians, Broadhaven Bay, Co. Galway.

Navicula veneta, (Kütz.) Brackish water.
Valve minute; length, ·0010; breadth, ·0003; lanceolate, ends slightly produced; transverse striæ faint, convergent in the middle; longitudinal striæ noticeable with good illumination; longitudinal free space narrow, linear. (Pl. 31, fig. 45.)
Kütz. Bac., p. 95, T. xxx., fig. 76. Donkin (N. H. Brit. Diat., p. 43, Pl. vi., fig. 13,) rightly observes that the form "is abundant in estuaries and harbours between tide marks." Rab. Süssw. Diat., p. 39, T. vi., fig. 83. Ralfs, in Pritch., p. 901. None of the above authors refer to the longitudinal striæ, which, however, by careful illumination may be easily detected if the valves be dry.

Mouth of Bray River, Co. Wicklow. Dollymount Strand, Co. Dublin. Galway Bay, near town of Galway.

Navicula johnsonii, (Wm. Sm.) Marine.

Valve long and narrow; length, ·0060; breath, ·0005; inflated in the middle and at the ends; transverse striæ very fine, parallel, longitudinal striæ more easily detected; colour of dry valve whitish. (Pl. 31, fig. 46.)

Pinnularia johnsonii, Wm. Sm. B. D., Vol. i., p. 58, Pl. xix., fig. 179. Rab. Fl. Eur. Alg., sect. i., p. 211. Rabenhorst considers the form identical with Navicula scopulorum, De Brébisson. In this opinion he agrees with Ralfs, in Pritch., p. 895, and Donkin, N. H. Brit. Diat., p. 73, Pl. xii., fig. 5. I cannot find any figure of De Brébisson's species, Navicula scopulorum, and consider the identification of the last named with the present species more than doubtful, inasmuch as Kützing regards that form as identical with Navicula mesotyla, figured by him, Bac., T. v., fig. 3, and T. xxviii., fig. 84. These figures are obscure as to details, but from the size and outline I would think it impossible to confound Navicula johnsonii with them, and therefore I attribute the species to Smith, who has described and figured it with unmistakable accuracy. This course commends itself the more to my judgment, inasmuch as Grunow has described and figured under the name of Navicula scopulorum a form which is obviously distinct from that under consideration.

Bannow, Co. Wexford. Malahide, Portmarnock, Co. Dublin. Mouth of the River Nannywater, Laytown, Co. Meath.

Navicula simulans, (Donkin). Marine.

Valve linear, with long cuneate ends; transverse striæ very faint; longitudinal striæ quite noticeable with good illumination, if the valve be dry; longitudinal free space narrow, except in the middle, where it spreads out to the margin in a narrow stauroform band; length ·0030, breadth ·0006. (Plate 31, fig. 47.)

The present species I consider to be identical with that so named by Donkin, N. H. Brit. Diat., p. 60, Pl. ix, fig. 3. Donkin considers it the same as Amphiprora constricta, Ehr., but in this opinion I cannot concur. Donkin does not notice the longitudinal striæ; but in all other respects the present form is, in my mind, not distinguishable from the species named Navicula simulans by that author.

Stomachs of Ascidians, Broadhaven Bay, Co. Galway. Malahide, Co. Dublin.

Navicula delginensis, N. S. Marine.

Valve rhomboid, gradually attenuated towards the broadly rounded ends; transverse striæ very faint; longitudinal striæ easily detected, more especially at the margin, where there is a strongly marked sulcus; intermediate free space narrow, lanceolate towards the ends, and slightly expanded in the middle; length ·0020; breadth in the middle ·0006. (Pl. 31, fig. 48.)

This form is in outline very similar to a species described and figured by Grunow as Navicula scopulorum, in Verhand. der K. K. Zool. Bot. Gesell., Band x., 1860, p. 547, T. iii. fig. 6. The present species, however, is shorter, broader, and more rhombic; the transverse striæ more obscure, and not reaching the median line, but leaving a distinct intermediate free space.

Seaweeds, Dalkey Island, Malahide, Co. Dublin.

(f) *Crassinerves.*

"*Forms for the most part lanceolate, with very strong median lines and very fine scarcely noticeable structure, in which the longitudinal striæ come out more distinctly than the transverse. These approach the group Limosæ, from which, however, they differ essentially by the colorless condition of the valves in a dry state. In the appearance of the median line there is an approximation to some forms of the group Cuspidatæ not to be mistaken.*"—Grunow.

Navicula rhomboides, (Ehr.) Fresh water.

Valve rhomboid; lanceolate; ends slightly rounded; median line distinct, with two longitudinal lines close to and nearly parallel with it; slightly expanded in the middle, united towards the ends; the median line extending slightly beyond the point of junction; striæ very faint; length about ·0045; breadth about ·0009. (Plate 31, fig. 49.)

With a high objective and very skilful illumination the striæ are found to be parallel. It is noteworthy that in a gathering made by me at Lough Awn, on the summit of the Slieveanciran Mountain, this form occurred in abundance, for the most part free, but frequently in mucous tubes, ever in single files, and in some cases the frustules were placed end to end, without any mucous investment.

Kütz. Bac., p. 94, T. xxviii., fig. 45; and T. xxx., fig. 44. This author attributes the species to Ehrenberg. Wm. Sm., B. D., vol. i., p. 46, Pl. xvi., fig. 129. Rab. Süssw. Diat., p. 38; T. v., fig. 13. This figure represents the form as much smaller than it is generally found to be. Ralfs, in Pritch., p. 903; Grunow, Verhand. der K. K. Zool. Bot. Gesell, Band x., 1860, p. 549. Donkin, N. H. Brit. Diat., p. 42, Pl. vi., fig. 11. Schumann, Die Diat. der Hohen Tatra., p. 68.

Pool, Glencar, near Glengariff, Bantry, Co. Cork. Lower Lake, Killarney, Arraglen, near Castlegregory, Co. Kerry. Friarstown, Piperstown, Co. Dublin. River Bann, near Coleraine, Co. Derry. Connemara, Co. Galway. Rathdrum, Glenchree, Co. Wicklow. Deposit, Tollymore Park, Co. Down.

Navicula serians, (De Bréb.) Fresh water.

Valve elliptical-lanceolate; ends slightly rounded; median line distinct, as are also the two longitudinal lines, close to and parallel to the same; transverse striæ obscure, slightly oblique; longitudinal striæ distinct; length about ·0038; breadth about ·0009. (Plate 31, fig. 50.) Kütz. Bac., p. 92; T. xxx., fig. 23; T. xxviii., fig. 43. This author considers the species identical with Frustulia serians, De Brébisson, and with Navicula lineolata, Ehr. He adds, "I have no doubt that the Ehrenbergian form, which has been described in our T. xxviii., fig. 43, according to Ehrenberg, is perfectly identical with that of De Brébisson." That form is rather smaller than Navicula serians, and therefore some doubt may reasonably be entertained on the subject. It seems better then, with Donkin, to attribute the species to De Brébisson than to abandon the specific name by which the species has been so long known. Wm. Sm., B. D., vol. i., p. 47, Pl. 16, fig. 130. Rab. Süssw. Diat., p. 38; T. vi., fig. 51; Ralfs, in Pritch., p. 904. Grunow, Verhand. der K. K. Zool. Bot. Gesell, Band x., 1860, p. 549; T. v., fig. 13. Cleve, Om Svenska och Norska Diat., p. 228. Donkin, N. H. Brit. Diat., p. 41, Pl. vi., fig. 10.

Pool, Cushendun, Co. Antrim. Piperstown, Co. Dublin. Glenchree, Co. Wicklow. Pool near town of Wicklow. Tollymore Park deposit, Co. Down.

Navicula crassinervia, (De Bréb.) Fresh water.

Valve small, elliptical-lanceolate; ends produced and slightly constricted; longitudinal sulci parallel to the median line, distinct; striæ obsolete; length about ·0024; breadth about ·0005. (Plate 31, fig. 51.) Wm. Sm., B. D., Vol. i., p. 47, Supp. Pl. xxxi., fig. 271, who describes and figures the species according to specimens furnished by De Brébisson. Ralfs, in Pritch., p. 900. Grunow, Verhand. der K. K. Zool. Bot. Gesell., Band x., 1860, p. 548, T. v., fig. 12. Cleve, Om Svenska och Norska Diat., p. 228. Donkin, N. H. Brit. Diat., p. 42, Pl. vi., fig. 12. This last named author considers this species identical with Frustulia saxonica, Rab. Fl. Eur. Alg., sect. i., p. 227.

Friarstown, Piperstown, Featherbed Mountain, Co. Dublin. Lough Gill, Co. Kerry. Bantry, Co. Cork. Rostrevor, Co. Down. Rathdrum, Glencree, Co. Wicklow.

Navicula dirhynchus, (Ehr.) Fresh water.

Valve nearly linear, narrow; ends produced, and slightly capitate. Longitudinal sulci parallel with median line, distinct. Transverse striæ obsolete; longitudinal striæ distinct; length, ·0022, breadth, ·0005. (Plate 31, fig. 52.)

Kützing, Bac., p. 95, T. xxviii., fig. 48, by whom the species is attributed to Ehrenberg. Rab. Süssw. Diat., p. 40, T. vi., fig. 48. Ralfs, in Pritch., p. 901. Donkin, N. H. Brit. Diat., p. 29, Pl. v., fig. 3. The last named author remarks that "in outline this species has a strong resemblance to Navicula affinis, but it is much smaller, and distinguished by the apparent absence of striæ." If the valve be examined in a dry state, the longitudinal striæ are distinct, but much less numerous and distinct than in Navicula affinis; the margin also, instead of being perfectly linear as it is in the last named species, is slightly elliptical.

Lough Mask, near Tourmakeady, Co. Mayo. Featherbed Mountain, Co. Dublin.

Navicula rostellum, (Wm. Sm.) Fresh water.
Valves broadly elliptical; ends produced into very short narrow apices; longitudinal sulci parallel to median line distinct; striæ obscure; length ·0020; breadth ·0010. (Plate 31, fig. 53.) Wm. Sm., B. D., Vol. ii., p. 93. Ralfs, in Pritch., p. 900. Grunow, Verhand. der K. K. Zool. Bot. Gesell., Band x., 1860, p. 550, T. iv., fig. 10. This form, as described by Grunow, is narrower, and the apices much wider than in my specimens; the transverse striæ as described, are very fine and parallel, but as my specimens were mounted in balsam, I could not detect the striæ. Donkin, N. H. Brit. Diat., p. 40, Pl. vi., fig. 7. Rab. Fl. Eur. Alg., sect. i., p. 195. The last named author describes the striæ as very delicate and parallel.—Navicula apiculata, Gregory Q. J. M. S., Vol. iv., 1856, Pl. i., fig. 13, who attributes the form to Wm. Smith.

Killakee, Co. Dublin.

Navicula lævissima, (Kütz.) Fresh water.
Valve colourless, slightly expanded in middle, slightly constricted towards the broad rounded ends; median line strongly developed; transverse striæ very fine, slightly radiate; longitudinal striæ distinct; intermediate free space narrow, except in the middle, where sometimes it seems to expand in a short narrow stauroform band; at the extreme end a distinct transverse line is noticeable at right angles with the median line; length ·0015, breadth ·0004. (Plate 31, fig. 54.)
Kütz. Bac. p. 96, T. xxi., fig. 14. Wm. Sm., B. D., Vol. ii., p. 91. Grunow, Verhand. der K. K., Zool. Bot. Gesell., Band x., 1860, p. 549, T. iv., fig. 5. Rab. Fl. Eur. Alg., sect. i., p. 188. Donkin, N. H. Brit. Diat., p. 28, Pl. v., fig. 2.

Lower Lake, Killarney, Co. Kerry. Derrylane Lough, Co. Cavan. Lough Neagh, near Antrim town. Ulster Canal, near Poyntzpass, Co. Armagh. Loughbrickland Lake, Co. Down. River Bann, near Coleraine, Co. Derry. Trinity College Botanic Gardens, Co. Dublin. Killeshin, Queen's Co. Feighcullen, Co. Kildare.

Navicula oblongella, (Naegeli?) Fresh water.
Valve small, linear, elliptical; ends rounded; longitudinal sulci close to median line, strongly developed, parallel; transverse striæ

fine, but easily detected, parallel; longitudinal striæ generally obscure; intermediate free space narrow, except in the middle, where it expands into a quadrangular area; length about ·0008, breadth about ·0008. (Plate 31, fig. 55.)

Grunow, Verhand. der K. K. Zool. Bot. Gesell., Band x., 1860, T. iv., fig. 4. Grunow, with a note of doubtfulness, refers the species to Naegeli. Schumann, Die Diat. der Hohen Tatra, p. 70. Rab. Fl. Eur. Alg., sect. 1, p. 185.

Lough Derg, Co. Galway. Killakee, Co. Dublin. Ditch near town of Galway.

Navicula incurva, (Greg.) Fresh water.

Valve slightly incurved in the middle; ends broadly produced, subcapitate; longitudinal sulci parallel, with median line distinct; striæ obscure; length about ·0020, breadth ·0005. (Plate 31, fig. 56.)

Gregory, Q. J. M. S. 1856, p. 8, Pl. i., fig. 26. Ralfs, in Pritch., p. 893. Rab. Fl. Eur. Alg., sect. i., p. 203. Donkin, N. H. Brit. Diat., p. 38, Pl. vi., fig. 2.

Portmarnock, Co. Dublin. Callows, near Ballinasloe, Co. Galway.

(g) *Moniliferæ*.

Valves more or less lanceolate; striæ obviously moniliform, not reaching the median line; free intermediate space narrow except in the middle, where it is generally more or less expanded.

Navicula punctulata, (Wm. Smith.) Brackish or marine.

Valve broadly elliptical, with slightly apiculate ends; intermediate free space narrow, slightly expanded in the middle; striæ close, radiate; length about ·0026, breadth ·0012. (Plate 32, fig. 1.)

Wm. Sm., B.D., vol. i., p. 52, Pl. xvi., fig. 151. Grunow, Verhand. der K. K. Zool. Bot. Gesell., Band x., 1860, p. 537.—*Navicula marina*, Ralfs, in Pritch., p. 903. Rab. Fl. Eur. Alg., sect. i., p. 202. Donkin, N. H. Brit. Diat., p. 19, Pl. iii., fig. 5. The last named author remarks, "Although this species is described as marine in the Synopsis of Prof. Smith, I have never found it in purely marine localities, where its congener N. granulata is found." Some of the undernamed localities in which I have found the species are decidedly marine.

Stomachs of Ascidians, Belfast Lough, Co. Antrim. Seaweeds, Bannow, Co. Wexford. Portmarnock, Co. Dublin. Rostrevor, Co. Down. Seaweeds, Kilkee, Co. Clare. Laytown, Co. Meath. Drehednamaud, near Castlegregory, Co. Kerry.

Navicula granulata, (De Brébisson). Marine.

Valve broadly elliptical, with slightly produced broad rounded ends; intermediate free space narrow, linear, except at the centre, where it expands considerably; expanded area somewhat rounded; striae moniliform, convergent in the middle, then strongly radiate; length ·0035; breadth ·0017. (Plate 32, fig. 2.)

Donkin, Q. J. M. S., 1858, p. 17, Pl. iii., fig. 19, who attributes the species to De Brébisson. Ralfs, in Pritch., p. 903. Cleve, Om Svenska och Norska Diat., p. 226. Rab. Fl. Eur. Alg., sect. i., p. 201. Donkin, N. H. Brit. Diat., p. 17, Pl. iii., fig. 1.

Drehednamaud, near Castlegregory, Co. Kerry. Stomachs of Ascidians, Roundstone Bay, Stomachs of Ascidians, Broadhaven Bay, Galway Bay, Co. Galway.

Navicula humerosa, (De Brébisson.) Marine.

Valve linear, elliptical, gradually contracted towards the broad, produced, rounded ends; slightly constricted in the middle; striae close, moniliform; puncta small, convergent in the middle, radiate towards the ends; intermediate free space narrow, except in the middle, where it is broadly and somewhat roundly expanded; length, about ·0032, breadth, about ·0013, and in middle about ·9012. (Plate 32, fig. 3.)

Wm. Smith, (B. D., Vol. ii., p. 93), who attributes the species to De Brébisson. Ralfs, in Pritch., p. 903. Rab. Fl. Eur. Alg., sect. i., p. 201.

Bannow, River Slaney, near Killurin. Co. Wexford. Portmarnock, Malahide, Co. Dublin. Seaweeds, Portrush, Co. Antrim. Caum Lough, near Tralee, Lough Gill, Co. Kerry. Kilkee, Co. Clare. Salt marsh, Kilcool, Co. Wicklow.

Var. fuscata, (Schumann). Marine.

Like the typical form, but having the ends slightly capitate, and the margins perfectly linear; length ·0038, breadth ·0014. (Plate 32, fig. 4.)

Likely the same as Navicula fuscata, Schumann, Die Preussische Diat., p. 57, T. ii., fig. 43.

Drehidnamaud, near Castlegregory: Lough Gill, Co. Kerry. Stomachs of Ascidians, Roundstone Bay, Co. Galway.

Var. quadrata, (Gregory). Marine.

Like the typical form, but much shorter and relatively broader; the margins linear; the ends, too, being broader and less produced; length ·0020, breadth ·0012. (Plate 32, fig. 5.)

Navicula quadrata, Gregory, Q. J. M. S., 1856, p. 41, Pl. v., fig. 5. Donkin (N. H. Brit. Diat., p. 18) considers this identical with Navicula humerosa, and Ralfs adopts the same opinion in Pritchard, p. 903.

Lough Gill, Co. Kerry. Stomachs of Ascidians, Broadhaven Bay, Co. Galway. Seaweeds, Portrush, Co. Antrim.

Navicula latissima, (Gregory). Marine.

Valve large, broadly elliptical; ends slightly produced, rounded; intermediate free space broad, lanceolate, greatly expanded around the central nodule; striæ linear, with moniliform striæ interposed, convergent in the middle, radiate towards the ends; length ·0060, breadth ·0032. (Plate 32, fig. 6.)

Gregory, Q. J. M. S., 1856, p. 40, Pl. v., fig. 4. Ralfs, in Pritch., p: 903, Pl. vii., fig. 70. Rab. Fl. Eur. Alg., sect. i., p. 201. Donkin, N. H. Brit. Diat., p. 17, Pl. iii., fig. 2.—*Pinnularia divaricata*, O'Meara, Q. J. M. S., 1867, p. 116, Pl. v., fig. 7.

Arran Islands, Stomachs of Ascidians, Roundstone Bay, Co. Galway.

Navicula meniscus, (Schumann). Fresh water.

Valve broadly elliptical; ends slightly produced, not capitate; intermediate free space narrow, except in the middle, where it expands into a large stauroform band, wider towards the margin than at the central nodule; striæ linear, with moniliform striæ interposed, convergent in the middle, radiate towards the ends; length ·0026, breadth ·0013. (Plate 32, fig. 7.)

Schumann, Die Preussische Diat., p. 55, T. ii., fig. 32. Schumann's account of the locality in which the form was found by him leaves some doubt as to whether the deposit in which the form was discovered was marine or fresh water; his words are: "In deposito Regimontano, in portu Pillawensi, in Mari Baltico. Lagerstedt, however, includes the form among fresh-water species, under the name of *Navicula punctata*, var. asymmetrica, Sötvat. Diat. från Spetsbergen, p. 29, T. ii., fig. 7." This figure so precisely corresponds in all respects with the form here described, as to render the identity perfectly certain. Lagerstedt states that the frustule on front view is slightly unsymmetrical on the longitudinal axis. This seems to me to have been accidental, arising perhaps from the valves having been separated at one end while adhering at the other; he adds, "only a single specimen of this variety was found." And I have precisely the same report to make. So distinct is this form in its leading characters that I consider it a perfectly independent species, and not to be regarded as a variety of Navicula punctata.

Pond near the city of Armagh.

Navicula lucida, N. S. Marine.

Valve broadly elliptical, with sub-lanceolate ends; intermediate free space lanceolate, narrow, except in the middle, where it expands considerably; a strongly marked submarginal sulcus is present; striæ moniliform; puncta very close; convergent in the middle; divergently radiate towards the apices; length ·0020; breadth ·0012. (Plate 32, fig. 8.)

Stomachs of Ascidians, Roundstone Bay, Co. Galway.

Navicula cluthensis, (Gregory). Marine.
Valve broadly elliptical, with rounded ends; intermediate free space narrow, linear, but slightly expanded at the central nodule; striæ moniliform; puncta small, close, nearly parallel in the middle, and divergently radiate towards the ends; length, ·0020; breadth, ·0013. (Plate 32, fig. 9.)

Gregory, Diat. of Clyde, p. 478, Pl. ix., fig. 2. Ralfs, in Pritch., p. 909, Pl. vii., fig. 73. Rab. Fl. Eur. Alg., p. 184.—Navicula erythræa, Grunow, Verhand. der K. K. Zool. Bot. Gesell., Band x., 1860, p. 539, T. v., fig. 17.

River Slaney, near Killurin, Co. Wexford. Stomachs of Ascidians, Roundstone Bay, Co. Galway.

Var. producta, (O'Meara). Marine.
Precisely as the typical species, but having the ends slightly produced; length ·0025, breadth ·0011. (Plate 32, fig. 9a.)

Stomachs of Ascidians, Broadhaven Bay, Co. Galway.

Navicula punctata, (Kütz.) Fresh water.
Valve elliptical, ends produced, narrow, capitate; intermediate free space narrow, except in middle, where it expands into a tolerably broad stauroform band, widening towards the outer end; striæ moniliform; puncta small; radiate; length ·0032, breadth ·0010. (Plate 32, fig. 10.)

Donkin, N. H. Brit. Diat., p. 36, Pl. v., fig. 12. Lagerstedt, Sötvat. Diat. från Spetsberger och Beeren Eiland, p. 29.—Stauroneis punctata, Kütz., Bac., p. 100, T. xxi., fig. 9. Wm. Sm., B. D., Vol. i., p. 61, Pl. xix., fig. 189. Ralfs, in Pritch., p. 912. Grunow, Verhand. der K. K. Zool. Bot. Gesell., Band x., 1860, p. 565. Castracane, Catalogo di Diat. raccolte nella Val Intrasca, p. 11. Cleve, Om Svenska och Norska Diat., p. 228. Rab. Fl. Eur., Alg., sect. i., p. 245.—Stauroptera punctata, Rab. Süssw. Diat., p. 50, T. ix., fig. 11.

River Slaney, near Killurin, Co. Wexford. Drumoughty Lough, near Kenmare, Lower Lake, Killarney, Lough Gill, Co. Kerry. Lough Mask, near Tourmakeady, Co. Mayo. Lough Mourne deposit, Co. Antrim.

Navicula lacustris, (Gregory). Fresh water.
Similar to Navicula punctata, but the striæ are very much finer; and the intermediate free space expanded roundly, instead of in a stauroform band; length about ·0020, breadth ·0006. (Plate 32, fig. 11.)

Gregory, (Q. J. M. S., 1856, p. 6, Pl. i., fig. 23.) describes two distinct varieties, one elliptical, the other with linear margin and produced ends. He also refers to an intermediate form, which latter, I presume, to be the present one. Ralfs, (in Pritch., p. 903), says the only species with which this could be confounded is Navicula firma, but it appears to me that it is more likely to be confounded with Navicula punctata. Rab. Fl. Eur. Alg., sect. i., p. 200.

Lough Mask, near Tourmakeady, Co. Mayo. Lough Neagh, near the town of Antrim. Lough Gill, Lower Lake, Killarney, Pedlass Lake, near Dingle, Co. Kerry.

Navicula maculosa, (Donkin). Marine.

Valve linear, elliptical; ends slightly produced and somewhat cuneate; intermediate free space linear, narrow, slightly expanded around the central nodule; striæ distinctly moniliform, parallel in the middle, and divergently radiate towards the ends; length ·0027, breadth ·0008. (Plate 32, fig. 12.)
Donkin, N. H. Brit. Diat., p. 25, Pl. v., fig. 1.

Piles of wooden bridge, Dollymount Strand, Co. Dublin.

Navicula scutelloides, (Wm. Sm.) Fresh water.

Valve nearly orbicular, minute; intermediate free space narrow, linear, slightly expanded in the middle; striæ distant, moniliform, divergently radiate; length, ·0009; breadth, ·0008. (Plate 32, fig. 13.)
Wm. Sm., B. D., Vol. ii., p. 91. Grunow, (Verhand. der K. K. Zool. Bot. Gesell., Band x., 1860, p. 533, T. v., fig. 15), places it in intimate connexion with Navicula lyra and Navicula hennedyi, but the position I assign to it seems to me more appropriate. Rafls, in Pritch., p. 909. Rab. Fl. Eur. Alg., sect. i., p. 185.

Lough Neagh, near Antrim. Lough Mask, near Tourmakeady, Co Mayo.

Navicula pusilla, (Wm. Sm.) Brackish water.

Valve small, broadly elliptical, ends produced; narrow, rounded; intermediate free space narrow, linear, expanded in the middle; striæ distinctly moniliform; convergent in the middle, and radiate towards the ends; more distant in the middle, closer towards the ends; length ·0015; breadth, ·0008. (Plate 32, fig. 14.)
Wm. Sm., B. D., Vol. i., p. 52, Pl. xvii., fig. 145. Ralfs, in Pritch., p. 900. Cleve, Om Svenska och Norska Diat., p. 227. It is likely that the form mentioned by Cleve may be a distinct species, as he attributes it to fresh water. Rab. Fl. Eur. sect. i., p. 193. Donkin, N. H. Brit. Diat., p. 20, Pl. iii., fig. 6.—Navicula tumida, var. subsalsa, Grunow, Verhand. der K. K. Zool. Bot. Gesell., Band x., 1860, p. 537, T. iv., fig. 43.

Brackish ditch near town of Wexford; Tacumshane, Co. Wexford. Ballysodare, Co. Sligo. Breaches near Newcastle, Co. Wicklow.

Lough Gill, Co. Kerry, River Bann, near Coleraine; Bellarena, Co. Derry. Brackish ditches near town of Galway. Portmarnock, Co. Dublin.

Var. lanceolata, (Grunow). Marine or brackish water.
Valve lanceolate, ends produced; relatively longer and narrower than the typical species. Length ·0024, breadth ·0008.
Navicula tumida, var. lanceolata, Grunow, Verhand. der K. K. Zool. Bot. Gesell., Band x., 1860, p. 537, T. iv. fig. 44. This as well as the preceding species, being both incidental to marine or brackish water, can scarcely be regarded as varieties of Navicula tumida, which is a fresh water species.

Portmarnock, Co. Dublin. Breaches near Newcastle, Co. Wicklow.

Navicula tumida, (Wm. Sm.) Fresh water.
Valve small, elliptical, with short capitate ends; intermediate free space narrow, slightly expanded in the middle; striæ close, moniliform; convergent in the middle, and radiate towards the ends; length varying from ·0013 to ·0020 ; breadth from ·0005 to ·0008. Wm. Sm., B. D., Vol. i., p. 53, Pl. xvii., fig. 146. Grunow, Verhand. der K. K. Zool. Bot. Gesell., Band x., 1860, p. 537, T. iv., fig. 43*a*. Cleve, Om Svenska och Norska Diat., p. 226.—Navicula Anglica, Ralfs, in Pritch., p. 900. Rab. Fl. Eur. Alg., sect. i., p. 193. Donkin, N. H. Brit. Diat., p. 35, Pl. v., fig. 11*a*.

Kilcool; streamlet in Powerscourt demesne, Co. Wicklow. Lough Mask, Tourmakeady, Co. Mayo. Ditch near town of Sligo.

Var. linearis, (O'Meara). Fresh water.
Similar to the typical form, but sides linear, ends slightly produced; striæ coarser, obviously moniliform, radiate; length ·0011, breadth ·0005. (Plate 32, fig. 15.)

Lough Gill, Co. Kerry. Lough Mask, Tourmakeady, Co. Mayo.

Navicula pulchra, (Gregory). Marine.
Valve lanceolate; intermediate free space narrow, expanded in the middle; striæ distinctly moniliform, radiate; length ·0027, breadth ·0008. (Plate 32, fig. 16.)
Gregory, Q. J. M. S., 1856, Trans., p. 42, Pl. v., fig. 7. Ralfs, in Pritch., p. 906. Rab. Fl. Eur. Alg., sect. i., p. 176.

Galway Bay near the town of Galway.

(h) *Fuscatæ.*

Valves more or less elliptical; striæ divided into two portions on each side of the median line, by two longitudinal sulci, forming a tolerably broad rhomboidal space about the median line.

Navicula fusca, (Gregory). Marine.
Valve oblong elliptical; striæ obviously moniliform, radiate; intermediate space lanceolate, divided into three compartments, one unstriate, and having the median line in the centre, and one on either side striate; central nodule large; length about ·0047, breadth about ·0022. (Plate 32, fig. 17.)
Ralfs, in Pritch., p. 898; Rab. Fl. Eur. Alg., sect. i., p. 179. Donkin, N. H. Brit. Diat., p. 7, Pl. i., fig. 5.—Navicula Smithii var. fusca, Gregory, Diat. of Clyde, p. 486, Pl. ix., fig. 15. Schmidt's Atlas der Diat., T. vii., fig. 1.

Arran Islands; stomachs of Ascidians, Roundstone Bay; stomachs of Ascidians, Broadhaven, Co. Galway. Rostrevor, Co. Down.

Navicula smithii, (De Breb.) Marine.
Valve broadly elliptical; striæ moniliform, slightly radiate; intermediate space narrow, lanceolate, consisting of three distinct portions, one unstriate about the median line, and one on either side of the latter striate; length about ·0027, breadth about ·0012. (Plate 32, fig. 18.)
Wm. Sm., B. D., Vol. ii., p. 92. Smith assents to the suggestion of De Brébisson, to change to Navicula smithii the form he had previously named Navicula elliptica, B. D., Vol. i., p. 48, Pl. xvii., fig. 152. For this reason Grunow, Heiberg, and Donkin rightly attribute the species to De Brébisson. Grunow, Verhand. der K. K. Zool. Bot. Gesell., Band x., 1860, p. 531. Heiberg, De Danske Diat., p. 81. Ralfs, in Pritch., p. 898. Rab. Fl. Eur. Alg., sect. i., p. 178. Donkin, N. H. Brit. Diat., p. 6, Pl. i., fig. 4. Schmidt's Atlas der Diat., T. vii., fig. 16.

Arran Islands; Stomachs of Ascidians, Roundstone Bay; Stomachs of Ascidians, Broadhaven Bay, Co. Galway. Rostrevor, Dundrum Bay, Co. Down. Bannow, Co. Wexford. Seaweeds, Kilcool, Co. Wicklow.

Var. subrotunda, (O'Meara). Marine.
Like the typical species, but nearly orbicular.
Schmidt's Atlas der Diat., T. vii., fig. 17, fig. 22 ?

Stomachs of Ascidians, Roundstone Bay; Arran Islands, Co. Galway.

Var. rhombica, (O'Meara). Marine.

Valve like that of the typical form in general structure, but differing in its distinctly rhombic outline, as well as in the rhombic form of the inner band of striæ.

A form which seems to me to be identical with this is described by Schmidt, Atlas der Diat., T. vii., fig. 18.

Arran Islands, Co. Galway.

Navicula collisiana, N. S. Marine.

Valve broadly elliptical. Nearly linear at the margin, with broadly rounded ends. Intermediate space wide, oblong, elliptical. Striæ costate. Marginal striate band wide, striæ distinctly moniliform, nearly parallel in the middle; more and more radiate towards the ends; length ·0026, breadth ·0016. (Plate 32, fig. 19.)

This form is distinguished from Navicula fusca, and Navicula smithii, which in other respects it strongly resembles, by the broad oblong elliptical outline of the inner striate band, and more specially by the fact that the striæ in this portion of the valve are distinctly costate, while in the others they are moniliform. It was first exhibited by me at a meeting of the Dublin Microscopical Club, some years since, at the house of the late Surgeon Maurice Collis.

Stomachs of Ascidians, Roundstone Bay, Arran Islands, Co. Galway. Kilcool, Co. Wicklow.

Navicula æstiva, (Donkin). Marine.

Valve linear, elliptical; striæ fine, obscurely moniliform, parallel in the middle, slightly radiate towards the ends; inner striate band narrow, elliptical; length about ·0022; breadth about ·0010. The distinctive character of this species is the fineness of the striæ. (Plate 32, fig. 20.)

Donkin, Q. J. M. S. Trans., 1858, p. 32, Pl. iii., fig. 18; and N. H. Brit. Diat., p. 6, Pl. i., fig. 3. Donkin's figures represent the species as much larger than my specimens would lead me to regard it. Ralfs, in Pritch., p. 899. Rab. Fl. Eur. Alg., sect. i., p. 184.

Arran Islands, Stomachs of Ascidians, Broadhaven Bay, Co. Galway.

Navicula elliptica, (Kütz.) Fresh water.

Valve elliptical; striæ of the marginal band distinctly moniliform, converging in the middle, radiate towards the ends; inner striate band very narrow; free space about the median line greatly expanded, forming a rounded rhombic outline; median line strongly developed; length about ·0020, breadth about ·0011. (Plate 32, fig. 21.)

Kütz. Bac., p. 98, T. xxx., fig. 55. Wm Sm., B. D., Vol. ii., p. 92. Ralfs, in Pritch., p. 899. Rab. Fl. Eur. Alg., sect. i., p. 179.

Donkin, N. H. Brit. Diat., p. 7, Pl. i. fig. 6. Grunow, Verhand. der K. K. Zool. Bot. Gesell., Band x., 1860, p. 531. Heiberg, De Danske Diat., p. 81. Cleve, Om Svenska och Norska Diat, p. 226. Schumann, Die Diat. der Hohen Tatra., p. 69. Lagerstedt, Sötvat. Diat. från Spetsbergen och Beeren Eiland, p. 27. Schmidt, Atlas der Diat., T. vii. figs. 31, 32.—Navicula ovalis, Wm. Sm., B. D., Vol. i., p. 48, Pl. xvii., fig. 153a.

Tacumshane, Co. Wexford. Lower Lake, Killarney, Co. Kerry. Glenchree, Powerscourt, Co. Wicklow. Lucan, Killakee, Boherna-brena, Co. Dublin. Feighcullen, Royal Canal, near Enfield, Co. Kildare. Pond, near the city of Armagh.

Var. costata, (O'Meara). Fresh, or brackish water.

Valve strongly resembling the typical species, but striæ distinctly costate, and intermediate free space included between the inner margins of the inner striate band lanceolate, but slightly expanded in the middle.

This variety has been found in localities where marine and fresh water forms are mixed.

Breaches near Newcastle, Co. Wicklow. Lough Gill, Co. Kerry.

Var. davidsonii, (O'Meara). Fresh water.

Valve ovate-elliptical. Striæ very fine, moniliform ; space included within the inner margin of the inner striate band linear, roundly expanded in the middle.

This variety was first brought under my notice by my valued correspondent, Rev. George Davidson, of Logie, Coldstone, near Aberdeen, who found it in his neighbourhood. It has since been noticed by me in various localities in Ireland. On first view this form would seem to belong to Navicula æstiva, and when first noticed by me in a fresh water gathering, I considered it was a stray form of the species mentioned, which had come there by accident ; but subsequent observation induced me to give up this view, and to consider the form a well marked variety. It is likely the same as that figured by Schmidt in his Atlas der Diat., T. vii., fig. 33.

Moist Rock, Portrush, Co. Antrim, Lough Mask, near Tourmakeady, Lough Neagh, near Lurgan, Co. Armagh.

Var. ovalis, (Wm. Smith). Fresh water.

Valve linear, oblong, with rounded ends ; striæ much finer than in the case of the typical form; length about ·0016, breadth about ·0005. (Plate 32, fig. 22.)

Navicula ovalis, Wm. Sm., B. D., Vol. i., p. 48, Pl. xvii., fig. 153 a. Under the impression that this form and Navicula elliptica were identical, Smith abandoned the specific name of ovalis, and merged the two forms under the one designation Navicula elliptica. However close the resemblance must be acknowledged to be, there is such a difference in the details of structure as to require notice. Ralfs, in Pritch., p. 899, regards the form as identical with Navicula elliptica, and the same view is adopted by the following authors: Cleve, Om Svenska och Norska Diat., p. 226. Rabenhorst, Fl. Eur. Alg., sect. i., p. 179. Donkin, N. H. Brit. Diat. Lagerstedt, Sötvat. Diat. fran Spetsbergen och Beeren Eiland, p. 27, and probably Grunow, Verhand. der K. K. Zool. Bot. Gesell., Band x., 1860, p. 531. Castracane includes the two forms under the designation of Navicula ovalis; Catalogo di Diat. raccolte nella Val. Intrasca, p. 12. Schmidt, treating the two forms as distinct species, describes the present as Navicula ovalis; Atlas der Diat. T. vii., figs. 34 and 35.

Camolin, Co. Wexford. Lough Neagh, near Lurgan, Co. Armagh. Lough Gill, Co. Kerry. Lough Mourne deposit.

Var. parva, (O'Meara). Fresh water.
Valve like the last variety, but very much smaller, and the striation extremely indistinct; length ·0008, breadth ·0004.

It seems not improbable that this variety is identical with that described as Navicula oblongella by Schmidt, Atlas der Diat., T. vii., fig. 53.

Camolin, Co. Wexford.

(i) *Clavatæ*.

Valves elliptical; striæ in two distinct bands, one marginal, another close to the median line, with a wide elliptical intervening space. Marginal band of striæ lunate on the inner margin.

Navicula clavata, (Gregory). Marine.
Valve broadly elliptical; ends broadly produced and rounded; striæ moniliform, marginal band broad, narrowing towards the ends; inner bands of striæ separated from the median line by a narrow unstriate space, bending outward near the central nodule, where they terminate sharply, making a wide free space about the central nodule; space intervening between the inner and outer bands of striæ unstriate, broad and lunate; length about ·0050, breadth about ·0026. (Plate 32, fig. 23.)

Gregory, Q. J. M. S. Trans. 1856, p. 46, 'Pl. v., fig. 17. Ralfs, in Pritch., p. 898. Donkin, N. H. Brit. Diat., p. 15, Pl. ii., fig. 8.—Navicula lyra, Rab. Fl. Eur. Alg., sect. i., p. 178.

Stomachs of Ascidians, Co. Clare. Stomachs of Ascidians, Roundstone Bay; stomachs of Ascidians, Broadhaven Bay, Arran Islands, Co. Galway.

Navicula hennedyi, (Wm. Sm.) Marine.

Valve broadly elliptical, ends not produced; striæ moniliform; inner and outward bands of striæ, narrower than in Navicula clavata, but in other respects very similar; length about ·0030, breadth about ·0020. (Plate 32, fig. 24.)

Wm. Sm., B. D., Vol. ii., p. 93. Gregory, Q. J. M. S. Trans., 1856, p. 40, Pl. v., fig. 3. Ralfs, in Pritch., p. 898. Rab. Fl. Eur. Alg. sect. i., p. 178. Donkin, N. H. Brit. Diat., p. 11, Pl. ii., fig. 3. Schmidt, Atlas der Diat., T. iii., figs. 17, 18.

Stomachs of Ascidians, Belfast Lough, Co. Antrim. Stomachs of Ascidians, Roundstone Bay; stomachs of Ascidians, Broadhaven Bay, Arran Islands, Co. Galway.

Navicula nebulosa, (Gregory). Marine.

Valves in outward form similar to those of Navicula hennedyi, but narrower; the space intervening between the outer and inner bands of striæ obscurely marked with very fine parallel lines of puncta, which do not extend throughout; length about ·0042, breadth about ·0020. (Plate 32, fig. 25.)

Gregory, Diat. of Clyde, p. 480, Pl. ix., fig. 8. Ralfs, in Pritch., p. 898. Rab. Fl. Eur. Alg. sect. i., p. 179. Donkin, N. H. Brit. Diat., p. 11, Pl. ii., fig. 2. Schmidt, Atlas der Diat., T. iii., fig. 14. The clouded appearance of the space intervening between the inner and outer bands of striæ, as represented in the figures of Gregory and Donkin, is found with good illumination to arise from the fine punctate striæ above referred to.

Stomachs of Ascidians, Roundstone Bay, Arran Islands, Co. Galway.

Var. suborbicularis, (O'Meara). Marine.

Valve shorter and relatively broader than that of the typical species; marginal band of striæ relatively broader; that next the median line relatively narrower; intermediate space between the inner and outer bands of striæ narrow, and occupied by irregularly disposed puncta; length ·0024, breadth ·0014. (Plate 32, fig. 26.)

Arran Islands, Stomachs of Ascidians, Roundstone Bay, Co. Galway.

Navicula prætexta, (Ehr.) Marine.

Valve broadly elliptical; marginal band of striæ broad, distinctly moniliform; median bands of striæ broad, distinctly moniliform; intermediate space between the outer and inner bands of striæ ornamented with irregularly arranged large, round puncta; free unstriate space between the median line and the inner margins of the inner band of striæ expanding in the middle, with a narrow stauroform band; length about ·0040, breadth about ·0025. (Plate 32, fig. 27.)

Ehrenberg, in Proceedings of Berlin Acad., 1840, p. 20. Kütz.

Bac., p. 98. Gregory, Diat. of Clyde, p. 481, Pl. ix., fig. 11. Ralfs, in Pritch., p. 898. Rab. Fl. Eur. Alg. sect. i., p. 183. Donkin, N. H. Brit. Diat., p. 10, Pl. ii., fig. 1. Schmidt, Atlas der Diat., T. iii., fig. 31.

Arran Islands, Stomachs of Ascidians, Roundstone Bay; stomachs of Ascidians, Broadhaven Bay, Co. Galway.

Navicula moreii, N. Sp. Marine.

Valve very large, broadly elliptical, somewhat rhombical; marginal band of striæ broad in the middle, diminishing towards the ends; median band of striæ narrow, terminating considerably short of the central nodule; intermediate space between the inner and outer bands of striæ broad, unstriate; striæ fine, but distinctly moniliform; nearly parallel in the middle, slightly radiate towards the ends; length ·0075, breadth ·0037. (Plate 32, fig. 28.)

Navicula kittoniana, Schmidt, Atlas der Diat., T. ii., fig. 10. The form having been exhibited by me some years ago at the Meeting of the Dublin Microscopical Club, under the name of Navicula moreii, the latter designation has the priority. Schmidt's locality is Rio Janeiro.

Stomachs of Ascidians, Broadhaven Bay; stomachs of Ascidians, Roundstone Bay, Co. Galway.

Navicula sandriana, (Grunow). Marine.

Valve nearly orbicular; marginal band of striæ narrow, of equal breadth till near the ends, where it widens, and then suddenly narrows; median band of striæ very narrow, not reaching the median line, and terminating at some distance from the central nodule; intermediate space between the inner and outer bands of striæ wide, ornamented with irregularly disposed indistinct puncta, and having in the middle a narrow, longitudinal lunate band of small, but distinct, puncta; striæ of the marginal band moniliform, radiate; striæ of the inner band punctate, and parallel; length about ·0040, breadth about ·0030. (Plate 32, fig. 29.)

This form was exhibited by me at a Meeting of the Dublin Microscopical Club as Navicula cœlata, but subsequently I discovered that the species had been described in 1863 by Grunow as Navicula sandriana, which designation, having the priority, must be permitted to stand.

Grunow, Verhand. der K. Zool. Bot. Gesell., Band xii., 1863, p. 153, T. iv., fig. 5. Schmidt, Atlas der Diat., T. iii., fig. 10. Grunow's locality for the species is the Adriatic Sea. I may here remark that my specimens differ from those figured by Grunow and Schmidt, by the fact that in mine the outer band of striæ expands perceptibly near the ends, a feature which is not noticeable in the figures referred to above.

Stomachs of Ascidians, Roundstone Bay, Co. Galway.

Navicula franciscæ, N. S. Marine.
Valve nearly orbicular; marginal band of striæ narrow; median band of striæ narrow, distant from median line, leaving a lanceolate, unstriate space between the inner margins; intermediate space between the inner and outer bands of striæ broad, unstriate; striæ moniliform, parallel in the middle, radiate towards the ends; length ·0033, breadth ·0030. (Plate 32, fig. 30.)

Stomachs of Ascidians, Roundstone Bay, Co. Galway.

Navicula hibernica, N. S. Marine.
Valve elliptical oblong; marginal band of striæ narrow, slightly broader in the middle than at the ends; inner band of striæ narrow, roundly expanded at the ends; intermediate space between the inner and outer bands of striæ broad, ornamented with irregularly disposed distinct puncta; striæ of the marginal band linear, with moniliform striæ interposed, parallel in the middle, radiate towards the ends; striæ of the inner band punctate, parallel. (Plate 32, fig. 31.)

Stomachs of Ascidians, Roundstone Bay; Arran Islands, Co. Galway.

Navicula nitescens. (Gregory). Marine.
Valve elliptical, lanceolate; striæ apparently strongly costate, divided by a longitudinal sulcus into two nearly equal compartments; free space between the inner margins of the inner bands of striæ narrow, lanceolate; slightly expanded in the middle. (Plate 32, fig. 32.)
Ralfs, in Pritch., p. 898. Rab. Fl. Eur. Alg. sect. i., p. 179. Donkin, N. H. Brit. Diat., p. 8, Pl. i. fig. 7.—Navicula smithii, var. nitescens, Gregory, Diat. of Clyde, p. 487, Pl. ix., fig. 16.—Pinnularia arraniensis, O'Meara, Q. J. M. S., 1867, p. 116, Pl. v., fig. 6.

Arran Islands. Stomachs of Ascidians, Roundstone Bay; stomachs of Ascidians, Broadhaven Bay, Co. Galway.

Navicula richardsoniana, N. S. Marine.
Valve narrow, elliptical; ends rounded; inner band of striæ broad outer band of striæ very narrow; striæ strongly costate, sub-distant, radiate; length ·0024. breadth ·0006. (Plate 32, fig. 33.)
This form strongly resembles Navicula nitescens, but differs so much as to be entitled to be regarded as a distinct species.

Stomachs of Ascidians, Broadhaven Bay, Co. Galway.

Navicula stokesiana, N. S. Marine.
Valve large, rhombic, lanceolate; marginal striate band wide; inner striate band narrow, elevated above the surface; free space in-

cluded within the inner margins of the inner striate bands narrow, linear, forming in the middle a very narrow stauroform line; space intermediate between the outer and inner striate bands occupied by lines of striæ, which are prolongations of the striæ of the marginal band; striæ close, punctate, radiate; length ·0045, greatest breadth ·0018.

This form is one of very rare occurrence, only three specimens having been noticed. The only forms I have seen figured which bear resemblance to this very striking species are those of Mastogloia jelininckiana, Grunow, Reise S. M. Novara um die Erde, T. i. A., fig. 11; and Navicula irrorata, Schmidt, Atlas der Diat., T. ii., fig. 19. As to the former, even a cursory examination suffices to show that this form is perfectly distinct. As to the latter, the inner and outer bands of striæ are separated by an intervening blank space, whereas in the present case the corresponding intermediate space is distinctly striate.

This beautiful species I wish to identify with the name of the present respected President of the Royal Irish Academy. (Plate 32, fig. 34.)

Stomachs of Ascidians, Roundstone Bay; stomachs of Ascidians, Broadhaven Bay, Co. Galway.

(j) *Lyratæ.*

Similar to the last sub-group, and distinguished by the bending in at the middle of the marginal striate band, which consequently is bilunate on the inner margin. The intermediate free space is more or less distinctly lyrate.

Navicula wrightii, (O'Meara). Marine.

Valve linear elliptical; ends broadly produced; marginal band of striæ tolerably wide, projecting inwards slightly in the middle; striæ moniliform, nearly parallel at the middle, slightly radiate towards the ends; inner band of striæ narrow, expanded at the ends; intermediate space between the inner and outer bands of striæ wide, unstriate; length ·0045, breadth ·0018. (Pl. 32, fig. 35.)

Navicula wrightii, var. Q. J. M. S., 1867, p. 116, Pl. v., fig. 46.—
Navicula caribea, Schmidt, Atlas, T. ii., fig. 17.

Arran Islands; Stomachs of Ascidians, Roundstone Bay; Stomachs of Ascidians, Broadhaven Bay, Co. Galway.

Navicula spectabilis, (Gregory). Marine.

Valve broadly elliptical; marginal band of striæ broad in the middle, and gradually decreasing towards the ends; inner band of striæ wide; striæ moniliform, nearly parallel in the middle, slightly radiate towards the ends; intermediate space between the inner and outer bands of striæ very wide, unstriate, but interrupted by a narrow longitudinal nebulous belt, which runs conformably with the inner edge of the marginal band of striæ; length ·0044, breadth ·0025.

Gregory, Diat. of Clyde, p. 481, Pl. ix., fig. 10. Ralfs, in Pritch., p. 898. Rab. Fl. Eur. Alg., sect. i., p. 178. Donkin, N. H. Brit. Diat., p. 12, Pl. ii., fig. 5. Cleve, Om Svenska och Norska Diat., p. 226.

Arran Islands; Stomachs of Ascidians, Roundstone Bay; Stomachs of Ascidians, Broadhaven Bay, Co. Galway.

Var. sub-orbicularis, (O'Meara). Marine.

In all respects resembling the typical species, but nearly orbicular; the marginal band of striæ relatively broader, the inner band of striæ; as well as the intermediate space between the inner and outer striate bands much narrower; length ·0024, breadth ·0018. (Plate 32, fig. 36.)

Navicula spectabilis, var.? Schmidt, Atlas der Diat., T. ii. fig. 31.

Arran Islands; Stomachs of Ascidians, Roundstone Bay; Stomachs of Ascidians, Broadhaven Bay, Co. Galway.

Navicula lyra, (Ehr.) Marine.

Valve linear elliptical; ends broadly produced; marginal band of striæ broad; inner band broad, incurved in the middle; intermediate free space between the inner and outer bands of striæ very narrow; ends pointed and directed outwards; striæ moniliform; length, about ·0040, breadth, about ·0014. (Plate 33, fig. 1.)

Kützing, Bac., p. 94, T. xxviii., fig. 55, who refers the species to Ehrenberg. Gregory, Diat. of Clyde, p. 485, Pl. ix., fig. 13*b*. Ralfs, in Pritch., p. 897, who remarks, "Either Navicula lyra is very variable, or more than one species has been included under the name." Heiberg, De Danske Diat., p. 80, who includes this form and the variety elliptica. Cleve, Om Svenska och Norska Diat., p. 226. Donkin, N. H. Brit. Diat., p. 14, Pl. ii., fig. 7. Schmidt, Atlas der Diat., T. ii., fig. 16.

River Slaney, Killurin, Bannon, Co. Wexford. Malahide, Portmarnock, Co. Dublin. Seaweeds, Portrush, Co. Antrim. Caum Lough, near Tralee, Lough Gill, Co. Kerry. Salt marsh, Kilcool, Co. Wicklow. Kilkee, Co. Clare. Arran Islands; Stomachs of Ascidians, Broadhaven Bay; Stomachs of Ascidians, Roundstone Bay Co. Galway. Stomachs of Ascidians, Belfast Lough.

Var. elliptica, (Wm. Smith). Marine.

Valve elliptical; greatly attenuated at the ends; marginal band of striæ very broad; inner band of striæ narrow; intermediate free space between the inner and outer striate bands narrow; incurved in the middle, converging at the attenuated extremities; striæ obviously moniliform; length, about ·0056, breadth, about ·0024. (Plate 33, fig. 2.)

This form was first described by Wm. Smith, who doubtfully considered it a sporangial variety of Navicula elliptica, B. D., Vol. i., p. 48, Pl. xvii., fig. 152 a. Subsequently the same author regarded it as identical with Navicula lyra, Ehr., B. D., Vol. ii., p. 93; but judging by the figure which Kützing has given of the latter, there can be little doubt that the forms are not altogether identical. Still, so similar are they, that it seems desirable to represent them as merely varieties. Schmidt, Atlas der Diat., T. ii. fig. 29.

Stomachs of Ascidians, Belfast Lough. Stomachs of Ascidians, Kilkee, Co. Clare. Arran Islands; Stomachs of Ascidians, Roundstone Bay; Stomachs of Ascidians, Broadhaven Bay, Co. Galway. Ballysodare, Co. Sligo. Bannow, Co. Wexford.

Var. grunovii, (O'Meara). Marine.

Valve broadly elliptical; marginal band of striæ very broad; inner band of striæ narrow; intermediate space between the inner and outer bands of striæ narrow, converging, and anastomosing at the ends; striæ very close, radiate, minutely punctate; length ·0028, breadth ·0015. (Plate 33, fig. 3.)

Grunow, Verhand. der K. K. Zool. Bot. Gesell., Band x., 1860, p. 532, T. v., fig. 22. The author just named regards the form as identical with Navicula Lyra, Ehr., as described by Kützing, Bac., p. 96, T. xxviii., fig. 55; but comparison of specimens of both will convince the observer that the forms are not identical; so distinct are their details that the present form might almost be regarded as entitled to a distinctive specific name.

Arran Islands; Stomachs of Ascidians, Broadhaven Bay; Stomachs of Ascidians, Roundstone Bay, Co. Galway.

Var. minor, (Grunow). Marine.

This variety resembles that last described, but differs from it in the following characters; the form is much smaller, the ends are broadly rounded, and the lyrate space between the two bands of striæ is much more convex; length ·0015, breadth .0009. (Plate 33, fig. 4.)

Grunow, Verhand. der K. K. Zool. Bot. Gesell., Band x., 1860, p. 532, Pl. v., fig. 23.

Stomachs of Ascidians, Roundstone Bay; Arran Islands, Co. Galway.

Var. forcipata, (Greville). Marine.

Valve elliptical, oblong; marginal and inner bands of striæ separated by a broad lyrate, blank space; convergent at the ends; striæ, minutely moniliform; length about ·0024, breadth about ·0010.

Greville, Q. J. M. S. 1859, p. 83, Pl. vi., figs. 10, 11. Ralfs, in Pritch., p. 897. Rab. Fl. Eur., Alg., sect. i., p. 178. Donkin, N. H.

Brit. Diat., p. 12, Pl. ii., fig. 4. And likely the same as that figured by Schmidt, Atlas der Diat., T. ii., fig. 36.

Arran Islands; Stomachs of Ascidians, Roundstone Bay; Stomachs of Ascidians, Broadhaven Bay, Co. Galway. Bannow, Co. Wexford. Malahide, Portmarnock, Piles of wooden bridge, Dollymount strand, Dalkey, Co. Dublin. Rostrevor, Dundrum Bay, Co. Down. Lough Gill, Co. Kerry.

Var. abrupta, (Gregory). Marine.
Like the last described variety, but the striæ are costate, and the intermediate lyrate free space does not extend so near the ends.
Gregory, Diat. of Clyde, p. 486, Pl. ix., fig. 14. Rab. Fl. Eur., Alg., sect. i., p. 178. Donkin, N. H. Brit. Diat., p. 13, Pl. ii., fig. 6. Gregory and Donkin figure the species with obscurely moniliform striæ; and therefore I have a doubt of the identity of the present variety with that so described. Supposing the figures referred to be exact in this particular, I could scarcely distinguish between the former and Navicula lyra, var. elliptica.

Arran Islands; Stomachs of Ascidians, Roundstone Bay; Stomachs of Ascidians, Broadhaven Bay, Co. Galway.

Var. costata, (O'Meara). Marine.
Valve broadly elliptical; marginal band of striæ broad; inner band of striæ narrow; striæ distinctly costate, close, parallel in the middle, slightly radiate towards the ends, which latter are slightly cuneate; intermediate lyrate space very narrow, convergent at the ends, and reaching to the apices; length ·0024, breadth ·0012.

Arran Islands; Stomachs of Ascidians, Broadhaven Bay; Stomachs of Ascidians, Roundstone Bay, Co. Galway.

Var. seductilis, (Gründler). Marine.
Valve narrow, linear-elliptical; marginal band of striæ relatively wide; inner band of striæ narrow; striæ very fine, linear, parallel in the middle, slightly, radiate towards the ends, lyrate smooth space very narrow; length about ·0020, breadth about ·0006.—Navicula seductilis (Gründl), Schmidt, Atlas der Diat., T. ii., fig. 35. Yokohama. (Plate 33, fig. 5.)

Stomachs of Ascidians, Roundstone Bay, Co. Galway.

Var. constricta, (O'Meara). Marine.
Valve linear, elliptical, slightly constricted in the middle, ends cuneate, rounded at the extremity; striæ, fine, moniliform, lyrate; free space narrow, converging at the ends; length ·0042, greatest breadth ·0016, breadth in the middle ·0015. (Plate 33, fig. 6.)

Stomachs of Ascidians, Broadhaven Bay, Co. Galway.

Navicula pygmæa, (Kütz..) Marine or brackish water.

Valve linear, elliptical; marginal band of striæ narrow, with a distinct ridge on the inner margin; inner band of striæ relatively broad, reaching the median line, and having a distinct ridge on the outer margin; striæ fine, linear, nearly parallel; space intermediate between the inner and outer bands of striæ narrow, lyrate; apparently unstriate, but on closer inspection it will be found that the striæ which seem to be interrupted are really pervious; length about ·0015; breadth about ·00066, but often of much larger dimensions. (Plate 33, fig. 7.)

Wm. Smith (B. D., Vol. ii., p. 91), who attributes the species to Kützing. Rabenhorst (Süssw. Diat., p. 39) refers to a form under this name without a figure; the species is not correctly included among those incidental to fresh water. Ralfs, in Pritch., p. 899, who says "the species occurs in brackish or fresh water;" but though often found by me in marine gatherings, it never once occurred to me in fresh water. Donkin, N. H. Brit. Diat. p. 10, Pl. i., fig. 10. Lagerstedt, Sötvat. Diat. från Spetzbergen och Beeren Eiland, p. 27.—Navicula minutula, Wm. Sm., B. D., Vol i., p. 48, Pl. xxxi., fig. 274.

Bannow, salt ditch near town of Wexford, River Slaney, near Killurin, Tacumshane, Co. Wexford. Malahide, Portmarnock, Piles of wooden bridge, Dollymount Strand, Co. Dublin. Galway Bay, near town of Galway. Portnacrush, Co. Donegal. Lough Gill, Co. Kerry. On seaweeds, Kilkee, Co. Clare.

Var. cuneata, (O'Meara). Marine.

Valve linear, elliptical, with cuneate ends; marginal band of striæ broad; inner band of striæ narrow; striæ coarse, linear, distant, parallel in the middle, slightly radiate towards the ends, lyrate; free space narrow, and sometimes difficult to detect; length ·0017; breadth ·0010. (Plate 33, fig. 8.)

Stomachs of Ascidians, Broadhaven Bay, Co. Galway.

(k) *Trifasciatæ.*

Distinguished by having the intermediate space between the inner margins of the marginal bands of striæ divided into three distinct longitudinal compartments, one about the median line, and one on either side of the same.

---

† *Not constricted in the middle.*

Navicula expleta. N. S. Marine.

Valve broadly elliptical; median compartment nearly linear, slightly incurved towards the ends, next compartments narrow, lunate; marginal band of striæ relatively wide; striæ linear, undulate, divided by about five longitudinal sulci; length about ·0018; breadth about ·0012. (Plate 33, fig. 9.)

This form appears to me obviously identical with that described under the name of Navicula notabilis, passing into the variety expleta, by Schmidt, Atlas der Diat., T. viii., figs. 50, 51 and 52. It seems to be perfectly distinct from Navicula notabilis, and deserving of being marked by a distinct specific name.

Stomachs of Ascidians, Roundstone Bay; Stomachs of Ascidians, Broadhaven Bay; Arran Islands, Co. Galway.

Navicula cynthia, (Schmidt). Marine.
Valves broadly elliptical; ends rounded; median compartment narrow, linear, slightly incurved at the ends, and slightly constricted in the middle compartment at either side, narrow, arcuate, upstriate; marginal striate band broad; striæ fine, close, linear, slightly radiate, divided into two nearly equal parts by a longitudinal sulcus; length ·0012, breadth ·0007. (Plate 33, fig. 10.)
Schmidt, Atlas der Diat., T. viii., fig. 41. This figure does not indicate the longitudinal sulcus which in my specimens divides the marginal band of striæ into two compartments; still I am disposed to regard the present form as at best a variety of the form described by Schmidt.

Stomachs of Ascidians, Broadhaven Bay, Co. Galway.

Navicula sansegana, (Grunow). Marine.
Valve linear, elliptical, ends rounded; median compartment narrow, linear throughout; compartments on either side narrow, very slightly arcuate, striate; marginal striate band relatively broad; striæ linear, sub-distant, parallel in the middle, slightly radiate towards the ends; length ·0020, breadth ·0009. (Plate 33, fig. 11.)
Schmidt, Atlas der Diat., T. viii., fig. 27, who attributes the species to Grunow, but I cannot find it noticed in any of the many papers of that author which I have had the opportunity of consulting.

Stomachs of Ascidians, Broadhaven Bay, Co. Galway.

Navicula arraniensis, N. S. Marine.
Valve small, elliptical; median compartment narrow, slightly constricted in the middle, slightly incurved at the ends; compartments at either side narrow, arcuate, striate; marginal band of striæ narrow; striæ strongly costate, distant, nearly linear. Length ·0012, breadth ·0006. (Plate 33, fig. 12.)
Arran Islands, Co. Galway.

Navicula schmidtii, N. S. Marine.
Valve broadly elliptical, ends rounded; middle compartment narrow, linear, strongly marked; very slightly constricted in the middle, very slightly incurved at the ends; compartments at either side

arcuate, unstriate; marginal band of striæ relatively broad; striæ coarse, costate, nearly parallel in the middle, but distinctly radiate towards the ends. (Plate 33, fig. 17.)

Navicula eugenia, Krit., form from Java, Schmidt, Atlas der Diat., T. viii. fig. 45. In my form the costæ are stronger and more remote than in the form described by Schmidt; still I have little hesitation in regarding them as the same species.

Arran Islands. Stomachs of Ascidians, Broadhaven Bay, Co. Galway.

Navicula eugenia, (Schmidt). Marine.

Valve linear elliptical; ends rounded; median compartment slightly constricted in the middle, slightly incurved at the ends; compartments at either side arcuate, nearly as wide as the marginal band of striæ, striate; striæ fine, linear, nearly parallel throughout; length ·0002, breadth, ·0007. (Plate 33, fig. 13.)

Schmidt, Atlas der Diat., T. viii., fig. 44. From Campeachy Bay.

Stomachs of Ascidians, Broadhaven Bay, Co. Galway.

Navicula scutellum, (O'Meara). Marine.

Valve broadly elliptical, narrowed and rounded at the ends; median compartment broad, linear, slightly incurved at the ends, slightly constricted in the middle; central nodule large, quadrangular, but slightly incurved at the ends; compartments at either side narrow, unstriate, the ends of the striæ of the marginal band sometimes appearing as beads on the outer edge; marginal striate band broad: striæ costate, nearly parallel in the middle, more and more radiate towards the ends; length about ·0025, breadth about ·0015. (Plate 33, fig. 14.)

Pinnularia scutellum, O'Meara, Q. J. M. S., 1869, p. 151, Pl. xii. fig. 5.

Arran Islands, Co. Galway.

Navicula suborbicularis, (Gregory). Marine.

Valve suborbicular, linear; median compartment wide, with margins distinctly marked, slightly inflexed at the ends, considerably constricted in the middle; compartments at either side tolerably broad; biluuate on the inner margin; marginal striate band broad, lunate on inner edge; striæ radiate, finely costate, with obscure moniliform striæ interposed; the costæ only continued across the contiguous compartment; length ·0025, breadth ·0016. (Plate 33, fig. 15.)

Ralfs, in Pritch., p. 898; Donkin, N. H. Brit. Diat., p. 9, Pl. i., fig. 9. Schmidt, Atlas der Diat., T. viii., fig. 5.—Navicula smithii, var. suborbicularis, Gregory, Diat. of Clyde, p. 15, Pl. ix., fig. 17.

Ascidians, Roundstone Bay; Arran Islands, Co. Galway.

Var. forficula, (O'Meara). Marine.
Valve elliptical, median compartment as in the typical species; compartments at either side very much narrower; marginal striate band wide, projecting towards the central nodule; inner margin bilunate; striæ radiate, costate, with obscure moniliform striæ interposed, the costæ only penetrating the contiguous compartment; length ·0023, breadth ·0014. (Plate 33, fig. 16.)
Schmidt, Atlas der Diat., T. viii., fig. 3.—Pinnularia forficula, O'Meara, Q. J. M. S., 1867, p. 117, Pl. v., fig. 9.

Arran Islands, Co. Galway.

Var. parva, (Schmidt). Marine.
Valve linear, elliptical; median compartment narrow, inflexed at the ends, slightly constricted in the middle; compartment at either side very narrow, bilunate; marginal striate band broad, bilunate on the inner margin; striæ fine, linear, nearly parallel throughout; length ·0014, breadth ·0008.
Schmidt, Atlas der Diat., T. viii., figs. 1 and 2.

Stomachs of Ascidians, Broadhaven Bay, Co. Galway.

Navicula coffeiformis, (Schmidt). Marine.
Valve small, broadly elliptical; median compartment narrow, inflexed at the ends, slightly constricted in the middle; compartments on either side narrow; median striate band relatively wide; striæ fine, linear, slightly radiate; length ·0010, breadth ·0005. (Plate 33, fig. 18.)
Schmidt, Atlas der Diat., T. viii., fig. 7.

Arran Islands, Co. Galway.

†† *Valve constricted to the middle.*

Navicula eudoxia, (Schmidt). Marine.
Valve elliptical, slightly constricted, ends broadly rounded; median compartment narrow, inflexed at the ends, slightly constricted in the middle; compartments at either side narrow, striate; striæ linear, nearly parallel and very faint; marginal striate band narrow; striæ linear, slightly convergent in the middle, slightly radiate towards the ends; length ·0016, breadth at the constriction ·0007, greatest breadth ·0008. (Plate 33, fig. 19.)
Schmidt, Atlas der Diat., T. viii., fig. 19.

Stomachs of Ascidians, Broadhaven Bay, Co. Galway.

Navicula donkinia, (O'Meara). Marine.

Valve slightly constricted; ends somewhat cuneate, rounded; median compartment narrow, slightly inflexed at the ends, slightly constricted in the middle; compartments at either side narrow, arcuate, having very faint striæ; marginal striate band narrow; striæ costate, coarse, sub-distant; nearly parallel in the middle, slightly radiate towards the ends; length ·0015, breadth at the constriction ·0006; greatest breadth ·00066. (Plate 33, fig. 20.)

Schmidt, Atlas, T. xii., fig. 63.—Navicula musca, Donkin, N. H. Brit. Diat., p. 50, Pl. vii., fig. 6, exclusive of Synonyms.

Arran Islands; Stomachs of Ascidians, Roundstone Bay; Stomachs of Ascidians, Broadhaven Bay, Co. Galway.

Navicula marginata, (O'Meara). Marine.

Valve very slightly constricted; median compartment broad, slightly inflexed at the ends, slightly expanded in the middle; compartments at either side nearly linear; striæ extremely faint; marginal striate band narrow; striæ costate, not reaching the margin, nearly parallel; length ·0036, breadth ·0011. (Plate 33, fig. 21.)

Pinnularia marginata, O'Meara, Q. J. M. S., 1869, p. 15, Pl. xii., fig. 4.

Arran Islands; Stomachs of Ascidians, Broadhaven Bay; Stomachs of Ascidians, Roundstone Bay, Co. Galway.

Navicula subcincta, (Schmidt). Marine.

Valve large, slightly constricted, ends somewhat cuneate, rounded; median compartment broad, inflexed at the ends, slightly constricted in the middle; compartments on either side broad, unstriate; marginal striate band divided into two equal portions by a longitudinal sulcus; striæ costate, close, parallel in the middle, slightly radiate towards the ends; length ·0042, breadth at the constriction ·0015; greatest breadth, ·0016. (Plate 33, fig. 22.)

Schmidt, Biolog. Untersuch. der Nordsee. Diat., p. 87., T. xi., fig. 7.

Arran Islands. Stomachs of Ascidians, Broadhaven Bay, Co. Galway.

Navicula archeriana, N. S. Marine.

Valve large, slightly constricted; ends somewhat cuneate, rounded; median compartment broad, inflexed at the ends, constricted in the middle; compartments at either side broad, arcuate; marginal striate band narrow; striæ costate, parallel in the middle, radiate towards the ends; length ·0026, breadth ·0012; at constriction, ·0011. (Plate 33, fig. 23.)

O'Meara, Q. J. M. S., 1874, p. 260, Pl. viii., fig. 9.—Navicula donkinii, Schmidt, Atlas, T. xii., fig. 64. This species is at first view extremely like Navicula donkinii; it is, however, considerably larger, the striæ finer and closer, and valve more deeply constricted.

Arran Islands; Stomachs of Ascidians, Broadhaven Bay, Co. Galway.

Navicula incurvata, (Gregory). Marine.

Valve slightly constricted; median compartment tolerably wide, slightly inflexed at the ends, very slightly inflexed in the middle; compartments at either side about the same width as the median, slightly arcuate, unstriate; marginal band of striæ narrow; striæ nearly parallel throughout, fine, tolerably close; indistinctly punctate; puncta very close; length ·0028, breadth ·0009; at constriction, ·0008. (Plate 33, fig. 24.)

Gregory, Q. J. M. S., 1856, p. 44, Pl. v., fig. 13. In this figure the marginal band of striæ is represented as very much wider than it appears to be in any of the very numerous specimens I have met with, and also the compartments on either side of the median line are much narrower; in consequence of this, I was induced to consider the form distinct from that of Gregory, and named it Navicula pellucida, Q. J. M. S., 1867, p. 115, Pl. v., fig. 3. Ralfs, in Pritch., p. 893. Donkin, N. H. Brit. Diat., p. 49, Pl. vii., fig. 4. This figure does not describe the incurved ends and middle of the median compartment. Donkin regards the species as = to Navicula interrupta, Grunow, Verhand. der K. K. Zool. Bot. Gesell., Band x., 1860, p. 531, T. iii., fig. 20. If so, Grunow's figure is liable to the same remark as that of Gregory. —Navicula splendida, var. incurvata, Rab. Fl. Eur. Alg., sect. i., p. 204. I think the form obviously distinct from Navicula splendida.

Arran Islands; Stomachs of Ascidians, Broadhaven Bay; Stomachs of Ascidians, Roundstone Bay, Co. Galway. Stomachs of Ascidians, Co. Clare.

Navicula musca, (Gregory). Marine.

Valve small, deeply and suddenly constricted; ends sharp; median compartment relatively broad, inflexed at ends, slightly constricted in the middle; compartments at either side narrow, arcuate, unstriate; marginal band of striæ narrow, obscurely punctate, extremely short in the middle, radiate towards the ends; length ·0012, breadth ·0006; at the constriction, ·0004. (Plate 33, fig. 25.)

Gregory, Diat. of Clyde, p. 479, Pl. ix., fig. 6. This figure by no means agrees with the description nor the measurements of the text. So that it is not at all to be wondered at that Donkin should have considered it identical with that which he has figured as Navicula musca. Donkin's form referred to was properly regarded by Schmidt as a distinct species, and named Navicula donkinii, the name which I had given to it in my list before the Atlas had come under my notice. The form here described agrees precisely with Gregory's description of Navicula musca, which may readily be distinguished from Navicula donkinii, by its much deeper constriction, and the sharp outline at the ends, in consequence of which it resembles the abdomen of a fly; the striæ, too, in this are punctate, while in the other they are costate.

Piles of wooden bridge on Dollymount Strand, Co. Dublin.

Navicula interrupta, (Kützing). Marine.

Valve deeply constricted; lobes suborbicular; median compartment broad, greatly inflexed at the ends, considerably constricted in the middle; compartments on either side very narrow, bilunate, unstriate; marginal band of striæ very narrow in the middle, where the striæ seem to fail, but tolerably wide in the middle of the lobes; striæ costate, nearly parallel in the middle, radiate towards the ends; length ·0023, breadth, ·0010; at constriction ·0007. (Plate 33, fig. 26.)
Kütz. Bac., p. 100, T. xxix., fig. 93. Ralfs, in Pritch., p. 894. Rab. Fl. Eur. Alg., sect. i., p. 205. Donkin, N. H. Brit. Diat., p. 47, Pl. vii., fig. 2. Schmidt, Atlas, T. xii., fig. 2.—Navicula didyma, Wm. Sm., B. D., Vol. i., p. 53, Pl. xvii., fig. 154a.

Ballysodare, Co. Sligo. Lough Gill, Co. Kerry. Arran Islands; Stomachs of Ascidians, Roundstone Bay; Stomachs of Ascidians, Broadhaven Bay, Co. Galway. Seaweeds, coast of Co. Clare.

Navicula apis, (Ehr.) Marine.

Valve deeply constricted, ends narrowed and rounded; median compartment broad, with well-defined boundary lines, slightly inflexed at ends, slightly constricted in the middle; compartments at either side unstriate, narrow, tapering to a point at the ends; marginal band of striæ narrow in the middle, increasing considerably, and then narrowing towards the ends; striæ in the middle apparently costate, convergent towards the ends, radiate, and having the appearance more of fine costæ interrupted by close longitudinal sulci, than of being moniliform; length ·0038, breadth ·0011; breadth at the constriction ·0008. (Plate 33, fig. 27.)

There is great difficulty in identifying the species so named, and with some hesitation have I come to my conclusion on the subject. Kützing's figure of Navicula apis is shorter and stouter than the present, and the striæ are so indistinct as to furnish no help. Donkin's figure in outline is precisely the same as in the form under consideration; the striæ, however, are represented as more decidedly punctate, and the compartments on either side of the median one are distinctly striate. In the present case, there is sometimes an appearance of striæ there, but with precise focusing they disappear, or, if they appear at all, are very faint. Schmidt's figure represents the species as more robust than mine, but the compartments on either side of the median one are just as in mine.

Arran Islands; Stomachs of Ascidians, Broadhaven Bay, Co. Galway.

Navicula bombus, (Ehr.) Marine.

Valves much constricted, lobes much inflated; median compartment very wide, the boundary lines strong, and having the edges milled, greatly curved at the ends, slightly constricted in the middle; compartments at either side narrow; scarcely striate, or if striate, the striæ very faint; marginal band of striæ very wide; striæ remote, distinctly moniliform, the beads being distant, parallel in the middle, more and more radiate towards the ends; length ·0036, breadth ·0016; breadth at the constriction ·0010. (Plate 33, fig. 28.)

Ralfs, in Pritch., p. 893, who attributes the species to Ehrenberg. Gregory, Diat. of Clyde, p. 484, Pl. ix., fig. 12. Rab. Fl. Eur. Alg., sect. i, p. 204. Donkin, N. H. Brit. Diat., p. 50, Pl. vii., fig. 7a. This figure fairly represents the characters of the species, but in my specimens the constriction is deeper, and the compartments at either side of the median one are much narrower. Cleve, Om Svenska och Norska Diat., p. 226.

Arran Islands; Stomachs of Ascidians, Broadhaven Bay; Stomachs of Ascidians, Roundstone Bay, Co. Galway. Ballysodare, Co. Sligo. Malahide, Portmarnock, Co. Dublin. Bannow, Co. Wexford. Stomachs of Ascidians, coast of Co. Clare. Stomachs of Ascidians, Belfast Lough, Co. Antrim.

Navicula entomon, (Ehr.) Marine.

Valves not so deeply constricted as in Navicula bombus; median compartment narrow, inflexed at the ends, slightly constricted in the middle; compartments at either side narrow, unstriate, or striæ very obscure; marginal band of striæ broad; striæ distinctly moniliform, distant, parallel in the middle, radiate towards the ends; length ·0030, breadth ·0012; breadth at the constriction ·0010.

This species strongly resembles Navicula bombus in the character of the moniliform striæ; the constriction is, however, not so deep, nor are the lobes so much expanded; the median compartment also is much narrower in this species than it is in the other.

Kütz. Bac., p. 100, T. xxviii., fig. 74. In this case, the figure is very obscure. Kützing attributes the species to Ehrenberg. Ralfs, in Pritch., p. 893. Donkin, N. H. Brit. Diat., p. 49, Pl. vii., fig. 5. This figure represents the species as much larger, and the compartments on either side of the median one wider than they appear in my specimens. Schmidt, Atlas der Diat., T. xii., fig. 51. In outline, this figure exactly represents the present species; the striation, however, seems different.

Arran Islands; Stomachs of Ascidians, Broadhaven Bay, Co. Galway.

Navicula didyma, (Ehr.) Marine.
Valves slightly constricted; median compartment wide, inflexed at the ends, greatly constricted in the middle; compartments on either side very narrow, exhibiting a row of moniliform dots on the inner margin; marginal striate band broad; striæ radiate throughout, closely moniliform; length about ·0030, breadth ·0011; breadth at the constriction ·0010. (Plate 33, fig. 29.)
Kütz. Bac., p. 100, T. iv., fig. 7, T. xxviii., fig. 75. In the former figure, the compartments at either side of the median one are represented as much wider than in my specimens; in the latter figure the striæ are represented as running up to the outer margin of the median compartment, the compartments at either side being thus wholly obliterated. Kützing attributes the species to Ehrenberg. Wm. Sm., B. D., Vol. i., p. 53, Pl. xvii., fig. 54. Ralfs, in Pritch., p. 893, Pl. xii., fig. 15. Ralfs' figure of the species, Pl. vii., fig. 61, is more like Navicula interrupta than Navicula didyma. Grunow, Verhand. der K. K. Zool. Bot. Gesell., Band x., 1860, p. 530. Cleve, Om Svenska och Norska Diat., p. 225. Donkin, N. H. Brit. Diat., p. 51, Pl. vii., fig. 8.
The form described by Rabenhorst as Pinnularia didyma, Süssw. Diat., p. 46, T. vi., fig. 26, is probably the same as the present species, but if so, its occurrence in fresh water must have been casual.

Bannow, River Slaney, at Killurin, Tacumshane, Co. Wexford. Malahide, Portmarnock, Piles of wooden bridge, Dollymount Strand, Co. Dublin. Lough Foyle, Co. Derry. Salt-marsh, near town of Wicklow. Kilkee, Co. Clare. Arran Islands; Stomachs of Ascidians, Roundstone Bay; Stomachs of Ascidians, Broadhaven Bay, seaweeds near Westport, Co. Galway. Stomachs of Ascidians, Belfast Lough, Co. Antrim.

Navicula splendida, (Gregory). Marine.
Valve large, deeply constricted; median compartment wide, greatly inflexed at the ends, greatly constricted in the middle; compartments at either side narrow, having the inner edge milled; marginal band of striæ narrow in the middle, widening in a graceful curve towards the middle of the lobe, then narrowing towards the somewhat lanceolate ends; striæ convergent in the middle, radiate towards the

ends, moniliform, the beads being quadrangular; length ·0040, breadth ·0012; breadth at the constriction ·0007. (Plate 33, fig. 30.) Gregory, Q. J. M. S., 1856, Pl. v., fig. 14. Ralfs, in Pritch., p. 893. Rab. Fl. Eur. Alg., sect. i., p. 204.—Navicula entomon. Donkin, N. H. Brit. Diat., p. 49, Pl. vii., fig. 5. The outline of this form greatly resembles that of Navicula incurvata, which Rabenhorst makes a variety of this species. So different, however, is the character of the striæ, that they cannot properly be considered as nearly related. The present form differs so much, both in outline and striation, from Navicula entomon, that it ought to be considered a very distinct species.

Arran Islands, Co. Galway.

Navicula gregorii, (O'Meara). Marine.

Valves considerably constricted, lobes much expanded, median compartment wide, greatly inflexed at the ends, slightly constricted in the middle; central nodule large, quadrangular, with three short spine-like projections at each side; compartments on either side narrow, attenuated to a point at the ends, roundly expanded in the middle; marginal band of striæ wide; striæ convergent in the middle, radiate towards the ends, moniliform; beads large, quadrangular; length ·0045, breadth ·0028; breadth at the constriction ·0016. (Plate 33, fig. 31.)

Navicula didyma, var. y. Gregory, Q. J. M. S., 1856, p. 45, Pl. v., fig. 16.

Arran Islands, Stomachs of Ascidians, Roundstone Bay, Co. Galway.

Navicula williamsonii, (Wm. Sm.) Marine.

Valve large; margin incurved, rather than constricted; median compartment wide, inflexed at the ends, constricted in the middle; compartments at either side scarcely so wide as the median one, narrowed to a point at the ends, greatly expanded, and anglewise in the middle, striate; marginal band of striæ wide; striæ slightly convergent in the middle, radiate towards the ends, moniliform; beads large, quadrangular; length ·0072, breadth ·0029; breadth at the middle ·0026. (Plate 33, fig. 32.)

Navicula didyma, sporangial var.? Wm. Sm., B. D., Vol. i., p. 53, Pl. xvii., fig. 154*.—Navicula smithii, Donkin, N. H. Brit. Diat., p. 6, Pl. i., fig. 4. This form on first view would appear to be an incurved variety of Navicula fusca, which it resembles much more than it does Navicula smithii. I believe it is only necessary to see the form, which is extremely rare, in order to be convinced that it is as distinct from Navicula didyma as it is from Navicula fusca. Professor Smith informs us that the species came under his observation in a collection made by Professor Williamson in the Isle of Skye.

Arran Islands; Stomachs of Ascidians, Roundstone Bay, Co. Galway.

Navicula incisa, N. S. Marine.

Valve deeply constricted; median compartment narrow; inflexed at ends, slightly contracted in the middle; compartments at either side narrow, striate; striæ faint; marginal band of striæ narrow in the middle, wide towards the middle of the lobes; striæ convergent in the middle, nearly parallel for some distance, and slightly radiate towards the ends; costate, divided into four distinct equal bands, by three deep sulci, which lie conformably with the outer margin; the costæ in each band appear slightly curved; length ·0035, breadth ·0015; breadth at the constriction ·0010. (Plate 33, fig. 33.)

This form somewhat resembles that figured by Schmidt, Atlas der Diat., T. xii., figs. 21 to 24, without a name, and which he thinks stands between Navicula apis and Navicula splendida, but I doubt its identity with either.

Arran Islands, Co. Galway.

Navicula crabro, (Ehr.) Marine.

Valves large, slightly constricted; median compartment narrow, slightly inflexed at ends, constricted in the middle; compartments on either side wider, gently tapering towards the ends; striate, the ends of the striæ appearing as large puncta on the elevated margin of the inner edge; marginal striate band wide; striæ convergent in the middle, radiate towards the ends; costate; length ·0073, breadth ·0021; breadth at constriction ·0015.

Wm. Sm., B. D., Vol. ii., p. 94. Donkin, N. H. Brit. Diat., p. 46, Pl. vii., fig. 1a. Ralfs, in Pritch., p. 894. Rab. Fl. Eur. Alg., sect. i., p. 204.—Diploneis crabro, Ehr., Mic., T. xix., fig. 29. —Navicula pandura, De Brébisson, Diat. du Littoral de Cherbourg, p. 16, Pl. i., fig. 4.—Pinnularia pandura, var. elongata, Gregory, Diat. of Clyde, p. 489, Pl. ix., fig. 22. Though Ralfs and Rabenhorst seem to regard this form as distinct from Navicula pandura, I am inclined to think with Donkin, that there is no distinction between them. Smith describes the striæ as obscurely moniliform; but all the figures I have seen represent the striæ as distinctly costate, and such I consider is their normal character. Donkin's figure represents the compartments at either side of the median compartment as unstriate, except on the inner edge, where there is a row of large bead-like detached puncta. In all the specimens I have seen, the costæ in this portion, though of a fainter colour, are clearly traceable all through; the large puncta described by Donkin being simply the ends standing out distinctly on an elevated ridge.

Arran Islands; Stomachs of Ascidians, Roundstone Bay, Co. Galway.

Var. intermedia, (O'Meara). Marine.

Valve considerably smaller than that of the typical form; the lobes are more expanded; the ends of the costæ on the inner edge of the compartments on either side of the median one are longer, the ridge seeming to be in this case wider, and not so much elevated.

This is, perhaps, identical with Navicula crabro, Grunow, Verhand. der K. K. Zool. Bot. Gesell., Band x., 1860, p. 524, T. v., fig. 21, and with Navicula nitida, Gregory, Q. J. M. S., 1856, p. 44, Pl. v., fig. 12.

Broadhaven Bay. Roundstone Bay.

Var. denticulata, (O'Meara). Marine.

Valve very much smaller than the preceding variety, not so much constricted, the ends of the striæ appearing on the inner edge of the compartments on either side of the median one being of the same breadth, or nearly so, as that of the costæ of the marginal band of striæ, which are very narrow. (Plate 33, fig. 34.)

Navicula denticulata, O'Meara, Q. J. M. S., 1867, p. 115, Pl. v., fig. 2. In the description at first given of this form it would appear as if the space between the two bands of costæ were unstriate; but upon more close examination, with better illumination than I then possessed, I have satisfied myself that the costæ pervade the interspace. They are indeed very indistinct, but still traceable.

Arran Islands; Stomachs of Ascidians, Broadhaven Bay; Stomachs of Ascidians, Roundstone Bay, Co. Galway.

Navicula pfitzeriana, N. S. Marine.

Valve small, slightly constricted; median compartment very narrow, lanceolate; compartments at either side become wider in middle than at ends; striate; marginal striate band relatively wide; striæ linear, close, convergent in the middle, thence finer, and nearly parallel; length ·0017, breadth ·0005; breadth at constriction ·0004. (Plate 33, fig. 35.)

This form was a considerable time ago exhibited by me among other interesting species collected by Mr. Mozely, H. M. S. Challenger, on the coast of Patagonia. It is identical with a specimen from Valparaiso, figured as Navicula divergens by Schmidt, Atlas der Diat., T. xii., fig. 53; but as my designation has the priority of publication, it has a right to stand.

Stomachs of Ascidians, coast of Co. Clare.

Navicula vickersii, N. S. Marine.

Valve very large, deeply constricted; median compartment linear, wide; compartments on either side wide, unstriate, bilunate on the outer margin; marginal striate band narrow in the middle, widening towards the broadest part of the heart-shaped lobes, and thence decreasing in width towards the rounded ends; striæ costate, nearly parallel in the middle, convergent towards the ends; a strongly developed submarginal, longitudinal sulcus appears conformable with the outer margin of the valve; length ·0055, breadth ·0020; breadth at the constriction ·0011. (Plate 33, fig. 36.)

This very striking form was exhibited by me some years ago, at a meeting of the Dublin Microscopical Club, at the house of Mr. Henry Vickers, with whose name it is associated.

Arran Islands; Stomachs of Ascidians, Roundstone Bay, Co. Galway.

(1.) *Perstriatæ.* Striæ reaching the median line.

† *Directæ.* Striæ parallel.

Navicula directa, (Wm. Sm.) Marine.

Valve narrow, lanceolate; median line distinct; striæ finely costate; length ·0025, breadth ·0003. (Plate 34, fig. 4.)

Ralfs, in Pritch., p. 906. Cleve, Om Svenska och Norska Diat., p. 224.—Pinnularia directa, Wm. Sm., B. D., Vol. i., p. 56, Pl. xviii., fig. 172. Rab. Fl. Eur. Alg., sect. i., p. 217.

Malahide, Co. Dublin. Stomachs of Ascidians, Co. Clare.

Navicula lanceolata, (Kütz.) Fresh water.

Valve lanceolate; striæ punctate; length ·0016, breadth ·0004.

Kütz. Bac., p. 94, T. xxviii., fig. 38; T. xxx., fig. 48. Neither of these figures indicates the character of the striæ; it is therefore impossible to identify Kützing's species with certainty. Wm. Sm., B. D., Vol. i., p. 46, suppl. Pl. xxxi., fig. 272. Rab. Fl. Eur. Alg., sect. i., p. 171. This author attributes the species to Wm. Smith, who has described it so that it can be easily recognised, and regards it as distinct from that so named by Kützing.

River Bann, near Coleraine, Co. Derry. Kilcool, Co. Wicklow. Adregoole, Co. Galway.

Navicula exilis, (Kütz.) Fresh water.

Valve small, narrow, elliptical; ends produced and slightly capitate; striæ obscure; length ·0013, breadth ·0003. (Plate 34, fig. 2.)

Kütz. Bac., p. 95, T. iv., fig. 6. This figure does not represent the striæ. Grunow, Verhand. der K. K. Zool. Bot. Gesell., Band x., 1860, p. 553, T. iv., fig. 30. Rab. Fl. Eur. Alg., sect. i., p. 198.

Lough Mask, near Tourmakeady, Co. Mayo.

† † *Radiosæ.* *Striæ more or less distinctly radiate.*

Navicula radiosa, (Kütz.) Fresh water.
Valve lanceolate, obtuse; striæ strongly costate; convergent in middle, radiate towards the ends; length about ·0020, breadth about ·0005. (Plate 34, fig. 3.)
Kütz. Bac., p. 91, T. iv., fig. 23. Ralfs, in Pritch., p. 905. Grunow, Verhand. der K. K. Zool. Bot. Gesell., Band x., 1860. Cleve, Om Svenska och Norska Diat., p. 225. Lagerstedt, Sötv. Diat. från Spitzbergen och Beeren Eiland, p. 25.—Pinnularia radiosa, Wm. Sm. B. D., Vol. i., p. 56, Pl. xviii., fig. 173. Rab. Fl. Eur., Alg., sect. i., p. 214.

Pool, Glengariff, Co. Cork. Lower Lake, Killarney, Co. Kerry. Stream Crossdoney, Co. Cavan. River Dodder, Bohernabreena, Glenasmole, Killakee, Co. Dublin. Lake near Castlewellan, Co. Down.

Navicula gracilis, (Ehr.) Fresh water.
Valve lanceolate, attenuated towards the ends, which are obviously produced; striæ costate, convergent in the middle, radiate towards the ends; length about ·0022, breadth about ·0005. (Plate 34, fig. 4.)
Kütz., Bac., p. 91, fig. 48, T. xxx., fig. 57, who regards the species described by him as identical with Navicula gracilis, Ehrenberg, Infus., 1838, p. 176, T. xiii., fig. 2. Smith is doubtful as to the identity of the form described and figured by him with that of Kützing just referred to and comparison of the figures of Kützing with specimens of the form, so accurately delineated by Smith will impress something more than doubt upon the observer's mind. Ralfs, in Pritch., p. 906. Grunow, Verhand. der K. K. Zool. Bot. Gesell., Band x., 1860, p. 526, T. iv., fig. 27. The species is broader, more attenuated at the ends, than this figure represents it. Schumann, Diat., der Hohen Tatra, p. 69. Rab. Fl. Eur., Alg., sect. i., p. 174.—Pinnularia gracilis, Wm. Smith, B. D., Vol. i., p. 57, Pl. xviii., fig. 174.

Drumoughty Lough, near Kenmare, Co. Kerry. Stream, Bellarena, Co. Derry. Stream near Crossdoney, Co. Cavan. Stream, Killiney, Stream, Ballybrack, Co. Dublin.

Navicula acuta, (Wm. Smith). Fresh water.
Valve, narrow, lanceolate; ends acute; striæ costate, convergent in the middle, radiate towards the ends; length ·0046, breadth ·0005. (Plate 34, fig. 5.)
Pinnularia acuta, Wm. Sm., B. D., Vol. i., p. 56, Pl. xviii., fig. 171.—Navicula radiosa, var. acuta. Grunow, Verhand. der K. K. Zool. Bot. Gesell., Band x., 1860, p. 526. There is a form described

and figured by Kützing under the name of Navicula acuta, the details of which are so indistinct that identification would be impossible, but the outline of the valve is such as to make it certain that it is distinct from the present form. Kütz. Bac., p. 93, T. iii., fig. 69.

In a fossil state, it occurs abundantly in the Lough Mourne deposit. In a living state, I have found it in the following localities: River Erne, near Crossdoney, Co. Cavan. Lower Lake, Killarney, Caumlough near Tralee, Co. Kerry. River Dodder, Pond in Botanic Gardens of Trinity College, Co. Dublin. Kilcool, Co. Wicklow.

Navicula acutiuscula, (Gregory). Marine.

Valve narrow, lanceolate, with acute ends. Striæ costate, slightly radiate throughout; length ·0040, breadth ·0005.

Ralfs, in Pritch., p. 906.—Pinnularia acutiuscula, Gregory, Q. J. M. S. 1856, Trans., p. 48, Pl. v., fig. 21. Rab. Fl. Eur. Alg., sect. i., p. 218.

Stomachs of Ascidians, seacoast, Co. Clare.

Navicula peregrina, (Ehr.) Marine or brackish water.

Valves broadly lanceolate, ends obtuse. Striæ costate, sub-distant, radiate; length ·0046, breadth ·0010. (Plate 34, fig. 6.)

Kütz. Bac., p. 97, T. xxviii., fig. 52. The form was considered by Kützing to be identical with Pinnularia peregrina of Ehrenberg. Ralfs, in Pritch., p. 906. Cleve, Om Svenska och Norska Diat., p. 225, Grunow, Verhand. der K. K. Zool. Bot. Gesell., Band x., 1860, p. 523.—Pinnularia peregrina, Wm. Sm., B. D., Vol. i., p. 56, Pl. xviii., fig. 170. Rab. Fl. Eur. Alg., sect. i., p. 213.

Salt ditch near the Town of Wexford, River Slaney, near Killurin, Tacumshane, Co. Wexford. Bellarena, mouth of the River Roe, Co. Derry. Rostrevor, Co. Down. Breaches near Newcastle, Co. Wicklow. Kilkee, Co. Clare. Lough Gill, Co. Kerry. Howth, Co. Dublin. Stomachs of Ascidians, Broadhaven Bay, Co. Galway. A small variety of this species occurred from stomachs of Ascidians Belfast Lough, Co. Antrim.

Navicula zostereti, (Grunow). Marine.

Valve, large lanceolate with sharp ends. Striæ strongly costate, sub-distant, radiate; length ·0056, breadth ·0002. (Plate 34, fig. 7.)

Grunow, Verhand. der K. K. Zool. Bot. Gesell., Band x., 1860, p. 528, T. iv., fig. 23. The locality in which this form was found by Grunow was the Adriatic Sea, from a depth of from two to four fathoms. I know of no other locality in which the species has been discovered save that specified below.—Pinnularia zostereti, Rab. Fl. Eur. Alg., sect. i., p. 218.

Stomachs of Ascidians, Broadhaven Bay, Co. Galway.

Navicula cleviana, N. S. Marine.
Valve narrow, elliptical. Striæ strongly costate, convergent, rounded, and sub-distant in the middle, radiate, linear, and closer towards the ends. Two very short costæ are interposed in the middle between the next which run to the median line; length ·0034 breadth ·0008. (Plate 34, fig. 8.)

From stomachs of Ascidians, Broadhaven Bay, Co. Galway.

Navicula digito-radiata, (Gregory). Fresh water.
Valve elliptical, with obtuse ends. Striæ costate, convergent, and distant in the middle, radiate towards the ends; length ·0028, breadth ·0008. (Plate 34, fig. 9.)
Ralfs, in Pritch., p. 904.—Pinnularia digito-radiata, Gregory, Q. J. M. S. 1856, p. 9, Pl. i., fig. 32. Rab. Fl. Eur. Alg., sect. i., p. 215.

Bowen's Court, Co. Cork. River Slaney, near Killurin, Co. Wexford, Lower Lake, Killarney. Caumlough, near Tralee, Co. Kerry. River Barrow, near Clonegal, Co. Carlow. Ditch near Kilcool, Co. Wicklow.

Navicula ergadensis, (Gregory). Marine.
Valve linear, elliptical, ends obtuse, rounded. Striæ costate, convergent in the middle, radiate towards the ends; length ·0026, breadth ·0006. (Plate 34, fig. 10.)
Ralfs, in Pritch., p. 907.—Pinnularia ergadensis, Gregory, Q. J. M. S. 1856, Pl. v., fig. 22. Rab. Fl. Eur. Alg., sect. i., p. 215.

Portmarnock, Malahide, Co. Dublin. Lough Gill, Co. Kerry. Salt ditches near the Town of Galway.

Navicula cyprinus, (Ehr.) Marine.
Valve rhombo-lanceolate, ends somewhat cuneate. Striæ costate, convergent in the middle, radiate towards the ends; length ·0025, breadth ·0007. (Plate 34, fig. 11.)
Kütz. Bac., p. 99, T. xxix., fig. 35. The species is here ascribed to Ehrenberg. The figure, it must be observed, is very inadequate to describe the species, the ends being rounded instead of cuneate, and the striæ parallel instead of being as above described.—Pinnularia cyprinus, Wm. Sm., B. D. Vol. i., p. 57, Pl. xviii., fig. 176. Rab. Fl. Eur. Alg., sect. i., p. 215.

Bannow, River Slaney, near Killurin, Co. Wexford. Lough Foyle. Mouth of River Roe, Co. Derry. Seaweeds near Town of Wicklow. Malahide, Portmarnock, Dalkey, Co. Dublin. Kilkee, Co. Clare.

Navicula galvagensis, N. S. Marine.
Valve oblong, elliptical, ends narrowed and rounded. Striæ costate, radiate; length ·0024, breadth ·0005. (Plate 34, fig. 12.)

Salt marsh near town of Galway; Stomachs of Ascidians, Broadhaven Bay, Co. Galway.

Navicula solaris, (Gregory). Marine.
Valve elliptical, with obtuse rounded ends. Striæ fine, linear, convergent in the middle, and very distinct, radiate towards the ends and less distinct. (Plate 34, fig. 13.)
Gregory, Q. J. M. S. 1856, Trans., p. 43, Pl. v., fig. 10. This figure represents the striæ as shortened in the middle so as to leave a blank space round the central nodule. And such is the appearance presented by the specimens that have come under my notice; but when well focused the blank space disappears, and the striæ are found to reach the median line. Ralfs, in Pritch., p. 904. Rab. Fl. Eur. Alg., sect. i., p. 181.

Ballarena, Co. Derry. Adregoole, Co. Galway. Malahide, Co. Dublin.

Navicula viridula, (Kütz. ?) Fresh water.
Valve elliptical, lanceolate, sometimes slightly produced. Striæ fine, linear, convergent in the middle, radiate towards the ends; length ·0016, breadth ·0005. (Plate 34, fig. 14.)
Kütz., Bac., p. 91, T. xxx., fig. 47; T. iv., figs. 10 and 15. The only one of these figures which at all resembles the present form is the last. Ralfs, in Pritch., p. 905. Cleve, Om Svenska och Norska Diat., p. 225. Lagerstedt, Sötv. Diat. från Spetsbergen och Beeren Eiland, p. 25.—Pinnularia viridula, Wm. Sm., B. D., Vol. i., p. 57, Pl. xviii., fig. 175. The description is accurate, but the figure represents the costæ as greatly coarser than they are in reality. The effect is to make this species appear scarcely to differ from Pinnularia gracilis. Lagerstedt indeed remarks, "I have considered it right to unite under the above name (Navicula viridula) the two species of Smith, Pinnularia viridula, and Pinnularia gracilis," p. 25. The striæ, however, in the former, are extremely fine, whereas in the latter they are very coarse. Rab. Fl. Eur. Alg., sect. i., p. 214. I think it not unlikely that this form is identical with that which Grunow has described as Navicula rhyncocephala, var. brevis. Verhand. der K. K. Zool. Bot. Gesell., Band x., 1860, p. 529, T. iv., fig. 31c.

Camolin, Co. Wexford. Lough Gill, Co. Kerry. Killakee, Stream near Clontarf, Co. Dublin. Ditch near town of Sligo. Well, Strokestown, Co. Roscommon.

Navicula heufleri, (Grunow). Fresh water.
Valve very small; lanceolate; central nodule large. Striæ fine; linear, radiate; length about ·0009, breadth about ·0003. (Plate 34. fig. 15.)
Grunow, Verhand. der K. K. Zool. Bot. Gesell., Band x., 1860, p. 528, T. iii., fig. 32. Schumann, Diat. der Hohen Tatra., p. 68. Rab. Fl. Eur. Alg., sect. i., p. 214.

Lough Gill, Co. Kerry. Powerscourt, Co. Wicklow.

Navicula fortis, (Gregory). Marine.
Valve small; broadly lanceolate; rounded at ends. Striæ costate, convergent in the middle, radiate towards the ends; on front view, frustule slightly constricted, with the angles slightly rounded; length ·0017, breadth ·0006.
Ralfs, in Pritch., p. 905. Donkin, N. H. Brit. Diat., p. 57, Pl. viii., fig. 8.—Pinnularia fortis, Gregory, Q. J. M. S., Trans., 1856, p. 47, Pl. v., fig. 19. Rab. Fl. Eur. Alg., sect. i., p. 215.

Lough Gill, Co. Kerry. Arran Islands, Co. Galway. Malahide, Co. Dublin.

Navicula northumbrica, (Donkin). Marine.
Valve narrow, lanceolate; ends acute. Striæ linear, convergent in middle, where they are strongly marked; length ·0019, breadth ·0004. Frustule on front view slightly constricted. (Plate 34, fig. 16.)
Donkin, Q. J. M. S., 1861, p. 9, Pl. i., fig. 5; N. H. Brit. Diat., p. 54, Pl. viii., fig. 1. Rab. Fl. Eur. Alg., sect. i., p. 175.

Bannow, Co. Wexford. Salt ditches near the town of Galway.

Navicula arenaria, (Donkin). Marine.
Valve lanceolate, narrow; ends acute, produced and slightly constricted. Striæ costate, convergent; length ·0019, breadth ·0004. Frustule on front view very slightly constricted. (Plate 34, fig. 17.)
Donkin, Q. J. M. S., 1861, p. 10, Pl. i., fig. 9; N. H. Brit. Diat., p. 56, Pl. viii., fig. 5. Rab. Fl. Eur. Alg., sect. i., p. 177.

Portmarnock, Co. Dublin.

Navicula inflexa, (Gregory). Marine.
Valve lanceolate; slightly depressed at the extremities. Striæ costate, convergent; length ·0018, breadth ·0004. (Plate 34, fig. 18.)
Ralfs, in Pritch., p. 905. Donkin, N. H. Brit. Diat., p. 54,

Pl. viii., fig. 2.—Pinnularia inflexa, Gregory, Q. J. M. S., 1856, Trans., p. 48, Pl. v., fig. 20. Rab. Fl. Eur. Alg., sect. i., p. 218. The depression of the valve at the ends is marked by a well-defined line which renders the species easy of identification.

Ballysodare, Co. Sligo. Lough Gill, Co. Kerry. Malahide, Co. Dublin.

Navicula hungarica, (Grunow). Fresh water.
Valve small, oblong; elliptical, ends rounded. Striæ subdistant, strongly costate, radiate; central nodule large; length ·0009, breadth ·0045. (Plate 34, fig. 19.)
Grunow, Verhand. der K. K. Zool. Bot. Gesell., Band x., 1860, p. 539, T. iii., fig. 30. Schumann, Diat. der Hohen Tatra, p. 76. Rab. Fl. Eur. Alg., sect. i., p. 190.

Lough Gill, Co. Kerry. Ditch near town of Sligo. Lough Mask, near Tourmakeady, Co. Mayo.

Navicula carassius, (Ehr.) Fresh water.
Valves small, broadly elliptical; ends broadly and shortly produced. Striæ costate; radiate; length ·0007, breadth ·0003. (Plate 34, fig. 20.)
Kütz. Bac., p. 95, T. xxviii., fig. 67. The description and figure represent the valve as unstriate, but the striæ are quite obvious. Grunow, Verhand. der K. K. Zool. Bot. Gesell., Band x., p. 537, T. iii., fig. 31, and T. iv., fig. 11. Ralfs, in Pritch., p. 900. Donkin, N. II. Brit. Diat., p. 20, Pl. iii., fig. 7. It is more than doubtful if the form described by Donkin as Navicula carassius belongs to this species. The figure represents the form as very much longer, the ends finer and more produced, than is the case in Navicula carassius; the striæ too, are described as granular, the striæ in Navicula carassius are linear. Donkin regards the species as identical with Navicula lacustris, Gregory, Q. J. M. S., 1856, p. 6, Pl. i., fig. 23 b., but the true Navicula carassius is broadly elliptical, and not linear, as the former is represented to be. Schumann, Diat der Hohen Tatra, p. 68.

Glenchree, Kilcool, Co. Wicklow. Kilcock, Royal Canal, Enfield, Co. Kildare. Dundrum, Co. Dublin. Killeshin, Queen's Co. Caum Lough, near Tralee, Arraglen, Co. Kerry.

Navicula mutica, (Kütz.) Fresh or brackish water.
Valve small, broadly elliptical. Striæ punctate, radiate; length ·0005, breadth ·0003. (Plate 34, fig. 21.)
Kütz. Bac., p. 95, T. iii., fig. 32, who found the form in rain pools mixed with salt water. Grunow, Verhand. der K. K. Zool.

Bot. Gesell., Band x., p. 538, T. v., fig. 16, who found the species in fresh water as well as in brackish. Ralfs, in Pritch., p. 905. Schumann, Diat. der Hohen Tatra, p. 69. Rab. Fl. Eur. Alg., sect. i., p. 185. It is not improbable that this species is identical with the form described by Gregory as Navicula lepida, var. B.? Q. J. M. S., 1856, p. 7, Pl. i., fig. 25, B.

Bannow, Co. Wexford. Lough Gill, Co. Kerry. In these, fresh water forms and marine were mingled. Glenchree, Killakee, Co. Dublin. Lough Mask, near Tourmakeady, Co. Mayo. The three last-named localities were wholly free from marine influences. Hence I consider that though the form has been found in brackish water, it is essentially a fresh water species.

Navicula semen, (Ehr.) Fresh water.
Valve linear, elliptical, broad; ends broadly and shortly produced. Striæ costate; convergent in middle, radiate towards ends; length ·0018, breadth ·0008. (Plate 34, fig. 22.)
Kütz. Bac., p. 99, T. xxviii., fig. 49, who attributes the species to Ehrenberg. Wm. Sm., B. D., Vol. i., p. 50, Pl. xvi., fig. 141. Heiberg, De Danske Diat., p. 82. Ralfs, in Pritch., p. 900. Donkin, N. H. Brit. Diat., p. 21. Pl. iii., fig. 8. Schumann, Diat. der Hohen Tatra, p. 68.

Stream, Bellarena, Co. Derry. Lough Mourne deposit, Co. Antrim.

Navicula humilis, (Donkin). Fresh water.
Valve small, inflated in the middle, with broad capitate ends. Striæ costate, coarse, subdistant, radiate; central nodule large; length ·0010, breadth ·0003. On front view, frustule quadrangular, slightly constricted in the middle; costæ divergent, leaving a considerable space about the central nodule, which latter appears very highly developed.
Donkin, N. H. Brit. Diat., p. 67, Pl. x., fig. 7. Donkin considers this form identical with Navicula inflata, var. Gregory, Q. J. M. S., 1855, Pl. ii., fig. 20 c.

Lough Gill, Co. Kerry. Lough Mask, near Tourmakeady, Co. Mayo.

Navicula inflata, (Kütz.) Fresh water.
Valve small, inflated in the middle; ends narrowed, produced, and scarcely capitate. Striæ closely granular, radiate; length ·0010, breadth ·00035. (Plate 34, fig. 23.)
Kütz. Bac., p. 99, T. iii., fig. 36. Wm. Sm., B. D., Vol. i., p. 50, Pl. xvii., fig. 158. Grunow, Verhand. der K. K. Zool. Bot. Gesell., Band x., 1860, p. 538, T. iv., fig. 41. Ralfs, in Pritch., p. 899. Hei-

berg, De Dansko Diat., p. 82. Donkin, N. H. Brit. Diat., p. 21, Pl. iii., fig. 9.

Lough Mask, near Tourmakeady, Co. Mayo. Ditch near town of Wexford. River near Glencar, Co. Kerry. Rock Mills, Co. Cork. Stream Bellarena, Co. Derry. Glenchree, Kilcool, Co. Wicklow. RiverDodder, Killakee, Co. Dublin.

Navicula mesolepta, (Ehr.) Fresh water.

Valve narrow, triundulate; ends narrowed, capitate; striæ costate, radiate. Length ·0025, breadth ·0006.

Kütz. Bac., p. 101, T. xxviii., fig. 33, and T. xxx., fig. 34, who attributes the species to Ehrenberg. Grunow, Verhand. der K. K. Zool. Bot. Gesell., Band x., 1860, p. 520. Ralfs, in Pritch., p. 894. Cleve, Om Svenska och Norska Diat., p. 225.—Pinnularia mesolepta, Wm. Sm., B. D., Vol. i., p. 58, Pl. xix., fig. 182.

Lough Mourne deposit. Common specially in mountain districts.

Navicula anglica, (Ralfs). Fresh water.

Valve broadly elliptical; ends produced; striæ costate; convergent in the middle, radiate towards the ends; length ·0015, breadth·00066, (Plate 34, fig. 24.)

Ralfs, in Pritch., p. 900, who considers the form identical with Navicula tumida, Wm. Smith. Donkin, N. H. Brit. Diat., p. 35, Pl. v., fig. 11. The latter author likewise coincides with Ralfs as to the identity of the species with that of Smith referred to. There is, however, a considerable difference between the forms. In Navicula anglica the valve is larger, the ends less capitate, the striæ more distant than in the case of Navicula tumida; and whereas in the latter the striæ are punctate, in the present form they are plainly costate. Schumann, Diat. der Hohen Tatra, p. 68.

Killakee. Trinity College Botanical Gardens, Co. Dublin. Ditch near Sligo. Lough Gill, Co. Kerry. Lough Mask, near Tourmakeady, Co. Mayo. Dundalk, Co. Louth.

Nav. sublinearis, (Donkin). Fresh water.

Valve in all respects like the tpyical species, except that the outline is nearly linear, and the produced ends wider; length ·0012, breadth ·0005.

Donkin, N. H. Brit. Diat., p. 35. Pl. v., fig. 11 b.

Killakee, Co. Dublin.

Navicula cryptocephala, (Kütz.) Fresh water.

Valve small, narrow, elliptical, with produced slightly capitate ends. Striæ fine, linear radiate; length ·0012, breadth ·0003. (Plate 34, fig. 25.)

Kütz. Bac. p. 95, T. iii., fig. 20. Wm. Sm., B. D., Vol. i., p. 53,

Pl. xvii., fig. 155, Ralfs, in Pritch., p. 901; Cleve, Om Svenska och Norska Diat., p. 228. Donkin, N. H. Brit. Diat., p. 37, Pl. v., fig. 14. Schumann, Diat. der Hohen Tatra, p. 68.

Tacumshane, Co. Wexford. Bowen's Court, Co. Cork. Lough Gill, Co. Kerry. Lough Mask, near Tourmakeady, Co. Mayo. Dysart, Co. Waterford.

Navicula angustata, (Wm. Smith). Fresh water.
Valve very narrow, elliptical; ends produced and slightly capitate. Striæ fine, linear, radiate; length ·0016, breadth ·0003. (Plate 34, fig. 26.)
Wm. Sm., B. D., Vol. i., p. 52, Pl. xvii., fig. 156. Ralfs, in Pritch., p. 901. Castracane, Cataloga di Diat. raccolte nella Val. Intrasca, p. 12. Schumann, Diat. der Hohen Tatra, p. 68.—Navicula cryptocephala, var. rhyncocephala, Grunow, Verhand. der K. K. Zool. Bot. Gesell., Band x., 1860, p. 527, T. iv., fig. 28*b*.

Bantry, Co. Cork. Black Castle, Co. Wicklow. Malahide, Co. Dublin. Lough Mask, near Tourmakeady, Co. Mayo.

Navicula lagerstedtii, N. S. Fresh water.
Valve small, rhombic; ends slightly produced. Striæ obviously punctate, radiate, sub-distant; when the centre is not exactly in focus, there is the appearance of a narrow stauroform band, which disappears when properly focused; length ·0010, breadth ·0005. (Plate 34, fig. 27.)

Lough Mask, near Tourmakeady, Co. Mayo. Lough Gill, Co. Kerry. In the latter, marine and fresh water species were mingled, but in the former locality marine influence was impossible; the form is therefore to be regarded as inhabiting fresh water.

Navicula gastrum, (Ehr). Fresh water.
Valve rhombic; ends scarcely produced. Striæ linear, convergent in the middle, radiate towards the ends; length ·0018, breadth ·0009. (Plate 34, fig. 28.)
Kütz. Bac., p. 94, T. xxviii., fig. 56, who regards the species as identical with Pinnularia gastrum, Ehrenberg. Ralfs, in Pritch., p. 900. Donkin, N. H. Brit. Diat., p. 22, Pl. iii., fig. 10. This figure represents the form as much narrower, and the ends more produced than is the case in my specimens.—Pinnularia gastrum, Rab. Süssw. Diat., p. 44, T. vi., fig. 15. This last figure represents the striæ as parallel, which is not accurate. Gregory, Q. J. M. S., 1855, p. 41. Plate iv., fig. 20.

Dundalk, Co. Louth. Lough Gill, Co. Kerry. Lough Mask, near Tourmakeady, Co. Mayo. Lough Mourne deposit.

Navicula binodis, (Ehr). Fresh water.

Valve small, narrow, incurved; ends produced, apiculate. Striæ fine, linear, radiate; length ·0012, breadth ·0004; breadth in the middle ·00035. (Plate 34, fig. 29.)

Kützing (Bac., p. 100, T. iii., fig. 35,) considers the form identical with that so named by Ehrenberg. Wm. Sm., B. D., Vol. i., p. 53, Pl. xvii., fig. 159. Rab. Süssw. Diat., p. 41, T. v., fig. 5, and Fl. Eur. Alg., sect. i., p. 203. Ralfs, in Pritch., p. 893. Castracane, Catalogo di Diat. raccolte nella Val. Intrasca, p. 12. Heiberg, De Danske Diat., p. 83. Cleve, Om Svenska och Norska Diat., p. 227. Donkin, N. H. Brit. Diat., p. 38, Pl. vi., fig. 3. Schumann, Diat. der Hohen Tatra, p. 77.

Powerscourt, Co. Wicklow. Lough Gill, Co. Kerry. Donkin considers this species as one which occurs frequently in England; it is, however, one of very rare occurrence in Ireland.

Navicula dicephala, (Ehr.) Fresh water.

Valve small, narrow, linear, narrowing towards the produced slightly capitate ends. Striæ obvious, convergent in the middle, radiate towards the ends; length ·0014, breadth ·00055. (Plate 34, fig. 30.)

Kütz. Bac., p. 96, T. xxviii., figs. 60 and 62; these figures incorrectly describe the striæ as parallel. Kützing attributes the species to Ehrenberg. Wm. Sm., B. D., Vol. i., p. 53, Pl. xvii., fig. 157. Grunow, Verhand. der K. K. Zool. Bot. Gesell., Band x,, p. 538, T. iv., fig. 45. Ralfs, in Pritch., p. 902.

Lough Gill, Co. Kerry. Lough Neagh, near Lurgan, Co. Armagh. Camolin, Co. Wexford. Friarstown, Lucan, Killakee, River Dodder, Co. Dublin. Cushendun, Co. Antrim. Powerscourt, Co. Wicklow. Lough Mourne deposit.

Navicula rhyncocephala, (Kütz.) Fresh water.

Valve narrow, elliptical; ends considerably produced, not capitate. Striæ distinct, closely moniliform, radiate; length ·0025, breadth ·0006. (Plate 34, fig. 31.)

Kütz. Bac., p. 152, T. xxx., fig. 35. Wm. Sm., B. D., Vol. i., p. 47, Pl. xvi., fig. 132. Grunow, Verhand. der K. K. Zool. Bot. Gesell., Band x., 1860, p. 530, T. iv., fig. 32. Heiberg, De Danske Diat., p. 82. Ralfs, in Pritch., p. 900, Pl. vii., fig. 68. Cleve, Om Svenska och Norska Diat., p. 227. Schumann, Diat. der Hohen Tatra, p. 68. Rab. Fl. Eur. Alg., sect. i., p. 196. Donkin, N. H. Brit. Diat., p. 38, Pl. vi., fig. 4.

River Dodder, ditch, Dundrum, Co. Dublin. Caumlough, near Tralee, Co. Kerry. Ulster Canal, near Poyntzpass, Co. Armagh. Kilcool, Co. Wicklow.

Navicula globifera, N. S. Fresh water.

Valve narrow, margin slightly constricted; ends constricted and broadly capitate. Striæ extremely fine, close, convergent; length ·0018, breadth ·0003. (Plate 34, fig. 32.)

This form is very similar to that described by Gregory as Pinnularia globiceps, Q. J. M. S., 1856, p. 10, Pl. i., fig. 34; but differs in the following respects: in Gregory's form the valve is obviously expanded in the middle; in this it is linear, with the appearance of a slight constriction in the middle; the striæ in this are much finer, and reach the median line, instead of leaving a central stauroform free band, as is the case with Pinnularia globiceps.

Camolin, Co. Wexford.

Navicula rostellifera, (Gregory). Marine or brackish water.

Valve minute, narrow, linear; narrowed towards the ends, which are apiculate. Striæ costate, convergent in the middle; frustule on front view constricted in the middle; length of valve .0013, breadth ·0003. (Plate 34, fig. 33.)

Pinnularia apiculata, Gregory, Q. J. M. S., 1856, p. 41, Pl. iv., fig. 21. This form appears to be the same which Donkin describes as Navicula apiculata, De Brèbisson, and Pinnularia rostellata, Gregory, Diat., of Clyde, p. 488, Pl. ix., fig. 20. See Donkin, N. H. Brit. Diat., p. 56, Pl. viii., fig. 6. Gregory himself evidently regarded the forms as distinct; and comparison of the two compels me to coincide with that eminent observer. Navicula apiculata, De Brèbisson, and Pinnularia rostellata, Gregory, are obviously identical, and quite different from the present, which is much smaller and narrower in proportion; the striæ being very strong, and reaching the median line, while in this other they leave a considerable blank space about the central nodule; the rostrate ends too in the latter are much produced, while in this species they are very short. Gregory's specific term apiculata having been appropriated by De Brèbisson, ought to drop, and the form so distinctly described by Gregory bear another designation, to avoid confusion.

Lough Gill, Co. Kerry. Portmarnock, Co. Dublin.

Navicula cancellata, (Donkin). Marine.

Valve large, narrow, linear, with cuneate ends. Striæ strongly costate; convergent in the middle, nearly parallel towards the ends; length ·0036, breadth ·0006. Frustule on front view slightly constricted, the costæ appearing in a broad band. (Plate 34, fig. 34.)

Donkin, N. H. Brit. Diat., p. 55, Pl. viii. fig. 4. Navicula truncata, Donkin, Q. J. M. S., 1861, p. 9, Pl. i., fig. 4, and changed for the present designation, the former name having been anticipated by Kützing.—Pinnularia truncata, Rab. Fl. Eur. Alg., sect. i., p. 217.

Arran Islands; Stomachs of Ascidians, Roundstone Bay; Stomachs of Ascidians, Broadhaven Bray, Co. Galway. Malahide, Portmarnock, Co. Dublin.

Navicula minor, (Gregory). Marine or brackish water.

Valve small; linear with cuneate ends, striæ linear, nearly parallel in the middle; slightly radiate towards the ends; length ·0012, breadth ·0004. (Plate 34, fig. 35.)

Gregory, Diat. of Clyde, p. 477, Pl. ix., fig. 1. Gregory mentions that in this species the striæ do not reach the median line. In this particular, the present form does not answer Gregory's description, inasmuch as the striæ plainly reach the median line, but in all other respects there is such agreement as to make me think the forms are identical. Ralfs agrees with Gregory in all particulars, p. 909. Donkin describes a form under this name which he regards as identical with that described by Gregory. See N. H. Brit. Diat., p. 57, Pl. viii., fig. 7. The forms, however, are obviously different, that of Donkin being elliptical, lanceolate, while Gregory's is linear, with cuneated apices.

Piles of wooden bridge, Dollymount Strand, Co. Dublin. Lough Gill, Co. Kerry.

(m) *Diaphanæ*. *Striæ not observable.*

Navicula perpusilla, (Grunow). Fresh water.

Valve minute, linear, oblong, with rounded ends, and slightly expanded in the middle; length ·0005, breadth ·0002. (Plate 34, fig. 36.)

Grunow, Verhand. der K. K. Zool. Bot. Gesell., Band x., 1860, p. 552, T. iv., fig. 7 *a*.

Lough Mask, near Tourmakeady, Co. Mayo.

Navicula seminulum, (Grunow). Fresh water.

Valve very minute, oblong, elliptical, with rounded ends; length ·0006, breadth ·00025. (Plate 34, fig 37.)

Grunow, Verhand. der K. K. Zool. Bot. Gesell., Band x., 1860, p. 552, T. iv., fig. 2.

Lough Mask, near Tourmakeady, Co. Mayo.

EXPLANATION OF CONTRACTIONS AND LIST OF REFERENCES.

Agardh, Conspect.—Conspectus Criticus Diatomacearum. 1830.
" Syst.—Systema Algarum. 1824.
A. N. H., or Ann. Nat. Hist.—Annals and Magazine of Natural History.
Bailey Mic.—Microscopical Observations in Smithsonian Contributions to Knowledge. 1850.
Berkeley.—Papers in Ann. Nat. Hist.
Brightwell.—Papers in Quarterly Journal of Microscopical Science.
Castracane, Catalogo, &c.—Catalogo de Diatomea raccolte nella Val Intrasca. Genova. 1866.
Cleve, Om Svenska, &c.—Om Svenska och Norska Diatomacéer Ofversigt af K. Vetenskaps-Akad. Förhandlingar. Stockholm. 1868.
De Brébisson, Notes on, &c.—Notes on some French Diatoms, Journal Queckett Club. April, 1870.
De Brébisson, Diat. du, &c.—Diatomées marines du Litoral de Cherbourg.
Donkin.—Papers in Quart. Jour. Micros. Science.
Donkin, N. H. Brit. Diat.—Natural History of the British Diatomaceæ. London. Van Voorst (in course of publication).
Ehr. Abh.—Ehrenberg, Abhandlungen, Berlin Akademie.
Ehr. Infus.—Ehrenberg, Die Infusionsthierchen. 1838.
Ehr. Mic.—Ehrenberg, Microgeologie.
Gregory.—Papers in Quart. Jour. Micros. Science.
Gregory, Diat. of Clyde.—New forms of Marine Diatomaceæ found in the Frith of Clyde. Edinburgh, 1857.
Greville.—Papers in Quart. Jour. Micros. Science.
Grev. Brit. Flora.—In Hooker's British Flora (Cryptogamia).
Grunow.—Verhand. &c., Ueber neue oder ungenügend gekannte Algen in Verhandlungen der K. K. Zoologisch-botanischen Gesellschaft in Wien.
Grunow.—Reise S. M. Novara um die Erde. 1868.
Harvey, Manual.—Manual of the British Algæ. London, 1841.
Heiberg.—De Danske Diatomeer. Kjobenhavn. 1863.
Kitton.—Papers in Science Gossip.
Kütz. Bac.—Kützing, Die Kieselschaligen Baccillarien. 1844.
Kütz. Sp. Alg.—Kützing, Species Algarum. 1849.
Lagerstedt, Sötv. Diat., &c.—Sötvattens-Diatomaceer från Spetsbergen och Beeren Eiland. Stockholm. 1873.
Lyngbye, Tentamen Hydrophytologie Danicæ. 1819.
Pfitzer.—Ueber Bau und Entwicklung der Bacillariaceen. Bonn. 1871.
Rab. Fl. Eur. Alg.—Rabenhorst, Flora Europæa Algarum. Leipsic. 1864.
Rab. Süssw. Diat.—Rabenhorst, Die Süsswasser Diatomaceen. Leipsig. 1853.
Ralfs.—Papers in Ann. Nat. Hist.
Ralfs in Pritchard's History of Infusoria. London. 1861.
Roper.—Papers in Quart. Jour. Micros. Science.
Schmidt, Atlas, &c.—Atlas der Diatomaceen Kunde. Parts 1 to 4. 1875.
Schmidt.—Die Diatomaceen aus den Grundproben der Nordsee fahrt. Berlin. 1875.
Schumann, Diat.—Die Diatomeen der Hohen Tatra. Wien. 1867.
Schumann, Die Preussische Diat.—Die Preussische Diatomeen, *vide* Schriften der Physik-Oek. Gesellschaft zu Königsberg. 1867.
Thwaites.—Papers in Ann. Nat. Hist.
W. S., B. D.—W. Smith, Synopsis of British Diatomaceæ. 2 Vols. 1853 and 1856.
Wallich.—Papers in Quart. Jour. Mic. Science.
Walker-Arnott.—Papers in Quart. Jour. Mic. Science.
Weisse.—Papers in Bull. de l'Acad. Imp. des Sciences St. Petersbourg. Tome xii. 1867.

INDEX TO REPORT, PART I., ON THE IRISH DIATOMACEÆ.

The Families, Sub-families, and Genera are printed in Small Capitals, the Species in ordinary type. Synonyms are marked with an asterisk.

abrupta, 293.
ACHLAMYDIÆ, 337.
acicularis, 304.
ACTINOCYCLUS, 268.
ACTINOPTYCHUS, 266.
acrosphœria, 346.
acuminata, 355.
acuta, 407.
acuta,* 282.
acutiuscula, 408.
adriaticum, 319.
æqualis, 282.
æstiva, 384.
affinis (Syn.), 311.
affinis (Nav.), 367.
affinis,* 367.
alpina, 342.
alternans, 278.
ambigua, 360.
amblyoceros, 278.
americana, 351.
amphicephala, 299.
amphiceros, 295.
amphigomphus, 367.
AMPHIPLEURA, 281, 320.
AMPHIPLEUREÆ, 320.
amphirhynchus, 307.
amphisbæna, 363.
AMPHITETRAS, 275.
anglica, 414.
anglicus, 270.
angulosa, 364.
angusta, 350.
angustata, 415.
anomalum, 287.
antediluviana, 275.
antiqua, 257.
apiculata (Mast.), 327.
apiculata (Nav.), 349.
apiculata,* 376, 416.
apis, 400.

ARACHNOIDISCUS, 265.
archeriana, 398.
arcuatum, 318.
arcus, 311.
arenaria (Orth.), 251.
arenaria (Nav.), 411.
areolata, 268.
argus, 269.
arraniensis, 395.
ASTERIONELLA, 281.
atmospherica,* 259.
AULACODISCUS, 270.
AULACOSEIRA,* 254.
AULISCUS, 270.
aurea,* 283.
aurichalcia, 251.
aurita, 274.

bacillum, 351.
baculus, 297.
bayleyii, 275.
balfouriana, 316.
barbatula, 310.
barkeriana, 362.
BERKELEYA, 331.
biceps, 302.
biceps,* 352.
biccapitata, 352.
BIDDULPHIA, 272.
biddulphia,* 275.
biddulphianum,* 275.
BIDDULPHIEÆ, 271.
binodis, 416.
boeckii (Breb.), 338.
boeckii (Nav.), 348.
bombus, 401.
borealis, 345.
borrerii, 246.
BREBISSONIA, 337.
brebissonii, 350.

Index to Report on the Irish Diatomaceæ.

cærulea, 358.
cancellata, 417.
capitata (Syn.), 305.
capitata (Mast.), 327.
capucina, 282.
carassius, 412.
cardinalis, 341.
centralis, 260.
CERATAULUS,* 271, 273.
CERATONEIS,* 281.
ceres, 347.
cervinus, 262.
chrystallinum, 297.
clavata, 386.
CLAVATÆ, 386.
clepsydra, 347.
cleviana, 409.
closeii, 326.
cluthensis, 380.
cocconeiformis, 370.
coffeiformis, 297.
COLLETONEMA, 329.
collisiana, 384.
comoides, 335.
concinnus, 261.
CONFERVA,* 248.
constricta (Nav.), 353.
constricta, var. (Nav.), 393.
construens, 283.
convergens, 325.
COSCINODISCUS, 259.
coscinodiscus, 255.
costata (Dent.), 285.
costata (Mast.), 328.
costata (Nav.), 393.
costatum, 290.
crabro, 404.
CRASPEDODISCUS, 266.
CRASSINERVES, 374.
crassinervia, 375.
crassus, 269.
crotonensis, 283.
crucifera (Nav.), var., 353.
crucifera (Nav.), 354.
crucigerum, 333.
chryptocephala, 414.
crux, 369.
cuneata, 355.
cuneata, var., 394.
cuspidata, 357.
CUSPIDATÆ, 357.
cuspis, 358.
CYCLOTELLA, 255.
CYMATOSEIRA, 281.
cynthia, 395.
cyprinus, 409.

dallasiana, 259.
danica, var. (Syn.), 309.

danica (Amph.), 322.
danseii, 326.
davidsoniana, 361.
davidsonii, 385.
debilis, 313.
decipiens, 359.
delginensis, 373.
delicatissima,* 300.
denarius, 267.
DENTICELLA,* 272.
DENTICULA, 280, 285.
denticulata, 405.
desmogonium, 281.
DIADESMIS, 337.
DIATOMA, 280, 281, 291.
dicephala, 416.
DICKIEA, 328.
dickieii, 252.
didyma, 402.
didyma,* 400, 403.
digito-radiata, 409.
dilwinii, 336.
DIMEREGRAMMA, 280, 281, 288.
directa, 406.
DIRECTÆ, 406.
dirhynchus, 375.
DISCOPLEA, *
distans (Mel.), 248.
distans (Dim.), 289.
distans (Nav.), 343.
divaricata,* 379.
divergens (Schiz.), 333.
divergens (Nav.), 345.
divergens,* 405.
donkinea, 389.
donkinii, 399.
DORYPHORA,* 281.
dubia, 367.
duodenarius, 267.

ehrenbergii (Cos.), 264.
ehrenbergii (Arach.). 265.
elegans (Odont.), 288.
elegans (Nav.), 363.
elliptica (Nav), 384.
elliptica, var., 391.
elongatum, 292.
emarginatus, 318.
enervis, 280.
entomon, 401.
entomon,* 403.
ergadensis, 409.
erythræa,* 380.
esox, 369.
EUCAMPIA, 271.
eudoxia, 397.
eugenia, 396.
EUPODISCUS, 269.
excentricus, 270.

exigium, 278.
exilis, 406.
eximium, 330.
expleta, 390.

fasciculata,* 305.
favus, 277.
fenestrata, 317.
fimbriatus, 264.
firma,* 366.
flocculosa, 317.
follis, 369.
forcipata, 392.
forficula, 397.
fortis, 411.
FRAGILARIA, 280, 281.
FRAGILARIEÆ, 280.
fragilis, 331.
franciscæ, 389.
frauenfeldii, 312.
FRUSTULIA,* 375.
fulgens, 298.
fulva, 358.
fulvus, 269.
fusca, 383.
fuscata, 378.
FUSCATÆ, 383.

GALLIONELLA,* 248.
gallionii, 310.
galvagensis, 410.
gastrum, 415.
gibba, 348.
gibberula,* 368.
giberrula, 368.
GIBBOSÆ, 347.
gigas, 261.
globifera, 417.
gracillima, 356.
gracillimum, 336.
gracilis (Syn.), 300.
gracilis, var., 303.
gracilis (Nav.), 407.
GRAMMATOPHORA, 315.
GRAMMONEMA,* 281.
grande, 291.
granulata, 254.
gregorii (Cos.), 263.
gregorii (Nav.), 403.
grevilleii (Mast.), 328.
grevilleii (Schz.), 334.
grundleriana, 366.
GRUNOWIA,* 286.
grunovii, 362.
grunovii, var., 392.

harrissonii, 296.
hebes, 364.
helmentosum, 334.

hemiptera, 349.
hennedyi, 387.
heufleri, 411.
hibernica, 389.
hibernicus, 271.
hormoides, 250.
humerosa, 378.
humilis, 413.
hungarica, 412.
hyalina, 293.
HYDROSERA, 272.
hyemale, 287.

icostauron, 350.
incisa, 404.
incurva, 377.
incurvata, 399.
inflata, 413.
inflata,* 369.
inflatum, 288.
integra, 356.
intermedia, 405.
interrupta (Tess.), 320.
interrupta (Nav.), 400.
investiens, 299.
iridis, 366.
ISTHMIA, 279.
ISTHMIEÆ, 279.

johnsonii, 373.
jurgensii, 283.

kittoniana, 388.
kotzschyi, 370.
kutzingiana, 256.

laciniatum, 335.
lacustris (Tetr.), 318.
lacustris (Nav.), 380.
lævissima, 367.
lagerstedtii, 415.
lanceolata, var. (Syn.), 304.
lanceolata (Mast.), 324.
lanceolata, var. (Nav.), 344.
lanceolata, var. (Nav.), 382.
lanceolata (Nav.), 406.
lata, 371.
latissima, 379.
latiuscula, 361.
LATIUSCULÆ, 361.
lepida,* 413.
leptoceros, 295.
liber, 365.
liburnica (Raph.), 296.
liburnica (Nav.), 372.
limosa, 368.
LIMOSÆ, 366.
linearis, var. (Syn.), 305.
linearis, var. (Nav.), 371.

linearis, var. (Nav.), 382.
lineata, 365.
lineatus, 264.
lineolata,* 375.
litoralis,* 361.
longa, 344.
longiceps, 306.
longissima, 307.
lorenziana, 296.
lucida, 379.
lunaris, 301.
LYRATÆ, 390.
lyra, 391.
LYSIGONIUM, 248.

macula, 357.
macilenta, 316.
maculata, 250.
maculosa, 381.
major, 341.
marginata, 398.
marginatus, 264.
marina, 315.
marina,* 252, 377.
marinum, 289.
MASTOGLOIA, 323.
maxima (Frag.), 283.
maxima (Nav.), 371.
MELOSIRA, 246.
MELOSIREÆ, 246.
menapiensis, 346.
meneghiniana, 256.
meniscus, 379.
MERIDION, 281.
mesodon, 287.
mesolepta (Frag.), 284.
mesolepta (Nav.), 414.
microstauron, 354.
minima, 293.
minor, 265.
minor, var. (Nav.), 392.
minor (Nav.), 418.
minor,* 262.
minus, 289.
minutissima,* 304.
minutula,* 394.
minutum, 319.
MONILIFERÆ, 377.
moniliformis, 268.
moniliformis,* 248
montagnei, 250.
moreii, 388.
mucosum, 333.
musca, 399.
musca,* 398.
mutabilis, 285.
mutua, 412.

nanum, 289.

NAVICULA, 339.
NAVICULEÆ, 322.
nebulosa, 387.
neglectum, 331.
nervosa, 279.
nitescens, 389.
nitidus, 263.
NITZSCHIA, 281.
nitzschiodes, 312.
NOBILES, 340.
nobilis, 340.
nodosa, 352.
normanni, 263.
northumbrica, 411.
notarisii,* 306.
nummuloides, 248.
nummuloides,* 250.

obliquata,* 280.
obliquatum,* 280.
oblonga, 344.
oblongella, 376.
obtusa (Dent.), 285.
obtusa (Syn.), 308.
obtusa,* 364.
obtusum, 336.
ocellata,* 287.
oculus iridis, 260.
ODONTELLA,* 272.
ODONTIDIUM, 280, 281, 286.
ODONTODISCUS, 270.
OMPHALOPELTA, 268.
operculata, 257.
orichalcea, 353.
ornatus, 266.
ORTHOSIRA, 250.
ovalis, 385.
ovulum, 361.
oxyrhynchus, 306.

pachyptera, 342.
palpebralis, 364.
pandura,* 404.
papillifera, 372.
papillosa, 258.
PARALIA,* 252.
parasiticum, 335.
parva, var. (Nav.), 348.
parva, var. (Nav.), 386.
parva, var. (Nav.), 397.
pectinalis,* 355.
personis,* 367.
pellucida, 321.
pellucida,* 399.
peregrina, 408.
perforatus, 261.
perfrusilla, 418.
PERSTRIATÆ, 406.
pfitzeriana, 405.

pinnata, 329.
PINNULARIA,* 339.
pinnularia, 354.
pixidicula,* 266.
PLAGIOGRAMMA, 280, 281, 290.
plumbicolor, 372.
PODOSIRA, 249.
prætexta, 387.
producta (Nav.), 370.
producta, var., 380.
pulchella (Bid.), 275.
pulchella (Syn.), 303.
pulchra, 382.
punctata (Orth.), 254.
punctata (Cyc.), 251.
punctata (Nav.), 380.
punctulata, 377.
punctulatus, 265.
pusilla, 381.
putealis, 312.
pygmœa, 394.

quadrata, 378.
quarnerensis, 361.
quinquelocularis, 275.

radians, 300.
radiata, 273.
radiatus, 262.
radiatus,* 273.
radiolatus, 262.
radiosa, 407.
RADIOSÆ, 407.
RALFSIA, 293.
ralfsii, 268.
ramosissimun, 334.
rectangulata, 343.
regina, 278.
retusa, 355.
RHABDONEMA, 318.
RHAPHONEIS, 280, 281, 294.
rhombica (Nav.), 358.
rhombica, var., 384.
rhomboides, 374.
rhombus (Bidd.), 274.
rhombus (Rhap.), 295.
rhyncocephala, 416.
rhyncocephala,* var., 416.
richardsonii, 389.
roeseana, 251, 255.
rostellata,* 349.
rostellifera, 417.
rostellum, 376.
rostrata, 359.
rotula, 258.
rupestris, 347.

salina, 310.
sandriana, 388.

sansegana, 395.
scalaris, 354.
schmidtii, 395.
SCHIZONEMA, 332.
scopulorum,* 373.
scotica, 259.
sculptus, 270.
scutelloides (Rhap.), 295.
scutelloides (Nav.), 381.
scutellum, 396.
sedenarius, 267.
seductilis, 393.
semen, 413.
seminalum, 410.
semiplena, 364.
senarius, 267.
septemlocularis, 275.
sorians, 374.
serpentina, 316.
simulans, 373.
sinuatum, 286.
smithii (Cos.), 262.
smithii (Syn.), 313.
smithii (Mast.), 327.
smithii (Schiz.), 333.
smithii (Nav.), 383.
smithii,* 403.
solaris, 410.
spathulata, 310.
spectabilis, 390.
sphærophora, 360.
spinosa,* 253, 255.
splendens, 308.
splendida, 402.
splendida,* 399.
staurophora, 352.
staurophorum, 290.
stauroptera, 350.
STAUROSIRA, 281.
stellaris, 261.
stokesiana, 389.
STRIATELLA, 319.
STRIATELLEÆ, 314.
striatula, 283.
sub-capitata, 356.
sub-cincta, 398.
sub-flexilis, 247.
sub-linearis, 414.
sub-orbicularis, var., 387.
sub-orbicularis, var., 391.
sub-orbicularis (Nav.), 396.
sub-rotunda, 383.
sub-salina, 363.
subula, 371.
sulcata, 252.
superba, 299.
SURIRELLEÆ, 281.
SYNEDRA, 280, 281, 296.
SYSTEPHANIA,* 271.

TABELLARIA, 317.
tabellaria (Ralfsia), 293.
tabellaria (Nav.), 346.
tabellaria,* 283, 284.
tabulata, 311.
tenera,* 300.
tenue (Odont.), 288.
tenue (Diat.), 292.
tenuicollis, 283.
tenuirostris, 360.
tenuissima, 300.
termes, 353.
TESSELLA, 320.
TETRACYCLUS, 317.
TOXARIUM, 301.
translucida, 372.
trevelyana, 344.
TRICERATIEÆ, 275.
TRICERATIUM, 275, 277.
TRIFASCIATÆ, 394.
trilocularis,* 275.
TRINACRIA, 275, 278.
TRIPODISCUS,* 269.
truncata, 368.
truncata,* 368, 417.
tumens, 359.
tumida, 382.
tumida var. sub-salsa,* 381.
tumida var. lanceolata,* 382.
turgida, 273.

ulna, 306.
ulvoides, 329.
undata, 284.
undosa, 369.
undulata (Syn.), 301.
undulata (Nav.), 343.
undulatus,* 267.
uni-punctata, 320.

varians, 247.
vaucheriæ,* 313.
veneta, 372.
vicenarius, 267.
vickersii, 405.
virescens, 282.
viridis, 341.
viridula, 410.
vulgare (Diat.), 291.
vulgare (Coll.), 331.

westii, 248, 249.
williamsonii (Diad.), 337.
williamsonii (Nav.), 403.
wrightii (Lys.), 249.
wrightii (Nav.), 390.

zellensis, 357.
zostereti, 408.
ZYGOCEROS,* 272, 274.

PLATES 26 TO 34.

ILLUSTRATIVE OF THE REV. EUGENE O'MEARA'S REPORT "ON THE IRISH DIATOMACEÆ." Part I.

Vide Proceedings R. I. Acad., Vol. 2, Ser. 2, p. 235.

PLATE 26.

Fig. 1. Melosira Borrerii, p. 246.
2.   ,,   subflexilis.
3.   ,,   distans.
4. Lysigonium nummuloides, p. 248.
5. Podosira montagnei, p. 250.
5a. ,,   maculata.
6. Orthosira arenaria, p. 251.
7.   ,,   sulcata.
8.   ,,   orichalcea.
9.   ,,   Roëseana.
10. Cyclotella Kützingiana, p. 256.
11. ,,   Meneghiniana.
12. ,,   operculata.
12b. ,,   ,,   var.
13. ,,   antiqua.
14. ,,   rotula.
15. ,,   papillosa.
16. ,,   Scotica.
17. ,,   punctata.
18. Coscinodiscus, oculus iridis, p. 260.
19. ,,   centralis.
20. ,,   perforatus.
21. ,,   gigas.
22. ,,   radiolatus.
23. ,,   Gregorii.
24. ,,   Ehrenbergii.
25. ,,   minor.
26. Craspedodiscus coscinodiscus, p. 266.

PLATE 27.

Fig. 1. Actinocyclus Ralfsii, p. 268.
    2.   ,,   moniliformis.
    3. Eupodiscus Argus, p. 269.
    4. Auliscus sculptus, p. 270.
    5. Odontodiscus excentricus, p. 270.
    6.   ,,   Anglicus.
    7.   ,,   Hibernicus.
    8. Biddulphia Baileyii, p. 275.
    8a.   ,,   aurita.
    9.   ,,   pulchella.
   10. Amphitetras antediluviana, p. 277.
   11. Triceratium alternans, p. 278.
   12.   ,,   amblyoceros.
   13.   ,,   exiguum.
   14. Trinacria regina, p. 278.
   15. Isthmia nervosa, p. 279.
   16. Fragilaria maxima, p. 283.
   17. Denticula mutabilis, p. 285.
   18. Odontidium mesodon, p. 287.
   19. Dimeregramma distans, p. 289.
   20. Plagiogramma costatum, p. 290.

PLATE 28.

Fig. 1. Diatoma grande, p. 291.
    2. Ralfsia tabellaria, p. 293.
    3. Rhaphoneis amphiceros, p. 295.
    4.   ,,   scutelloides.
    5.   ,,   liburnica.
    6. Synedra crystallina, p. 297.
    7.   ,,   fulgens.
    8.   ,,   baculus.

9. Synedra superba.
10. ,, amphicephala.
11. ,, investiens.
12. ,, acula.
13. ,, gracilis.
14. ,, undulata.
15. ,, lunaris.
16. ,, biceps.
17. ,, pulchella.
18. ,, ,, var. gracilis.
19. ,, ,, ,, acicularis.
20. ,, ,, ,. lanceolata.
21. ,, ,, ,, linearis.
22. ,, capitata.
23. ,, ,, var. longiceps.
24. ,, ulna.
25. ,, ,, var. oxrhynchus.
26. ,, ,, ,, amphirhynchus.
27. ,, longissima.
28. ,, obtusa.
29. ,, splendens.
30. ,, ,, var. radians.
31. ,, ,, ,, danica.
32. ,, salina.
33. ,, gallionii.
34. ,, spathulata.
35. ,, barbatula.
36. ,, tabulata.
37. ,, arcus.
38. ,, affinis.
39. ,, Nitzschiodes.
40. ,, Frauenfeldii.
41. ,, putealis.
42. ,, Smithii.
43. ,, debilis.

PLATE 29.

Fig. 1. Grammatophora marina, p. 315.
    2.   ,,   serpentina.
    3. Tabellaria flocculosa, p. 317.
    4. Tetracyclus lacustris, p. 318.
    5. Rhabdonema arcuatum, p. 318.
    6. Striatella unipunctata, p. 320.
    7. Tessella interrupta, p. 320.
    8. Amphipleura pellucida, p. 321.
    9. Mastogloia convergens, p. 325.
   10. ,,   Closeii.
   11. ,,   porticrana.
   12. ,,   Smithii.
   13. ,,   costata.
   14. Dickieia ulvoides, p. 328.
   15. Colletonema neglectum, p. 331.
   16. Berkeleya fragilis, p. 331.
   17. Schizonema crucigerum, p. 333.
   18. ,,   Smithii.
   19. ,,   Grevillii.
   20. ,,   obtusum.
   21. Diadesmis Williamsonii, p. 337.
   22. Brebissonia Boeckii, p. 338.

PLATE 30.

Fig. 1. Navicula nobilis, p. 340.
    2. ,,   cardinalis.
    3. ,,   viridis.
    4. ,,   alpina.
    5. ,,   pachyptera.
    6. ,,   distans.
    7. ,,   undulata.
    8. ,,   rectangulata.
    9. ,,   Trevelyana.
   10. ,,   oblonga.

11. Navicula longa.
12. ,, tabellaria.
13. ,, divergens var.
14. ,, borealis.
15. ,, menapiensis.
16. ,, clepsydra.
17. ,, rupestris.
18. ,, ceres.
19. ,, gibba.
20. ,, ,, var. Boeckii.
21. ,, ,, ,, parva.
22. ,, hemiptera.
23. ,, apiculata.
24. ,, Brebissonii.
25. ,, ,, var. angusta.
26. ,, nodosa.
26a. ,, ,, var. staurophora.
27. ,, icostauron.
28. ,, stauroptera.
29. ,, bacillum.
30. ,, Americana.
31. ,, isocephala.
32. ,, bicapitata.
33. ,, ,, var. crucifera.
34. ,, ,, ,, constricta.
35. ,, termes.
36. ,, microstauron.
37. ,, crucifera.
38. ,, pinnularia.
39. ,, scalaris.
40. ,, cuneata.
41. ,, acuminata.
42. ,, retusa.
43. ,, integra.
44. ,, pachycephala.
45. ,, subcapitata.
46. ,, gracillima.
47. ,, macula.
48. ,, zellensis.

PLATE 31.

Fig. 1. Navicula cuspidata, p. 357.
    2. ,, fulva.
    3. ,, cuspis.
    4. ,, rhombica.
    5. ,, cœrulea.
    6. ,, decipiens.
    7. ,, tumens.
    8. ,, rostrata.
    9. ,, tenuirostris.
    10. ,, ambigua.
    11. ,, sphœrophora.
    12. ,, quarnerensis.
    13. ,, Davidsoniana.
    14. ,, ovulum.
    15. ,, latiuscula.
    16. ,, Barkeriana.
    17. ,, Grunovii.
    18. ,, amphisbæna.
    19. ,, elegans.
    20. ,, palbebralis.
    21. ,, hebes.
    22. ,, lineata.
    23. ,, liber.
    24. ,, lacuneata.
    25. ,, Gründleriana.
    26. ,, iridis.
    27. ,, ,, var. amphigomphus.
    28. ,, ,, ,, affinis.
    29. ,, dubia.
    30. ,, limosa.
    31. ,, ,, var. truncata.
    32. ,, undosa.
    33. ,, esox.
    34. ,, trochus.
    35. ,, producta.

36. Navicula cocconeiformis.
37.   ,,   Kotzchyi.
38.   ,,   maxima.
39.   ,,   ,,   var. linearis.
40.   ,,   subula.
41.   ,,   translucida.
42.   ,,   papillifera.
43.   ,,   liburnica.
44.   ,,   plumbicolor.
45.   ,,   veneta.
46.   ,,   Johnsonii.
47.   ,,   simulans.
48.   ,,   Delginensis.
49.   ,,   rhomboides.
50.   ,,   serians.
51.   ,,   crassinervia.
52.   ,,   dirhynchus.
53.   ,,   rostellum.
54.   ,,   laevissima.
55.   ,,   oblongella.
56.   ,,   incurva.

PLATE 32.

Fig. 1. Navicula punctulata, p. 377.
2.   ,,   granulata.
3.   ,,   humerosa.
4.   ,,   ,,   var. fuscata.
5.   ,,   ,,   ,, quadrata.
6.   ,,   latissima.
7.   ,,   meniscus.
8.   ,,   lucida.
9.   ,,   cluthensis.
9a. ,,   ,,   var. producta.
10. ,,   punctata.
11. ,,   lacustris.
12. ,,   maculosa.

13. Navicula scutilloides.
14. ,, pusilla.
15. ,, tumida, var. linearis.
16. ,, pulchra.
17. ,, fusca.
18. ,, Smithii.
19. ,, Collisiana.
20. ,, æstiva.
21. ,, elliptica.
22. ,, ,, var. ovalis.
23. ,, clavata.
24. ,, Hennedyi.
25. ,, nebulosa.
26. ,, ,, var. suborbicularis.
27. ,, prætecta.
28. ,, Morei.
29. ,, Sandriana.
30. ,, Franciscæ.
31. ,, Hibernica.
32. ,, nitescens.
33. ,, Richardsoniana.
34. ,, Stokesiana.
35. ,, Wrightii.
36. ,, spectabilis, var.

PLATE 33.

Fig. 1. Navicula lyra, p. 391.
2. ,, ,, var. elliptica.
3. ,, ,, ,, Grunovii.
4. ,, ,, ,, minor.
5. ,, ,, ,, seductilis.
6. ,, ,, ,, constricta.
7. ,, pygmæa.
8. ,, ,, var. cuncata.
9. ,, expleta.
10. ,, cynthia.

11. Navicula sansegana.
12. ,, Arraniensis.
13. ,, Eugenia.
14. ,, scutellum.
15. ,, suborbicularis.
16. ,, ,, var. forficula.
17. ,, Schmidtii.
18. ,, coffeiformis.
19. ,, eudoxia.
20. ,, Donkiniana.
21. ,, marginata.
22. ,, subcivita.
23. ,, Archeriana.
24. ,, incurvata.
25. ,, musca.
26. ,, interrupta.
27. ,, apis.
28. ,, bombus.
29. ,, didyma.
30. ,, splendida.
31. ,, Gregorii.
32. ,, Williamsonii.
33. ,, incisa.
34. ,, crabro, var. denticulata.
35. ,, Pfitzeriana.
36. ,, Vickersii.

PLATE 34.

Fig. 1. Navicula directa, p. 406.
2. ,, exilis.
3. ,, radiosa.
4. ,, gracilis.
5. ,, acuta.
6. ,, peregrina.
7. ,, zostereti.

8. Navicula Cleviana.
9. ,, digito-radiata.
10. ,, Ergadensis.
11. ,, cyprinus.
12. ,, galvagensis.
13. ,, solaris.
14. ,, viridula.
15. ,, Heufleri.
16. ,, Northumbrica.
17. ,, arenaria.
18. ,, inflexa.
19. ,, Hungarica.
20. ,, Carassius.
21. ,, mutica.
22. ,, semen.
23. ,, inflata.
24. Anglica.
25. ,, cryptocephala.
26. ,, angustata.
27. ,, Lagerstedtii.
28. ,, gastrum.
29. ,, binodis.
30. ,, dicephala.
31. ,, rhyncocephala.
32. ,, globifera.
33. ,, rostellifera.
34. ,, cancellata.
35. ,, minor.
36. ,, perpusilla.
37. ,, seminulum.

N. B.—All the figures in the preceding Plates of Diatoms are magnified 400 diameters, unless otherwise indicated.
Fig. 10, Plate 29.—The Striæ should be radiate.

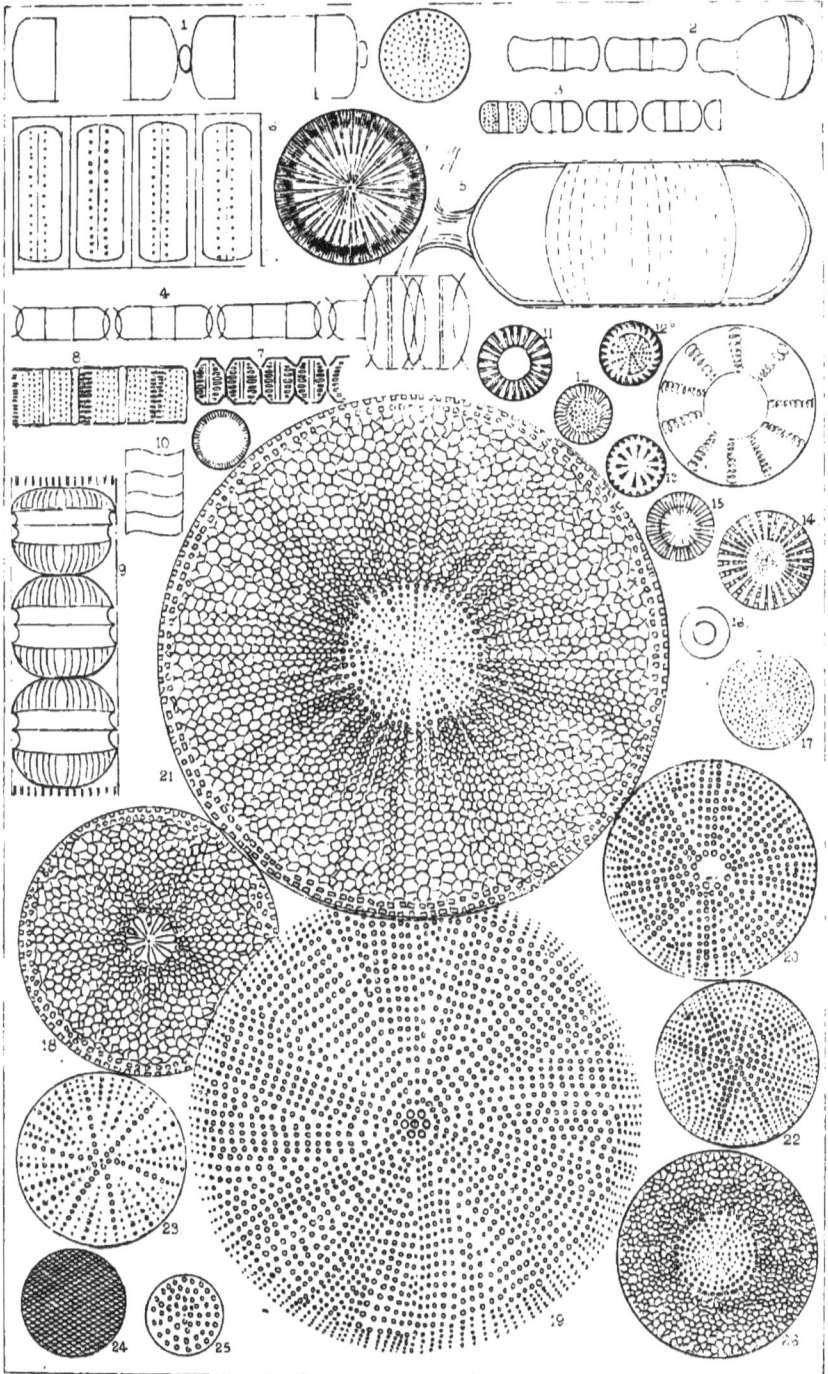

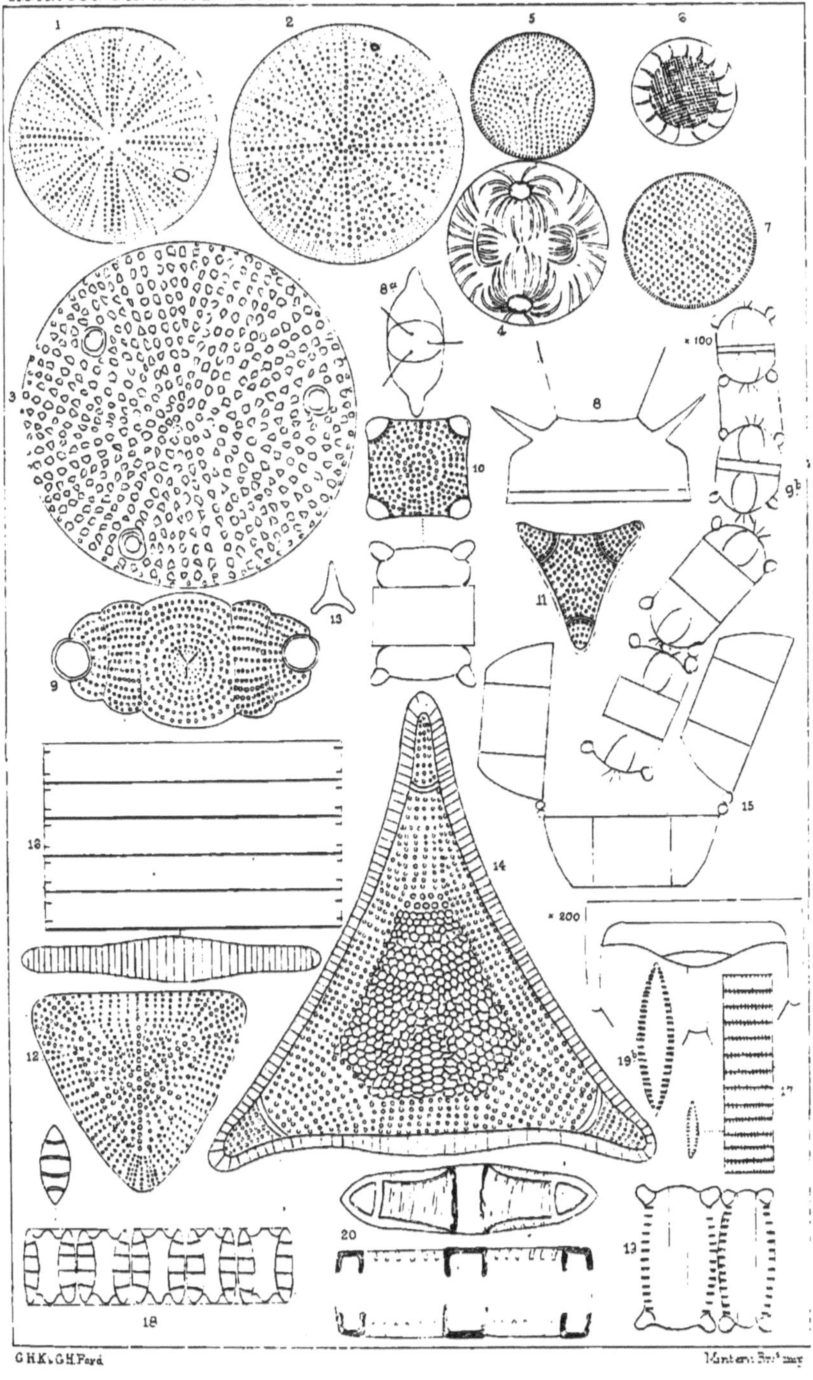

G.H.K. & G.H. Ford. Mintern Bros imp.

R.I.A. Proc. Ser. II. Vol. II. Science. ×200 Plate 28.

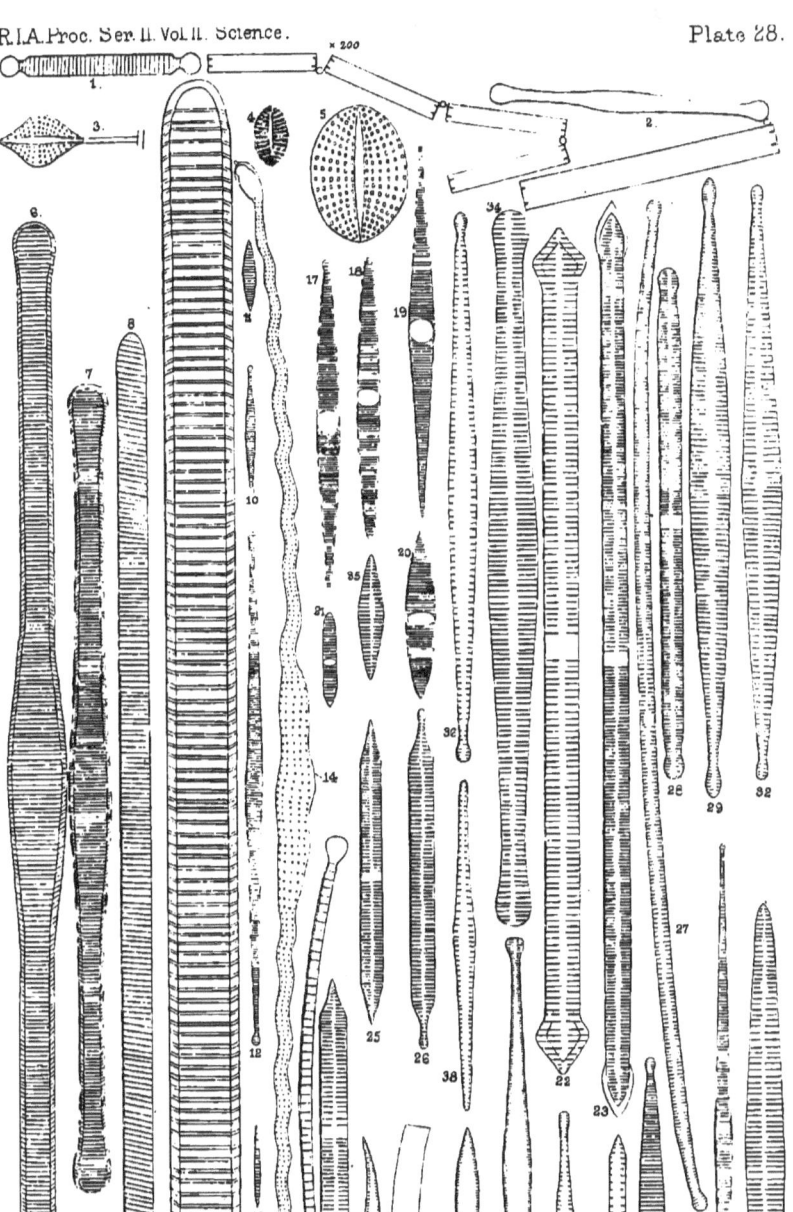

Plate 29

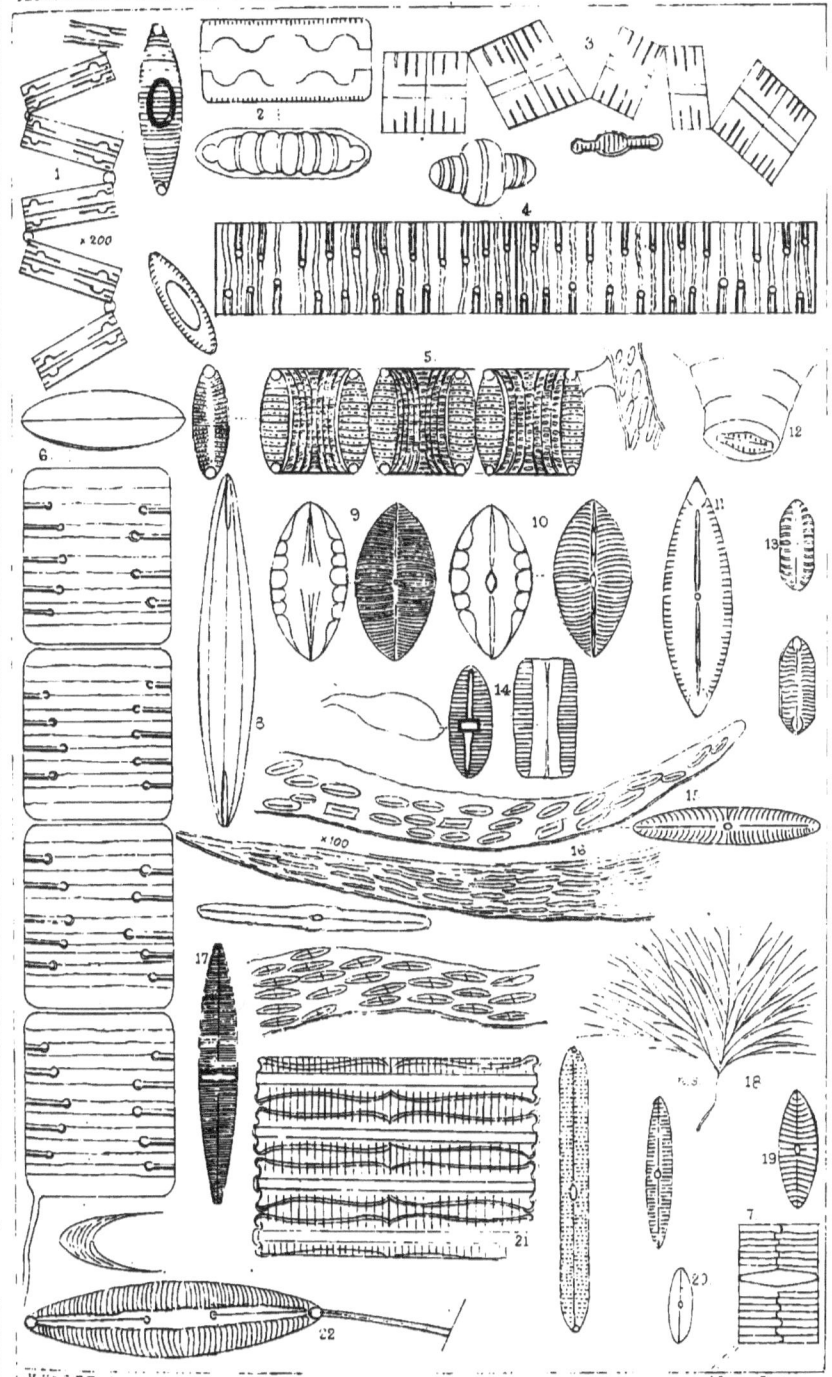

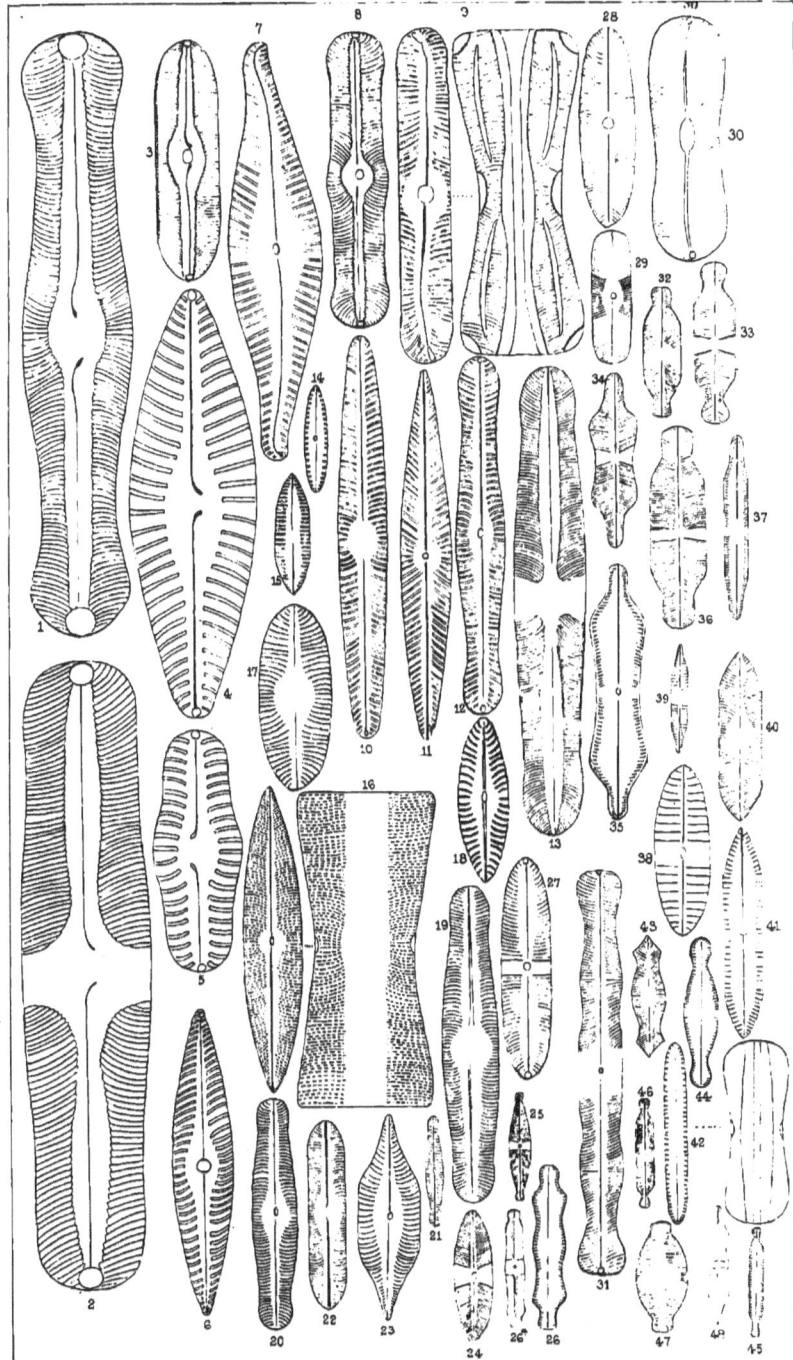

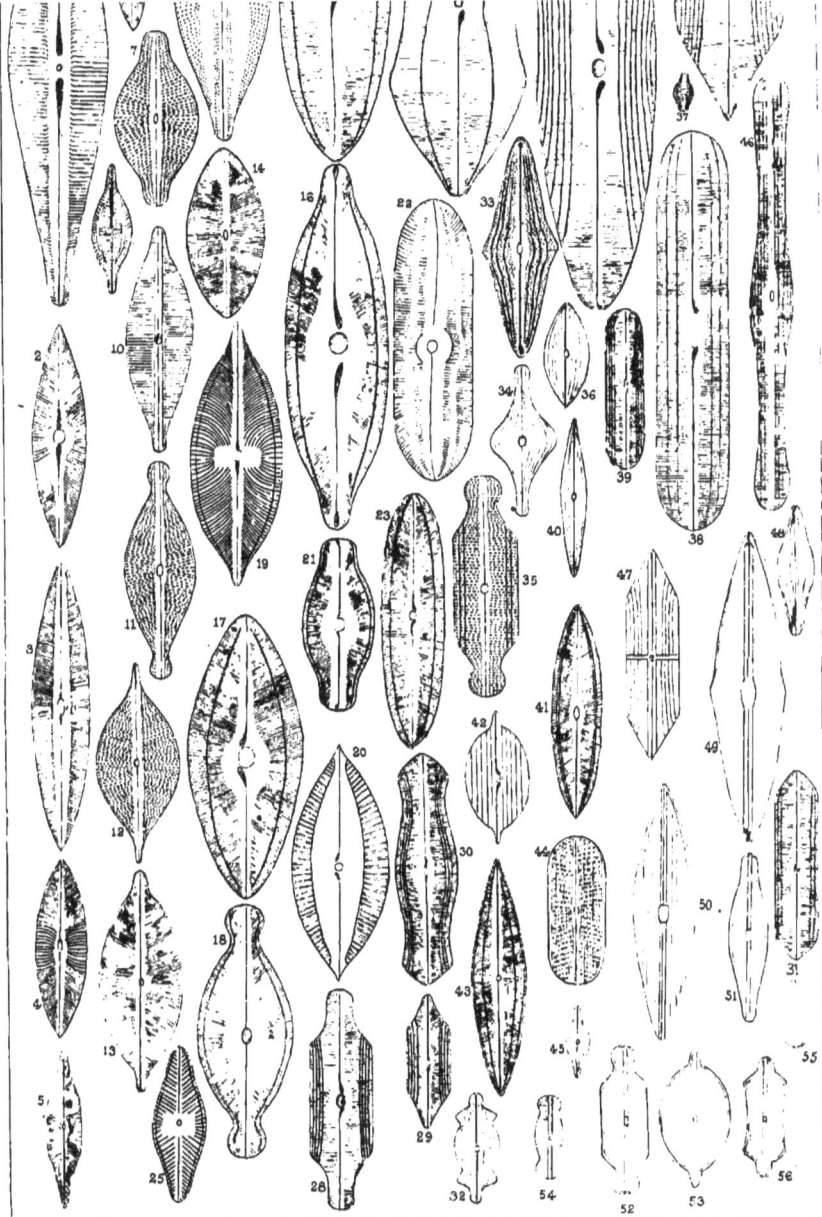

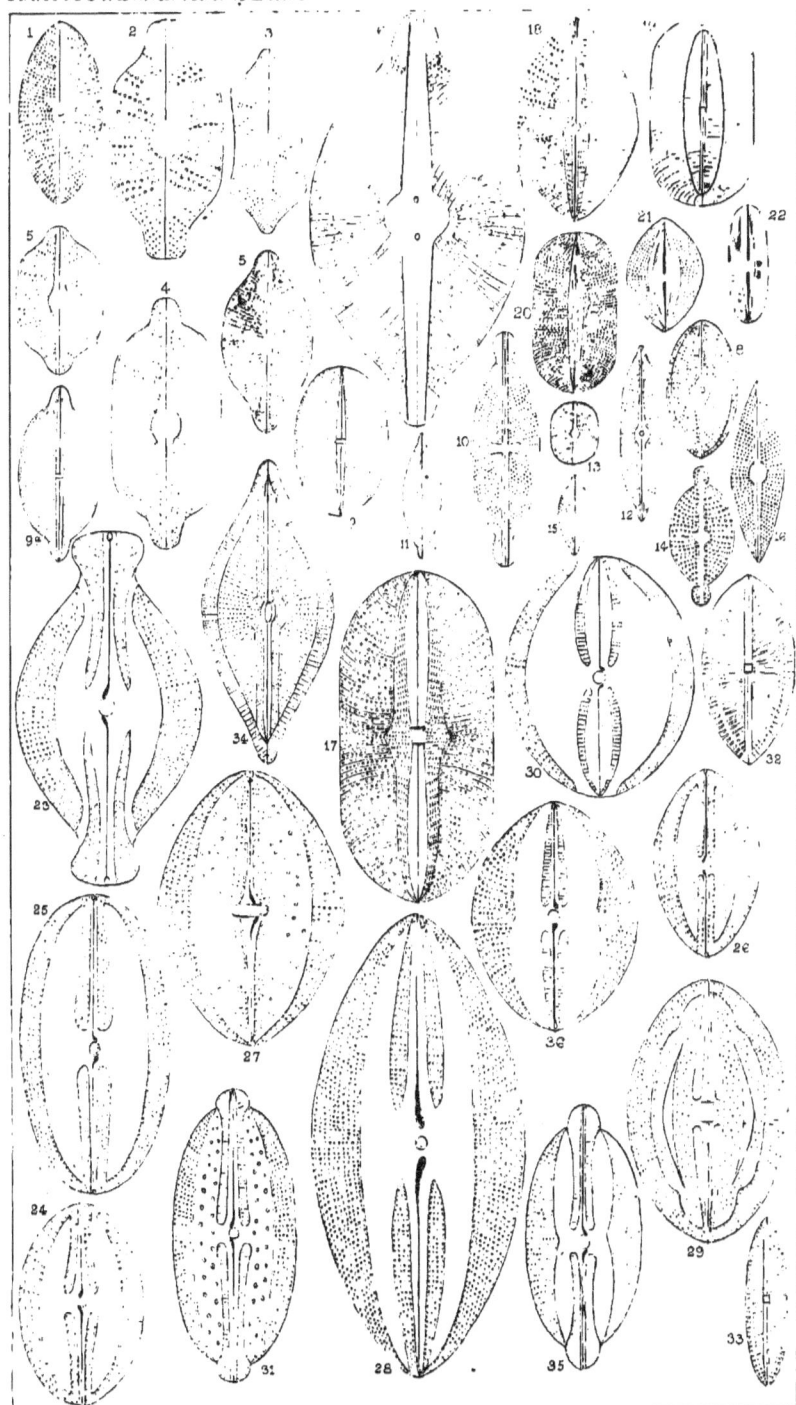

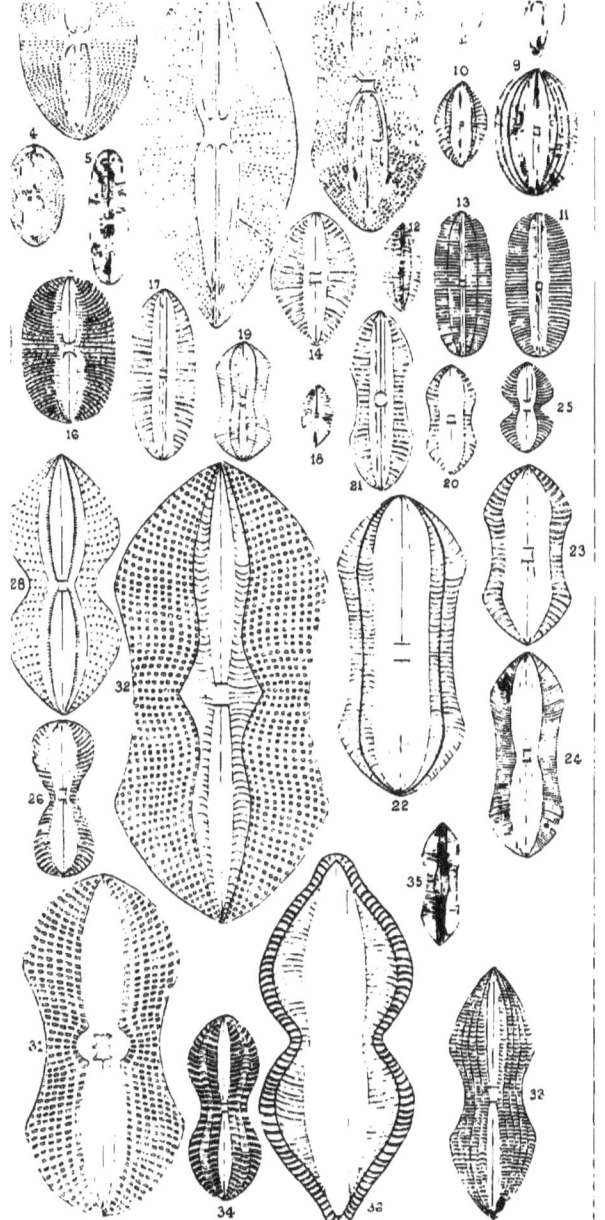

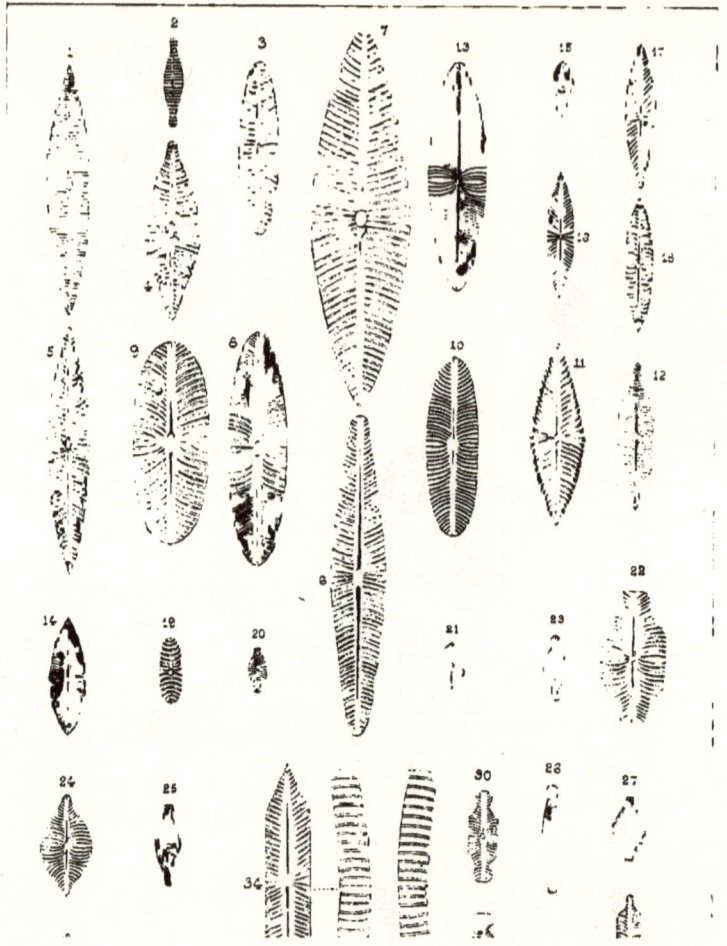

www.ingramcontent.com/pod-product-compliance
Lightning Source LLC
Chambersburg PA
CBHW031830230426
43669CB00009B/1292